The
War on Conservatives

Mark Dice

The War on Conservatives
© 2023 by Mark Dice
All Rights Reserved
Published by The Resistance Manifesto
San Diego, CA

No part of the text within this book may be reproduced or transmitted in any form and by any means, graphic, electronic, or mechanical, including photocopying, recording, taping, or by any information storage retrieval system, without the written permission of the author.

Printed in the United States of America

Visit www.MarkDice.com

ISBN: 978-1-943591-12-1

Cover design by Ben Garrison

Table of Contents

Introduction	1
Public Schools	13
The Family	45
American Symbols and Holidays	71
Christianity and Churches	105
The LGBTQ+ Agenda	155
Immigration	197
Antiwhiteism	223
Censorship	257
Cowardly Conservatives	301
Conclusion	323

Also by Mark Dice:

- *The True Story of Fake News*

- *Liberalism: Find a Cure*

- *The Liberal Media Industrial Complex*

- *Hollywood Propaganda: How TV, Movies, and Music Shape Our Culture*

- *The Bohemian Grove: Facts & Fiction*

- *The Bilderberg Group: Facts & Fiction*

- *The Illuminati: Facts & Fiction*

- *The New World Order: Facts & Fiction*

- *Big Brother: The Orwellian Nightmare Come True*

- *The Resistance Manifesto*

- *Inside the Illuminati: Evidence, Objectives, and Methods of Operation*

Introduction

Conservatives, or who should really just be called normal humans who maintain the basic values, traditions, and social norms that individuals, families, and communities have lived by since ancient times, are under attack by a barrage of deeply disturbing ideologies and well-funded institutions that can only be described as insane—or evil.

Instead of being relegated to a fringe group in a dark corner of the Internet or the subjects of a documentary looking into the lives of degenerate weirdos for viewers' entertainment, these insane people and their agendas are being promoted in public schools and Universities, by Hollywood celebrities and award-winning shows and films, and boosted by the algorithms on the Big Tech social media platforms.

Even major food brands and retailers are awash in this new breed of Leftist propaganda. The onslaught of wokeness is even gaining support in the legal system with draconian laws being snuck through Democrat-controlled state legislatures which undermine the very foundation of what America once stood for.

We now have Marxists in our own Congress calling for the removal of American symbols, the erasure of our history, and the systemic demonization of White people. The communication tools our society now relies on are being used to censor those who push back against their agenda too loud, and countless activist media outlets exist for the sole purpose of being attack dogs for the regime and smear its enemies as "racists," "transphobes,"

INTRODUCTION

"antisemites," and an array of other defamatory labels they hope will stick.

Children, being impressionable and vulnerable, are one of the enemy's prime targets. And in recent years it's become common in public schools across the country for teachers to sexualize their students as young as preschoolers—having kids engage in LGBTQ Pride parades at school, and the mainstream media now promotes pre-teen boys dressing in drag and young girls getting their breasts surgically removed if they feel uncomfortable with their body or unsure of their gender.[1]

Freaks, who in past generations you would only see featured on the *Jerry Springer Show,* are now credentialed teachers and proudly post videos on TikTok bragging about what they're doing with their students. The U.S. Military is openly recruiting and celebrating gays, lesbians, and transgenders.[2] Kids' cartoons are promoting gender bending drag queens to their young impressionable audiences on Disney+ and Nickelodeon.[3] What had always been seen as an adult form of entertainment at gay night clubs in seedy parts of the inner city is now being performed for small children at schools and libraries across the country.[4]

Many of our cherished holidays are even under attack from those within our own country. Such disgruntled

---

[1] WPDE ABC 15 "Miami surgeon performs 'top surgery' for 15-year-old transgender kids" by Alec Schemmel (September 26th 2022)

[2] Military Times "Pentagon officials defend diversity and inclusion at Pride Month event" by Zamone Perez (June 7th 2023)

[3] Washington Examiner "*Blue's Clues* song shows drag queen teaching children about gay, transgender, and nonbinary characters" by Lawrence Richard (May 29th 2021)

[4] New York Times "Drag Queen Story Hour Continues Its Reign at Libraries, Despite Backlash by Lisa Stack (June 6th 2019)

INTRODUCTION

citizens (and illegal aliens) were once relegated to shouting on the street corner, but now their anti-American ideas have taken root and mainstream Marxist Democrats are openly calling for the destruction of statues of the Founding Fathers, abolishing the national anthem, and even replacing the American flag.[5]

They hate the foundation of our country, including the Bill Rights and the freedoms Americans have enjoyed since 1776. And there's not just an ongoing assault on our nation's symbols and founders, but on Capitalism itself with many Democrats continuously nudging us toward socialism. The COVID lockdowns of 2020 and 2021 warmed millions of Americans up to the idea of getting free handouts from the government while they sit at home instead of going to work. And calls for issuing a Universal Basic Income, or UBI—free money to those unwilling to work, are increasing.[6]

Antifa, the Marxist foot-soldiers who show up to intimidate, threaten, and attack attendees at Conservative events, are now commonplace in cities across the country, and they're allowed to act with impunity and face no legal consequences for the violence they carry out, which is either ignored by the media or blamed on Trump supporters for "inciting it" by simply existing.

In their efforts to overthrow the United States and collapse us into the New World Order, our country has been flooded with a steady stream of millions of illegal aliens from third world countries for decades. These people aren't just future Democrat voters, but they further reduce the White majority and erode patriotism in

---

[5] Washington Examiner "Millennials in San Diego sign petition to remove American flag" by Emilie Padgett (June 30th 2015)

[6] CNBC "More Americans now support a universal basic income" by Annie Nova (February 26th 2018)

INTRODUCTION

America because most of them aren't interested in becoming *Americans* and don't care about our history, values, or customs—they just simply want to take advantage of what America has. They'll never assimilate, and instead just further weaken the bonds that hold our cultural fabric together.

To entice the caravans of migrants to continue coming, Democrats offer them free housing, free healthcare, free education, and an endless list of welfare benefits which further stresses our sputtering financial system. We're already so far in debt as a nation that it's impossible to repay, and things are getting to the point where even paying the interest on the national debt may be impossible.[7] The only way out of such a financial hole is to print more money—a lot more. Which means hyperinflation—drastically eroding the value of the dollar and skyrocketing prices, which will likely lead to what some call the Great Reset.

A primary tactic to sow discontent and foment social unrest is the promotion of antiwhiteism (anti-White racism) under the banner of Critical Race Theory, which is a scholarly sounding veneer used to cause racial strife by opening old wounds that healed long ago and blaming White people for all the current problems and shortcomings Black people have today. Critical Race Theory disguises antiwhiteism as supposed "history" and promotes the conspiracy theory that White supremacy is woven into the fabric of America and at the heart of our institutions.

While we've had racial injustices in the past (as with every multicultural country or region throughout history)

---

[7] Fox Business "The US is paying a record amount of interest on its national debt" by Megan Henny (August 17th 2023)

INTRODUCTION

and struggled to overcome the conflicts between different ethnic groups living among each other, by the end of the 20th century race relations were quite harmonic in the United States—only to begin deteriorating in the 21st century under President Obama who constantly stoked the embers of what was nearly an extinguished fire, reigniting racial and class conflicts and using Black Lives Matter to fan the flames.

They're "woke" they say, which just means they blame others for their own personal failures under the guise of "oppression" which is either imaginary or self imposed so they can portray themselves as victims who insist deserve special treatment. Wokeness is just another synonym for Marxism and is used to gather more supporters for the cause.

And of the Conservatives being targeted in this current culture war, Christians are enemy number one because of their adherence to traditional (normal) family values and customs. The Left's vicious hatred for Christianity has no bounds with Christian holidays, symbols, and businesses now under constant attack.[8]

The forces manipulating our society are more than just social media algorithms amplifying absurdities, perverts, and antiwhiteism; although the Big Tech platforms are a large part of the problem. There's also Operation Mockingbird secretly pulling the strings behind the scenes of the "news" networks, Wikipedia masquerading as an "encyclopedia," Google curating search results and burying websites and articles containing information they don't want the general public to know; and now various artificial intelligence "chatbots" which present just as

---

[8] Christianity Today "Christian Baker Sued Again for Refusing to Bake a Cake" by Colleen Slevin via Associated Press (March 24th 2021)

biased information because their programmers have placed strict parameters on the kinds of answers they can give and the content they can generate.[9]

Of course the high priests of Hollywood are in lockstep, building up false idols whose behaviors and ideologies are modeled by millions of mentally enslaved morons. What most people mindlessly consume as "entertainment" is carefully crafted political propaganda designed to incrementally desensitize the population to various ideas and activities; slowly shifting sensibilities and encouraging radical new notions.

The advent of social media proved to be a powerful tool against mainstream media, ultimately revolutionizing countless industries—from how customer service is conducted by businesses, to how people consume TV shows, movies, and music. Through Facebook, Twitter, and YouTube (the first three massive platforms to become centerpieces in society), various "personalities" and independent media companies organically grew massive audiences by utilizing the new technology which allowed anyone to post and distribute their reports to millions (for free), which had previously required enormous and expensive infrastructure to accomplish.

It wasn't until after Donald Trump's 2016 election victory that mainstream media conglomerates fully realized the average individual in their kitchen on a laptop was now on an even playing field with them, and their information monopoly had slipped through their fingers. What was once seen as a technological novelty that people used to keep in touch with old friends also meant they could share a local news story that may end up being

---

[9] Forbes "ChatGPT Has Liberal Bias, Say Researchers" by Emma Woollacott (August 17th 2023)

INTRODUCTION

seen by so many others it becomes a national story by going viral.

People also couldn't help but notice how the mainstream media acted as gatekeepers and purposefully ignored crime patterns and other issues that should have been widely covered. So the mainstream media struck back, co-opting the Big Tech social media platforms, partnering with them—and they were soon transformed into extensions of the mainstream media instead of alternatives, and the good old days were over. The brand name conglomerates weaseled their way back into a position of dominance over the flow of information.

Donald Trump winning the 2016 Presidential Election shocked much of the country, if not the world. Hillary Clinton had been expected to win and most of the media portrayed her victory as inevitable—as if it was her "right" to be the next president, which compounded Democrats' disappointment when she ultimately failed. Once the shock began to wear off, instead of coming to grips with the outcome, a vicious war was launched in hopes of destroying the Trump administration by any means necessary. Plans to impeach him were drawn up before he was even inaugurated.[10]

Then throughout his administration, he and his associates were relentlessly attacked by Deep State operatives in the intelligence agencies, frivolous lawsuits in the courts, Operation Mockingbird mouthpieces in the "news" media, and his supporters faced increasing censorship on social media.

Trump would have been banned from Twitter shortly after the 2020 election even if the January 6th protest

---

[10] The Washington Post "The campaign to impeach President Trump has begun" by Matea Gold (January 20th 2017)

hadn't turned into a riot because the media and the Democrats had manufactured an image of him as a dangerous monster, and numerous politicians including Kamala Harris had been demanding he be banned from social media even before the election.[11]

But the provocateured and staged false flag "insurrection" was the pretense they were looking for to finally purge him from all the Big Tech platforms and further crackdown on his supporters. Republicans who doubted the outcome of the 2020 election or voiced concerns about Democrats stealing it were now censored on social media, despite Democrats making the same allegations for four straight years prior. But now any talk of a stolen election was "dangerous," and "undermines our Democracy." Only in communist countries and other dictatorships are citizens not allowed to question the legitimacy of the ruling party, and that's what happened in America.

They're also engaging in what's called *lawfare* (legal warfare), which means using the legal system to harass and persecute one's enemies. Donald Trump, his associates, and his supporters have all been swept up in crippling legal entanglements—while the justice system allows the Biden and Clinton crime families, and Black Lives Matter and Antifa foot soldiers to operate above the law. Many January 6th defendants who weren't even accused of assaulting police or vandalism during the infamous protest at the Capitol that day were denied bail and held in jail for several *years* until their trials.[12]

---

[11] CNN "Kamala Harris calls on Twitter CEO to suspend Donald Trump" by Donie O'Sullivan (October 2nd 2019)

[12] Politico "Judge to revoke bail for Proud Boy leaders involved in Capitol riot" by Kyle Cheney and Josh Gerstein (April 19th 2021)

INTRODUCTION

Many of these same political prisoners were then sentenced to extremely harsh and unfair prison time for technically just trespassing if they happened to be members of the Proud Boys, or became symbols of the protest like the "QAnon Shaman" and the guy who was photographed with his feet resting on Nancy Pelosi's desk. They were all sentenced to *years* in prison[13]

One of the first actions the Justice Department took once Joe Biden was sworn into office was indicting a Twitter user named Douglas Mackey for posting a meme five years earlier back in 2016 joking that Democrats could "skip the lines" on election day by "texting" in their vote instead.[14] A common joke posted every election year by people from both political parties, along with the one about the "friendly reminder" that the opposing political party votes on *Wednesday*.

Nobody is fooled by such posts because they're obvious jokes. And not a single person took the meme about Democrats being able to "text" in their vote for Hillary Clinton seriously, but Douglas Mackey (who went by "Ricky Vaughn" on Twitter) was still indicted for "election interference!"[15] He was later sentenced to *seven months in federal prison.*[16]

---

[13] The "QAnon Shama" was sentenced to 41 months (nearly 3 and a half years), and Proud Boys leader Enrique Tarrio (who wasn't even in Washington D.C. on January 6th) was sentenced to 22 years, and Proud Boys member Joe Biggs who only entered the Capitol and walked around with the other protesters was sentenced to 17 years.

[14] The Hill "DOJ: Social media influencer charged with interference in 2016 election" by John Bowden (January 27th 2021)

[15] Washington Examiner "Pro-Trump Twitter influencer found guilty of conspiracy against rights over 2016 memes" by Brandy Knox (March 31st 2023)

[16] Washington Post "Trump supporter sentenced to 7 months after tweeting false voting ads" by Praveena Somasundaram (October 20th 2023)

Legal battles often take years and easily cost hundreds of thousands of dollars, even millions to defend. Those found innocent (or not liable in a civil case) usually can't recoup any of those costs. They may win the case, but are still destroyed financially.

The head of Joseph Stalin's secret police force in the Soviet Union infamously said, "Show me the man and I'll show you the crime," and the power of prosecutors to abuse their authority is widely known even in western Democracies. Former Supreme Court Justice Robert Jackson admitted in some cases, "it is not a question of discovering the commission of a crime and then looking for the man who has committed it, it is a question of picking the man and then searching the law books, or putting investigators to work, to pin some offense on him."[17]

He goes on, "It is in this realm—in which the prosecutor picks some person whom he dislikes or desires to embarrass, or selects some group of unpopular persons and then looks for an offense, that the greatest danger of abuse of prosecuting power lies. It is here that law enforcement becomes personal, and the real crime becomes that of being unpopular with the predominant or governing group, being attached to the wrong political views, or being personally obnoxious to or in the way of the prosecutor himself."[18]

The U.S. Supreme Court has found that even though the law may be "fair on its face, and impartial in appearance" it can still be "applied and administered by public authority with an evil eye and an unequal hand,"

---

[17] Journal of The American Judicature Society [vol. 24] "The Federal Prosecutor" by Robert H. Jackson (June 1940)

[18] Ibid.

allowing prosecutors to make "unjust and illegal discriminations between persons in similar circumstances," thus violating their civil rights by using the very mechanisms of government that are supposed to protect them.[19]

The FBI used disinformation to get a FISA warrant to spy on the Trump campaign in order to create the false narrative he conspired with Russians to "steal" the 2016 election. After his administration was bogged down for years, the Mueller investigation found no evidence of wrongdoing and when Robert Mueller finally testified about his investigation, he proved to be an embarrassing and bumbling old man who couldn't even convincingly articulate why it was launched in the first place.[20]

But the lawfare continued, with prosecutors ultimately indicting Trump for paying Stormy Daniels to sign an NDA to keep quiet about their alleged affair (claiming it was an unreported campaign expense), then for keeping some documents at his Mar-a-Lago residence from his time in the White House; and soon after that for other trumped up charges (no pun intended) claiming he orchestrated a "criminal conspiracy" trying to steal the 2020 election. All signs of a banana republic and a collapsing society.

And sadly, we aren't just opposed by a matrix of enemies on the Left, but also from within our own ranks. Brand name "Republicans" and corporate "Conservatives" have been too cowardly for years to stand up against what's happening to our culture—afraid of being called "homophobic" or "racist." Only recently

---

[19] Understanding Lawyer's Ethics (Third Edition) by Monroe H. Freedman and Abbe Smith page 309

[20] PBS "White House calls Mueller hearing embarrassment for Democrats" via Associated Press (July 24th 2019)

since the insanity has boiled over and infected elementary school children's cartoons and soiled advertisements from big box retailers and the U.S. military have they dared say anything.

And it wasn't until censorship of Conservatives had snowballed out of control and swept up mainstream figures (culminating in the seated President at the time, Donald Trump, being banned from all Big Tech platforms) that brand name Conservative news outlets, pundits, and Republican members of Congress finally began speaking out about what many of us independent YouTubers had been shouting from the rooftops about for years.

You've seen what's happening. And even though you may try to keep up with the news, there's only so much time in the day for that among all the other obligations of life. Unless your full-time job is following politics or pop culture, it's impossible to know the full extent of the damage being done to society, but it's clear to anyone that we are facing relentless assaults on numerous fronts. And as the weeks, months, and years fly by, we tend to lose perspective on where things are and how much they've changed. The shock wears off, and the "new normal" sets in.

Like the proverbial frog slowly boiling in the pot unaware of what's happening because of the small but incremental temperature increases, most people won't see the big picture of what the Marxists are doing to America until it's too late. So before we get to the point of no return (which hopefully we haven't already crossed) mute your phone, schedule some quiet time for yourself, and let's take a close look at how the pieces of the puzzle all fit together in *The War on Conservatives*.

Public Schools

Public schools (which should really be called *government* schools) were once a place for kids to learn the basic knowledge needed to get through life: reading, writing, and arithmetic; along with history, geography, science, and a few others; but in recent years they have become indoctrination centers where Leftists use the captive audience of young and impressionable minds to shape future generations into the mold of Marxism.

"Give me a child when he's seven, and we'll have him for life," is an old maxim attributed to numerous individuals throughout history from the Greek philosopher Aristotle to Adolf Hitler and Vladimir Lenin. Whoever said it doesn't matter because the statement conveys the obvious importance of early education and how what a child is taught when they're young can shape their character and beliefs for the rest of their lives.

It's now commonplace in public schools across the country for teachers to not just hang LGBTQ+ rainbow "Pride" flags up in their classrooms, but stock their libraries with sexually explicit queer books, and countless teachers are now "coming out" to their students as gay, lesbian, and gender non-binary—even posting the videos on TikTok.[21]

Many schools are inviting drag queens to put on "performances" for the kids and hold "Pride" parades

---

[21] Media Entertainment Arts World Wide "Who is Jadzia Watsey? Philly teacher trolled for coming out as lesbian to her students" by Sayantani Nath (December 13th 2021)

every June to kick off queer Pride Month.[22] Activities that had previously always been contained in seedy gay bars have now been imported into elementary schools across America.[23]

Most LGBT teachers who have infiltrated the schools are openly grooming young students hoping to convince them to question their own gender and experiment with their sexuality. And instead of just teaching history (which contains atrocities, and embarrassing actions carried out by every culture around the world), the woke system is intent on indoctrinating students to think that not much has changed from 1850s until now in the United States.

And even though slavery ended after the Civil War they still insist that America has "White supremacy" woven into the very fabric of our society. Every institution—from the legal system and schools to businesses and sports are supposedly secretly being run by "White supremacists" and keeping Black people down![24]

It's all being done under the cover of Critical Race Theory which is further disguised under the label of "history," but the agenda is the same. As countless proponents of Critical Race Theory have openly admitted, the principles and concepts are the same ones teachers are using to indoctrinate children with while avoiding the term itself in hopes of hiding their motive.

---

[22] CBS Los Angeles "Pride event sparks tense protest outside North Hollywood Elementary School" by KCAL News Staff (June 2nd 2023)

[23] NBC New York "Elementary Kids Get 'Special Surprise' Drag Performance at School Talent Show" by Roseanne Colletti (June 2nd 2017)

[24] New York Post "NYC public school asks parents to 'reflect' on their 'whiteness'" by Selim Algar and Kate Sheehy (February 16th 2021)

"Critical Race Theory" is really just a code word for antiwhiteism (anti-White racism), and it's now common for teachers to have Black Lives Matter flags hanging in their classrooms. Project Veritas was able to give everyone a close look at the mindset of these teachers when they caught one on hidden camera during an undercover investigation in Sacramento, California where he admitted he was trying to turn his students into "revolutionaries."[25] He had a poster of Chinese communist dictator Mao Zedong on the wall in his classroom as well—not as an educational tool about history or communism, but because the teacher himself is an avowed communist.

When Project Veritas later confronted him while he was out walking his dog to ask about what they had captured him on video saying, he was literally wearing a giant hammer and sickle communist tank top! A school board meeting held the next day was packed with parents who demanded he be fired.[26] Surprisingly he was, but how many other *literal* communists are working as teachers doing the same thing and go unnoticed by school officials and parents?

During a meeting of the American Federation of Teachers Union, a Colorado teacher boasted that there were fellow Marxists in the crowd and called for a

---

[25] Fox News "Pro-Antifa teacher brags about turning students into 'revolutionaries,' undercover video shows" by Jessica Chasmar (August 31st 2021)

[26] Sacramento Bee "See heated Natomas Unified School District meeting regarding Inderkum High School teacher" (September 1st 2021)

"forceful cultural revolution" in America against "whiteness."²⁷

FBI Investigates Parents

After a wave of parents began showing up to school board meetings and telling off the administrators for mandating children wear COVID masks in school all day and subjecting the students to gender bending propaganda and Critical Race Theory (antiwhiteism), the National School Boards Association sent a letter to the Biden administration literally comparing parents who were slightly aggressive or a bit rowdy during the meetings to domestic terrorists.²⁸

Less than a week later the Department of Justice sent a memo to the FBI instructing them to investigate alleged "threats" made to school boards by parents, and so the FBI's counterintelligence division began opening investigations. One case involved a mother who told her local school board "we're coming for you" during a meeting, which was interpreted as a threat (when it was an obvious figure of speech about exposing them and voting them out) but an investigation was launched into her anyway.²⁹

---

[27] Fox News "Colorado teacher calls for 'FORCEFUL cultural revolution' targeted at 'whiteness': 'This is sacred'" by Hannah Grossman (May 18th 2023)

[28] Fox News "Whistleblowers: FBI targeted parents via terrorism tools despite Garland's testimony that it didn't happen" by Bradford Betz (May 11th 2022)

[29] Fox News "Whistleblowers: FBI targeted parents via terrorism tools despite Garland's testimony that it didn't happen" by Bradford Betz (May 11th 2022)

Another investigation was launched after someone reported a parent to the FBI because he "rails against the government" and "has a lot of guns."[30] Joe Biden's Attorney General Merrick Garland testified to Congress that antiterrorism tools (like spying on their social media activity) had not been used against any of the protesting parents, but seven months later an FBI whistleblower revealed that they actually had.[31]

The New York Times even blamed the Proud Boys (a right-wing men's social club, similar to a Moose Lodge or The Elks) for the increasing turnout at school board meetings by angry parents who got fed up with their children being indoctrinated with queer theory and antiwhiteism. Their headline read, "Proud Boys Regroup, Focusing on School Boards and Town Councils," and the article detailed in horror that "The far-right nationalist group has become increasingly active at school board meetings and town council gatherings across the country."[32]

Others like MSNBC host Jason Johnson suggested the pushback against school boards was being fueled by "white nationalists" as well.[33] *Mother Jones*, a Leftist online outlet warned, "School boards have long been a tool of White supremacy" and that the "once-innocuous local gatherings have become anti–critical race theory

---

[30] House Judiciary Committee "Whistleblowers: The FBI has labeled dozens of investigations into parents with a threat tag created by the FBI's Counterterrorism Division" via Press Release (May 11th 2022)

[31] Fox News "Whistleblowers: FBI targeted parents via terrorism tools despite Garland's testimony that it didn't happen" by Bradford Betz (May 11th 2022)

[32] New York Times "Proud Boys Regroup, Focusing on School Boards and Town Councils" by Sheera Frenkel (December 14th 2021)

[33] Newsbusters "MSNBC Warns Parents Pushing Back Are Mentally Ill, White Nationalists" by Kristine Marsh (October 6th 2021)

caucuses administered by white people."[34] *The Columbus Dispatch* in Ohio echoed this sentiment telling their readers that "racists may be coming to a school board near you."[35]

"Cultural Discipline"

Some schools are even adopting a practice called "Cultural Discipline" or "Transformative Education Professional Development & Grading," which means they're allowing Black students to get away with causing trouble and handing out lesser punishments to them if they are disciplined because of concerns the school may be perceived as being "racist" since more Black students *cause* trouble than White students (because they statistically tend to come from fatherless homes and don't grow up with the proper discipline) and thuggery is often glorified and celebrated in Black culture.[36]

The schools adopting this practice are framing it as taking an "equitable" approach to punishment and discipline.[37] Notice the Orwellian change of terms recently from *equality* to *equity*. Marxists don't want people to be treated *equally*. They want special privileges granted to non-White people (and queers) to supposedly

---

[34] Mother Jones "School Boards Have Long Been a Tool of White Supremacy" by Anthony Conwrighte (March+April 2022 Issue)

[35] The Columbus Dispatch "Beware! 'Very fine' racists may be coming to a school board near you" by Ricky L. Jones (October 29th 2021)

[36] CBS Atlanta "CNN Of The Ghetto': WorldStarHipHop Becoming YouTube For Urban Violence" by Peter V. Milo (March 29th 2012)

[37] KTTH 770 "WA schools adopt race-based discipline, white students to get harsher punishment" by Jason Rantz (March 21st 2022)

"make up" for past "injustices" they claim haven't been remedied.[38]

Schools are even adopting policies of not docking students' grades for missing class, misbehavior, and failing to turn in their assignments on time because those methods "disproportionately hurt the grades of Black students," they say.[39]

Not issuing detentions and suspensions to Black students who deserve them and letting their bad behavior go unpunished is rationalized by the same ridiculous argument we see from people who claim there must be "systemic racism" in police departments across the country because Black people are arrested for committing violent crime at levels nearly ten times that of White people (*per capita*).[40] It's uncomfortable for most people to face the fact that Black men commit astonishingly more crimes per capita than White people, so of course they're going to get arrested more!

And an important side note about what per capita means, since most Liberals don't know anything about statistics. Often when people point out the Black Crime statistics and mention the fact that Black people are 13% of the U.S. population, but commit 50% of the total violent crimes, some Liberals will look up the murder statistics in the United States and claim "that's not accurate." But it is.

Those who deny the facts about Black Crime are only comparing the *total* number of murders committed by White people to the *total* number committed by Blacks,

---

[38] This is what they mean by demanding *equity* now, not equality.

[39] West Cook News "OPRF to implement race-based grading system in 2022-23 school year" by LGIS News Service (May 30th 2022)

[40] *Per capita* means the average per person, and is calculated by dividing a measurement by the population of a specific group.

but don't take into consideration that Blacks are only 13% of the U.S. population.[41] The term *per capita* means *per person*, or the average number per group, and is a more accurate way of reporting statistics, but because Liberals are ignorant about most things—they just don't get it. Since the White population is still an extremely higher percentage of the overall population in the United States, it would be common sense that White people would account for a higher number of murders, but we're talking about *percentages per group* here. And the uncomfortable reality is that Black people make up only 13% of the U.S. population, but commit half of all violent crime as a whole.[42]

And the vast majority of those perpetrators are Black *males*, so if you really want to get down to specifics, 6% of the US population (since half of the total Black population are males, and they're the ones who commit virtually all the violent crime compared to females out of the group) the scary reality is that a tiny demographic of the American population (6%—the Black males) are responsible for *half* of the violent crime in the country!

Nobody would argue that police are being "sexist" because men are arrested far more often than women for committing violent crime, because everyone knows that men commit more violent crime than women! But admitting the obvious facts about Black Crime is deemed "racist."

And when the figures of students who are punished for misbehaving and causing disruptions in school are broken down by race, it shouldn't be surprising to find the

---

[41] U.S. Department of Justice "Homicide Trends in the United States, 1980-2008" by Alexia Cooper and Erica L. Smith (November 2011)

[42] It used to be half of the violent crime, but recent statistics show that it's now almost 60% according to victim surveys.

same patterns that are shown in crime statistics. But the actual reason for such a wide disparity raises uncomfortable questions, so instead of addressing the root of the problem, "racism" is blamed.

Removing Honors Classes

Schools across the country have been ending honor classes along with gifted and talented programs because administrators are worried that they may appear as if they're "discriminating" against Black and Latino students because the programs tend to be dominated by White and Asian students.[43] Proponents of such idiocy are calling it a more "equitable" education, the social justice buzzword meaning there are too many White students in the programs.[44]

In San Diego, the entire school district changed the grading system because Hispanic students' grades were on average significantly lower than White students because of the language barrier since so many of them are illegal aliens or anchor babies born and raised by Mexican parents who speak little to no English themselves.[45] Before the change, 23% of D or F grades went to Hispanics, another 23% went to Native Americans, and

---

[43] Associated Press "New York public schools to end gifted and talented program" by Michelle L. Price and Bobby Caina Calvan (October 8th 2021)

[44] Fox News "Rhode Island parents enraged at school board for removing honors classes in 'equity obsession' by Hannah Grossman (May 9th 2022)

[45] CBS 8 San Diego "San Diego Unified revamps grading system after minority students disproportionately impacted" by Shannon Handy (October 21st 2020)

20% to Black students, while only 7% went to White students."[46]

In hopes of making the grades more "equitable" the district stopped docking students' grades for assignments that are turned in late. So now there are basically no deadlines for homework which will just further incentivize students not to schedule their time properly to do it, and they'll just keep watching TikTok videos or playing videogames all night instead.

A Minnesota school announced they were no longer going to be giving students F's in order to "combat systemic racism."[47] And homework doesn't get marked down if it's turned in late anymore there too, and students' grades are no longer effected by tardiness or detentions for bad behavior either.

Standardized tests have been deemed "racist" as well. The National Education Association says, "Since their inception almost a century ago, the tests have been instruments of racism and a biased system. Decades of research demonstrate that Black, Latin(o/a/x), and Native students, as well as students from some Asian groups, experience bias from standardized tests administered from early childhood through college."[48]

Of course the whole point of a standardized test is that all students take the same test! But now the Marxists want affirmative action-style tests so Black and Hispanic students can get different questions (easier questions) in order to artificially and unfairly boost their test scores!

---

[46] NBC San Diego "San Diego Unified School District Changes Grading System to 'Combat Racism'" by Alexis Rivas (October 15th 2020)

[47] Fox News "Minnesota middle school will eliminate 'F's to combat 'systemic racism'" by Pilar Arias (October 1st 2021)

[48] NEA.org "The Racist Beginnings of Standardized Testing" by John Rosalas and Tim Walker (March 20th 2021)

"We still think there's something wrong with the kids rather than recognizing there's something wrong with the tests," said race hustler Ibram X. Kendi, who heads up the laughable "Antiracist Research & Policy Center at Boston University."[49] He says that, "standardized tests have become the most effective racist weapon ever devised to objectively degrade Black and Brown minds and legally exclude their bodies from prestigious schools."[50] During the 2020 election cycle, at a town hall event Joe Biden was asked by a lunatic in the audience if he would promise to put an end to "racist" standardized tests, and he responded "yes."[51]

Teachers Coming Out as Gay to Their Class

Until very recently, teachers would never talk about their personal lives in the classroom. Students didn't know if they were single, dating someone, married, or divorced, because their personal relationships have no bearing on the material students need to learn at school. But now it's commonplace for teachers who are LGBTQ to announce their sexual preferences to their students in hopes of getting the kids to start talking with them about sex or experiment with homosexuality themselves.

The *Libs of TikTok* Twitter account, which is dedicated to finding videos posted publicly on TikTok by Liberal teachers and other odd individuals who keep coming up

---

[49] NEA Today "The Racist Beginnings of Standardized Testing" by John Rosales and Tim Walker (March 20th 2021)

[50] Ibid.

[51] The Daily Caller "Joe Biden Says He'll End Standardized Testing In Public Schools After Questioner Calls Them 'Rooted In A History Of Racism" by Peter Hasson (December 14th 2019)

with new "genders," has highlighted countless teachers who don't just make TikTok videos talking about how they've "come out" to their students as LGBTQ. Some of them actually record their speech on their phones and then post those videos on TikTok!

One teacher made the announcement she was a lesbian to every class that day so all of her students heard her speech.[52] Many of the students cheered since they've been conditioned to celebrate such behavior.

Another TikTok video posted by a teacher shows her explaining that she took down the American flag in her classroom and hid it because it's an "offensive symbol," but has an LGBT Pride flag hanging in her room and when a student asked what they were supposed to do during the Pledge of Allegiance she told them to pledge allegiance to the Pride flag.[53]

One queer high school teacher posted a video he recorded inside his classroom bragging about how "most days" he comes to school wearing stilettos, "and the reason why is so I can create an explicitly queer space for all my students. That way they know this place is a place for them, by them, and cuz I never had one of these growing up."[54] In the video he showed off his high heels.

It's important to understand that these aren't just a few rare or isolated instances. The *Libs of TikTok* Twitter account regularly reposts videos that are found on TikTok to raise awareness about just how widespread the problem

---

[52] Media Entertainment Arts World Wide "Who is Jadzia Watsey? Philly teacher trolled for coming out as lesbian to her students" by Sayantani Nath (December 13th 2021)

[53] NBC News "Teacher faces backlash for suggesting student pledge allegiance to Pride flag" by Jo Yurcaba (August 30th 2021)

[54] His TikTok username was @JustAQueerTeacher -but he later deleted his account after going viral.

is and to show how many teachers are talking with their students about their sexuality or trying to confuse the kids about which gender they are.

"Gender Non-Binary" Teachers

But it's not just gay and lesbian teachers who feel they need to "come out" to their students these days. *Libs of TikTok* has also uncovered numerous teachers (many of whom are elementary school teachers), "coming out" as "gender non-binary" to the kids (someone who doesn't consider themselves to be a man *or* a woman, but *neither!*)

Blue and green-haired freaks who were once only found loitering in the streets of inner cities or working at adult video stores are now teaching elementary school children and preschool across the country.

One woman (with green hair as usual) explains, "So I'm a non-binary elementary school teacher, and my kids know I'm non-binary, they know I'm not a girl or a boy, I use 'they' 'them' pronouns in the classroom. We work on it. Not all the kids get it. That's okay. And I go by Mx. Gray in the classroom, not Miss or Mister—Mx. And today one of the kids goes, 'hey, we've got two boy teachers in the classroom because the other teacher in the classroom at the time was a guy. And I go, no there's not. I'm not a girl or a boy, remember? And she goes 'oh my God. Wait, does that mean you're dead? So, I think that's my new gender now."[55]

Of course a three-year-old doesn't understand what the hell her lunatic teacher means by saying she's not a

---

[55] https://twitter.com/libsoftiktok/status/1480723017713864705.

boy or a girl. How could any child begin to comprehend such nonsense? And what kind of school wouldn't escort the teacher from the property immediately after learning that they're saying they aren't a man or a woman and trying to confuse the children with such mentally deranged insanity?

One polyamorous gender-fluid witch (polyamorous meaning in open relationships with numerous different sexual partners) who teaches preschool in Florida posted a video on TikTok saying how proud she is to talk with her 4-year-old students about her sexuality.[56] And that's not a typo, she also identifies as a witch. The list goes on and on of preschool and elementary school teachers who post TikTok videos boasting that they're teaching children about "transness" and "queerness."[57]

One preschool teacher explained that she hands out "pronoun pins" to the 4-year-olds she teaches every day so they can choose which "gender" they want to be that day. "We have some that pick, like, 'she' / 'her' every single day, and we have some that change it up."[58]

When I was in high school in the 1990s if a teacher put up a gay Pride flag, we would have torn it down every time they stepped out of the classroom into the hallway, and no one would have said who did it. And if they replaced it, the same thing would happen every single day until they gave up. And if a teacher came out as a "gender non-binary" and started talking about they weren't a man or a woman, the parents in the community wouldn't have

---

[56] The Blaze "Preschool teacher — and 'polyamorous, gender-fluid witch' — goes viral for admitting how she teaches her young students about sexuality and identity" by Sarah Taylor (April 12th 2022)

[57] https://twitter.com/libsoftiktok/status/1521183077967417344

[58] Twitchy "Teacher says she has her preschoolers pick a pronoun pin every day to wear" by Brett T. (April 12th 2022)

even needed to get involved because we the students would have run them out of town ourselves. Virtually any community in America would have run such freaks out of town in previous generations (or even hung them in the town square depending how far back it was) if they started telling elementary school children that boys could be girls and girls could be boys or made an announcement that they were queer, but today these creatures are allowed to make children participate in their fetishes and delusions by affirming their "identity" and most schools and parents are doing nothing to stop them![59]

Sexual Predator Teachers Now Allowed

Teachers even vaguely hinting at anything sexual with their students has always been a major red flag that they were a predator, and even the most subtle reference to anything sexual would have immediately been condemned by administrators and a dark cloud of suspicion would have hung over them for the rest of their career. Each year students would pass on word of the incident to the incoming students in the freshman class and such behavior would become part of school lore. The rumors would never stop.

Students with younger siblings would tell them what happened and they would tell their friends, and the teacher would never live it down, and in most cases would have been fired immediately. But now if the teacher is gay or bisexual, they often openly brag in

---

[59] These are most likely in California and New York, but with almost all other degenerate social contagions, it may not be much longer until such teachers start popping up in other parts of the country.

TikTok videos about what they're doing and the grooming agenda has gone full speed ahead. All while the media runs stories defending the practice and accusing Conservatives of being "homophobic" and going on a "witch hunt."[60]

The Government Accountability Office [GAO] published a report back in 2014 warning about the dangers of sexual predator teachers in public schools, recommending administrators be on the lookout for "grooming behaviors" that are "part of a pattern of behavior and are done with the intent to perpetrate future sexual abuse or misconduct."[61]

In 2015 *The Washington Post* ran the headline, "More teachers are having sex with their students. Here's how schools can stop them."[62] The article noted that the previous year there were 781 teachers or school employees were accused or convicted of sexual relationships with students, and cites social media as the primary method perpetrators use to first start communicating with their victims.

In 2019 the Iowa Department of Education published a guidebook to help teachers and administrators identify grooming in public schools, listing one of the red flags as (obviously) "talking about student sexuality" and having "inappropriate and personal conversations with

---

[60] New York Magazine "The Long, Sordid History of the Gay Conspiracy TheoryToday's right-wing campaign against 'groomers' is America's latest moral panic." by James Kirkchick (May 31st 2022)

[61] United States Government Accountability Office "Child Welfare. Federal Agencies Can Better Support State Efforts to Prevent and Respond to Sexual Abuse by SchoolPersonnel" page 5 (January 2014) Available online here https://www.gao.gov/assets/gao-14-42.pdf

[62] Washington Post "More teachers are having sex with their students. Here's how schools can stop them." by Terry Abbot (January 20th 2015)

students."[63] But now queer teachers grooming students using these exact same methods is widely acceptable behavior.

Gay Pride Parades in Schools

Once something that was always confined to inner city streets in places like New York and Los Angeles, gay Pride parades and "celebrations" are now regular occurrences in public schools across America.[64] They call them "Pride" parades now instead of gay Pride parades, because that name wasn't inclusive enough for the transgenders, pansexuals, and all the rest of the gender-bending degenerates who all fall under the queer umbrella.

And young children who don't yet know what differentiates gay and transgender people from normal people are being deceived about what the events are for. They're told that "Pride" celebrations are just about people celebrating "who they are" and anyone who is "different," or that it's about "diversity," while masking what is actually being celebrated.

Teachers are using classical conditioning techniques to associate the rainbow "Pride" flag with positive feelings—and like new members of a cult, the kids aren't being told what the group actually believes in hopes of incrementally indoctrinating them in order to make them more receptive to what's really going on so it won't

---

[63] Twitchy.com "People are mad at Christopher Rufo for exposing child sex predators in public schools" by Brett T. (April 20th 2022)

[64] US News & World Report "At School Pride Event Students Destroyed Decorations, Chanted 'USA Are My Pronouns,' Officials Say" via Associated Press (June 13th 2023)

appear as a sudden shock, causing them to possibly turn away.

Girls have always loved rainbows, and to innocent children they symbolize magic because they're such a rare occurrence. Most people only see naturally occurring rainbows a few times throughout their lives, but the LGBTQ movement has turned it into a sexual kink fetish symbol.

In 2022 "Pride Month" debauchery went supernova with countless schools across the country holding drag queen events for children. It's not just one or two, or even a handful of isolated instances—it's now a common occurrence. And not just in high schools. Drag queen "Pride" events targeting children as young as two years old are now commonplace.[65]

Schools regularly host drag queen story hour, and other drag queen themed events, like "drag queen bingo" night, and drag queen talent shows.[66] A middle school in New York even welcomed a drag queen to teach boys how to apply drag makeup.[67] There are too many such events to list here.

And many public schools are now forcing kids to study "gay history." As of 2023 at least six states require schools to teach it, including California (which was the first, as usual), along with New Jersey, Illinois, Oregon, Colorado, and Nevada.[68] And not just in high schools, but

---

[65] Fox News "Oklahoma State University hosts 'Drag Queen Story Hour' for kids as young as 2-years-old" by Adam Sabes (April 15th 2022)

[66] CNN "Middle school invites drag queens to encourage students to be themselves " by Lauren M. Johnson (May 18th 2019)

[67] Post Millennial "NYC public school teaches middle schoolers how to do 'drag makeup'" by Ashley St. Clair (May 31st 2022)

[68] The Wall Street Journal "More States Weigh How to Add LGBT History to Classroom Lessons" by Ben Chapman (June 2nd 2023)

middle schools and elementary schools too.[69] In one Illinois school, pre-kindergarten children are given an "introduction" to the rainbow flags and gender identity, and third graders are taught that White European colonizers "forced two-spirit people to conform to the gender binary."[70] A Florida school took elementary students on a field trip to a local gay bar to teach them about Pride Month.[71]

Michigan's Democrat attorney general said she wants "a drag queen for every school."[72] But the Leftists aren't satisfied with "Pride" month events now being the norm at schools across the country throughout the month of June so some schools now have "Back to School Pride Festivals" to celebrate queerness as the new school year begins.[73] Some people are now calling summer "Pride season" because they're not satisfied with "just" one month dedicated to them.[74]

Project Veritas caught the dean of students at a Chicago area high school on undercover video bragging that he had dildos, butt plugs, and lube passed around to students (as young as 14) and was excited they were

---

[69] Fox News "New Jersey to require 2nd graders learn about gender identity in fall, alarming parents" by Houston Keene (April 7th 2022)

[70] City Journal "Radical Gender Lessons for Young Children" by Christopher Rufo (April 21st 2022)

[71] New York Post "Florida school board member under fire for field trip to known gay bar" by Mark Lungariello (October 28th 2021)

[72] WWMT Channel 3 News "A drag queen for every school': Michigan AG reportedly dismisses concerns over kids, drag" by Zachary Rogers (June 16th 2022)

[73] The Daily Universe "RaYnbow Collective hosts first BYU Back-to-School Pride Night" by Ally O'Rullian (September 4th 2021)

[74] Washington Times "Biden official Rachel Levine wants to prolong Pride Month to Summer of Pride" by Valerie Richardson (June 26th 2023)

interested in how to use the butt plugs.[75] Of course the dean is a queer himself. It's nobody's business what two consenting adults do in the privacy of their bedroom they used to say, but now the queers won't shut up about it and insist on sharing their lifestyles with children and demand they celebrate it with them.

A math teacher in Huntington Beach, California forced students to watch an LGBTQ Pride Month propaganda video and many of them revolted. One student caught this on video and posted it online showing them booing, making barfing sounds, and asking "Why are you showing this to kids?" The teacher then threatened them with a Saturday detention, claiming they were being "inappropriate."[76]

Drag Queen Story Hour Pedagogy

Drag shows have always been considered adult entertainment because of their inherent sexual nature. And it's always been gay—there has never been a single heterosexual drag queen in the history of the world, with the exception of some men dressing in drag as a joke because of the absurdity of it—something that has always been viewed as such, with depictions in popular films and sketch comedy bits on TV.

But the Marxists are now using drag as a way to indoctrinate children into gender bending and other queer activities instead of making people laugh at how odd it is for men to dress as women. On one hand they try to

---

[75] New York Post "Elite Chicago prep school dean brags about kids handling sex toys in class" by Lee Brown (December 9th 2022)

[76] Fox News "California high school teacher allegedly threatens punishment after students protest Pride video in math class" (June 13th 2023)

claim it's just "entertainment" for the kids and there's "nothing sexual about it," while on the other admit that they are strategically using it as a pedagogy, meaning a method of teaching, in hopes of sparking "queer imagination" in the children, "strategic defiance against social norms" and the "destigmatization of shame."[77]

In an article published in the educational journal *Curriculum Inquiry* they admit, "Drag queens have historically been relegated to the realm of the night. In the past few years, however, drag performers have made their way from the dimly lit bars of gayborhoods [gay neighborhoods] and into the fluorescent lights of libraries and classrooms."[78]

It goes on to say "positioning queer and trans cultural forms" are "valuable components of early childhood education" and they encourage teachers to use Drag Queen Story Hour "as a way of bringing queer ways of knowing and being into the education of young children" and "create spaces for young children and families to immerse themselves in LGBT-themed stories."[79]

It was cowritten by a drag queen who goes by the name of "Little Hot Mess" who was featured in an Associated Press video about drag queen story hour where he is seen asking the children "Who wants to be a drag queen when they grow up?"[80]

---

[77] Curriculum Inquiry "Drag pedagogy: The playful practice of queer imagination in early childhood" by Harper Keenan and Lil Miss Hot Mess (Volume 50, 2020 - Issue 5)

[78] Ibid.

[79] Ibid.

[80] Associated Press YouTube Channel "NY Library Brings Drag Queens to Kids Story Hour" (May 16th 2017)

Transition Closets

An increasing number of public schools are now offering what are called "Transition Closets" which include clothes, makeup, and jewelry that students can change into once they arrive at school so they can "transition" their "gender" into something else while hiding it from their parents.[81] The idea seems to have been popularized on TikTok (as with nearly all socially toxic tends) and now some schools are receiving grants to fund them.[82]

An organization called Valid USA aims to "support schools interested in creating gender-affirming wardrobe spaces for trans and nonbinary affirming clothing" by donating clothes and makeup in what they call their Schools Affirming Wardrobe program.[83] Their website notes, "We offer a range of complimentary services, including free chest binders, bras, underwear, packers, referrals, and compassionate support from fellow trans peers."[84]

These "transition closets" don't just stock ordinary clothes though. They supply children with binders (not three ring binders, but breast binders to flatten girls' breasts tight against their chests to help them look more like a boy), as well as "tucking" underwear which help hide the penis and testicles of males who want to look like "girls." They also include "packing underwear" which

---

[81] The Post Millennial "Oakland school launches 'Transition Closet' to help students hide gender dysphoria from parents" by Libby Emmons (February 16th 2022)

[82] Spectrum News 1 "Gender Affirming Closet gives free clothes to transgender, queer students" by Ariel Wesler (August 25th 2021)

[83] https://www.instagram.com/p/CefYzntrAsy/

[84] https://www.validusa.org/

contain prosthetic penises and testicles to give girls who wear them the appearance of a bulge in their crotch as if they have male genitalia.[85]

Many schools are now issuing guidelines to teachers demanding they not tell parents about such activities. A Conservative activist group called Empower Wisconsin obtained a copy of training materials given to teachers in the state's Eau Claire district which says that "Parents are not entitled to know their kids' identities. That knowledge must be earned," meaning they aren't supposed to tell parents if their child starts gender bending at school.[86]

New Jersey's "Transgender Student Guidance for School Districts" says that teachers aren't allowed to tell a parent if their child "comes out" as "transgender" and mandates all school officials use whatever name or pronoun students want.[87]

"A school district shall accept a student's asserted gender identity; parental consent is not required. Further, a student need not meet any threshold diagnosis or treatment requirements to have his or her gender identity recognized and respected by the district, school or school personnel. Nor is a legal or court-ordered name change required. There is no affirmative duty for any school district personnel to notify a student's parent or guardian of the student's gender identity or expression," it says.[88]

---

[85] CBN "CA Public School Bypasses Parents with 'Transition Closet' for Teens Who Want to Cross-Dress in Class" by Steve Warren (February 25th 2022)

[86] The Federalist "Wisconsin School District: Parents Are Not 'Entitled To Know' If Their Kids Are Trans" by M.D. Kittle (March 8th 2022)

[87] https://www.nj.gov/education/safety/sandp/climate/docs/Guidance.pdf

[88] Ibid.

"Schools are advised to work with the student to create an appropriate confidentiality plan regarding the student's transgender or transitioning status," it goes on to say. And "a school district shall keep confidential a current, new, or prospective student's transgender status."[89]

Such rules are probably in place in countless districts across the country by now. Parents in Massachusetts sued their child's school after they found out that teachers were secretly encouraging students to change their gender and use different pronouns while keeping the "transitions" secret from the children's parents.[90] And it's up to parents to find out whether their children's schools are engaging in this same behavior. Most parents have no idea because few (normal) people could have imagined such policies would even be considered, let alone actually implemented.

LGBT Children's Books

The first LGBT children's books appear to have been published in the early 2000s, such as *King and King* (2003) about a prince who's supposed to be marrying a princess, but instead catches the eye of her brother and marries him instead. Another one called *And Tango Makes Three* (published in 2005) is about two gay penguins who adopt a baby penguin as "their" child, and was written to teach kids about same sex couples. Back then the books barely made any waves with only a few

---

[89] Ibid.

[90] Fox News "Massachusetts parents sue school, say officials encouraged children to use new names, pronouns without consent" by Timothy Nerozzi (April 16th 2022)

people denouncing them like Bill O'Reilly on his primetime show on Fox News at the time. And most Conservatives who heard of them thought, while they may be strange, they were no cause for alarm and quickly forgot about them. But these LGBT children's books weren't rare novelties, they were just the start of an onslaught of this kind of material. And the books that would soon follow weren't designed to supposedly help parents explain what gay people are and why some children have "two mommies" or why their uncle has a "special friend." This new wave of LGBTQ children's books teach children it's cool for boys to wear dresses and makeup and that they should try dressing in drag and experiment with homosexuality.

Jacob's New Dress, which came out in 2014, encourages young boys to wear dresses. "Jacob loves playing dress-up, when he can be anything he wants to be," the description on Amazon reads. "Some kids at school say he can't wear 'girl' clothes, but Jacob wants to wear a dress to school. Can he convince his parents to let him wear what he wants? This heartwarming story speaks to the unique challenges faced by children who don't identify with traditional gender roles."[91]

Sparkle Boy (2017) also encourages boys to wear dresses, even if they're not transgender and still identify as a boy. The book's description reads, "Casey loves to play with his blocks, puzzles, and dump truck, but he also loves things that sparkle, shimmer, and glitter. When his older sister, Jessie, shows off her new shimmery skirt, Casey wants to wear a shimmery skirt too."[92]

---

[91] https://www.amazon.com/Jacobs-New-Dress-Sarah-Hoffman/dp/0807563757

[92] https://www.amazon.com/Sparkle-Boy-Leslea-Newman/dp/1620142856

And so he does, and he also starts painting his nails like his older sister too. The parents embrace his new "gender expression," but his older sister is uncomfortable with it at first, but at the end she accepts his new style and respects it since dresses and "sparkly things" are "for everyone to enjoy."

Julian is a Mermaid (2018) is another book aimed at grooming boys to wear dresses. *Big Wig* (2022) is another one about a young boy who becomes a drag queen, and was even promoted by Pizza Hut's *Book It!* program which encourages young children to read.[93]

Others are sexually explicit, and unimaginably obscene. One such book titled *Lawn Boy* by Jonathan Evinson is so explicit that in 2021 when a mother who checked it out from the school's library and started reading it out loud to the school board meeting they tried to get her to stop. She began, "What if I told you I touched another guy's dick? What if I told you I sucked it? I was 10 years old, but it's true. I sucked Doug Goble's dick, the real estate guy, and he sucked mine, too."[94]

A school board member interrupted her, saying, "There are children in the audience here."[95] She responded that if it's too offensive to read out loud at a school board meeting, then why is it in the school library? Other parents in the audience at the school board meeting cheered her when she was finished speaking.

And others across the country began showing up at school board meetings too and reading *Lawn Boy* and

---

[93] Fox News "Pizza Hut facing boycott calls after promoting 'drag kids' book for kindergartners" by Emma Colton (June 5th 2022)

[94] Fairfax County Times "Mother exposes sexually graphic books available in FCPS libraries" by Heather Zwicker (October 1st 2021)

[95] Ibid.

other books like it out-loud, all of which are also found in the schools' libraries. Videos of the incidents went viral on social media since most schools, like city councils, record their meetings and post the archives online.

A graphic novel titled *Let's Talk About It,* written by a bisexual man named Matthew Nolan, encourages boys to play with each other's buttholes, saying "When you're starting out, explore your butt solo till you get used to it. Lube up and don't rush," and tells them, "a great place to research fantasies and kinks safely is on the Internet. There are tons of people and communities out there who share your interests and have all kinds of advice."[96] It also recommends sex toys for kids and promotes sexting.

One of the reviews on Amazon reads, "This is NOT appropriate for teenagers. Some of the content had me and my husband absolutely shocked and horrified! Read this book before you let your children touch it! The book starts off great and about half way through it's extremely inappropriate, things I don't even want to detail on this review."[97]

A book called *Seeing Gender* by Iris Gottlieb, which is aimed at teens, contains a chapter titled "Sex work is not a bad term" (meaning prostitution) and glowingly says it's "one of the oldest jobs in history" and explains that "A person may exchange sex or sexual activity for things they need or want, such as food, housing, hormones, drugs, gifts, or other resources."[98] A school librarian at a

---

[96] Fox News "Alaska board members brawl over silencing dad exposing book on kinks and sexting: 'I'm going to interrupt you'" by Hannah Grossman (February 16th 2023)

[97] https://www.amazon.com/Lets-Talk-About-Teens-Relationships/dp/1984893149

[98] Washington Stand "Loudoun Co. School Library Book Promotes Prostitution, Authorities Investigate" by Marjorie Jackson (May 31st 2022)

middle school in Loudoun Country, Virginia defended the book being on the shelf, saying many of the students "are sex workers" and the book "makes them feel validated."[99] The list of degenerate books aimed at children could fill an entire book in and of itself.

Of course many Leftists these days are furious that Conservative parents don't want these kinds of books in school libraries, denouncing so-called "book bans," but these same people would be screaming bloody murder if copies of *The Turner Diaries* were included in school libraries, the novel that inspired Timothy McVeigh to bomb the Oklahoma Federal Building in 1995.

And if that book was in a school library, it should outrage parents because obviously certain books are inappropriate for children. Would the parents who claim banning LGBTQ books in school libraries is reminiscent of Nazi Germany want copies of *The Anarchist Cookbook*, the infamous bomb-making manual, available to the students?

What about *Playboy* magazine or *Penthouse*? Any reasonable person can admit that some ideas can be dangerous (like books about how to build bombs) and measures *should* be taken to ensure such materials aren't planting seeds into the minds of impressionable and irresponsible children.

Anti-Grooming Laws

After the general public became of aware of how pervasive the problem of teachers grooming their students

---

[99] The Daily Wire "Cops Probe After Middle School Librarian Allegedly Says Students Are 'Sex Workers' To Justify Pro-Prostitution Book" by Luke Rosiak (May 28th 2022)

PUBLIC SCHOOLS

is, discussing their sex lives with them, and encouraging gender bending; Florida passed an anti-grooming bill forbidding teachers from discussing sexuality or gender identity with students from preschool through third grade.[100] Later expanded through 12th grade.[101]

It was dubbed the "don't say gay bill" by Democrats who falsely claim the laws forbid gay teachers from talking about their partners at all. Similar legislation was then introduced in other states, including Alabama, Georgia, Ohio, and Louisiana.[102] Sixteen states would eventually move to prohibit teachers from talking about sexual orientation or gender identity with students in the early grades.[103] Word finally got out about what the LGBTQ teachers were doing, and parents and state legislatures knew they had to stop them.

A major reason Florida's legislature introduced the bill is because of the *Libs of TikTok* Twitter account which simply searched TikTok for publicly available videos posted by teachers who were openly bragging about discussing their sexuality with their students and then reposted them on Twitter, bringing them to the attention of others.

These videos of the fluorescent-haired freaks often went viral and caught the attention of Florida Governor Ron DeSantis and others who decided to draft legislation to stop the groomers. *The Washington Post* admitted,

---

[100] Post Millennial "Florida passes anti-groomer law banning gender identity indoctrination in schools" by Mia Cathell (March 8th 2022)

[101] The Washington Post "Florida bans teaching about gender identity in all public schools" by Hannah Natanson (April 19th 2023).

[102] The Hill "Red states consider Florida-style 'Don't Say Gay' bills" by Reid Wilson (April 5th 2022)

[103] Associated Press "Other states are copying Florida's "Don't Say Gay" efforts" by Andrew Demillo (March 23rd 2023)

"Libs of TikTok has become an agenda-setter in right-wing online discourse, and the content it surfaces shows a direct correlation with the recent push in legislation and rhetoric directly targeting the LGBTQ+ community."[104]

Media Matters, the George Soros funded Leftist smear merchant, told the *Washington Post*, "Libs of TikTok is shaping our entire political conversation about the rights of LGBTQ people to participate in society...It feels like they're single-handedly taking us back a decade in terms of the public discourse around LGBTQ rights. It's been like nothing we've ever really seen."[105]

Cameras In Classrooms?

In 2020 and 2021 when word spread about the extent of the child grooming and Critical Race Theory (antiwhiteism) in public schools, some parents started pushing for cameras in all classrooms that would livestream what's happening so they could check in and listen to what the teachers were doing. Conservative lawmakers in Florida and Iowa even introduced bills to mandate them, but so far none of the bills have passed.[106]

Of course, Leftists are opposing the idea, but why shouldn't parents have access to a password-protected livestream of the classrooms? Many parents set up nanny cams in their house to monitor their nanny and baby sitters so they can see what they're doing with their children when they're gone. Even many dog kennels

---

[104] The Washington Post "Meet the woman behind Libs of TikTok, secretly fueling the right's outrage machine" by Taylor Lorenz (April 19th 2022)

[105] Ibid.

[106] NBC News "Iowa bill would require cameras in public school classrooms" by Adam Edelman (February 2022)

have livestreams so people can have some peace of mind by checking in on their pet when they're out of town if they have to put them into a doggie daycare center. So why shouldn't parents be able to see what's happening in their child's classroom?

Homeschooling Makes Big Comeback

Once seen as fringe or something only extremely religious parents did, homeschooling is now seeing widespread acceptance by many Conservatives who don't want to turn their children over to government schools to be indoctrinated by some crazy leftist who's going to incorporate Critical Race Theory into their math class somehow. If you live in a small town or a city in a Republican state and know the teachers and people in the community, the schools might be somewhat safe, but if you live in a Democrat controlled region, then God help you!

Of course putting your kids in a private Christian school is a great idea, but not everyone can afford that. If you're just starting a family, these are things to consider, and you need to plan ahead. Start investing for your children's education in a private school, or move to a different town or even a new state to raise your kids so you won't plant any roots in a Liberal community and then get stuck there.

MSNBC deemed this growing trend racist (of course), saying, "It may seem harmless, but the insidious racism of the American religious right's obsession with homeschooling speaks volumes."[107] Actor Kirk Cameron, who has been a vocal Christian and critic of Hollywood's war on our culture, has been attacked by the media for encouraging more parents to start homeschooling their kids.[108] And if the Liberal media is against something, then you can be sure that whatever it is—it's the right thing to be doing.

Author's Note: Please take a moment to rate and review this book on Amazon.com, or wherever you purchased it from if you're reading the e-book, to let others know what you think. This also helps to offset the trolls who keep giving my books fake one-star reviews when they haven't even read them.

Almost all of the one-star reviews on Amazon for my previous books are from NON-verified purchases which is a clear indication they are fraudulent hence me adding this note.

It's just more proof that Liberals are losers and can't play fair, so if you could help me combat them as soon as possible since you actually bought this book, that would be great! Thank you!

---

[107] Foundation for Economic Education "MSNBC Claims Homeschooling Is Driven By "Insidious Racism," But the Facts Show Otherwise" by Kerry McDonald (May 16th 2022)

[108] Fox News "Police in Alabama stop noisy protesters from disrupting Kirk Cameron library event" by Christine Rousselle (August 5th 2023)

The Family

Since the beginning of the human race, families have been the foundation of our species' survival. Mothers, fathers, grandparents, aunts, uncles, cousins, and siblings have helped feed, protect, and educate their fellow humans who they share common ancestry with. Families maintain cultural norms and customs, and offer emotional and even financial support if one of their members falls on hard times. Families have been the center point of civilization and everyone instinctually knows they are the most important thing in life.

But now our modern society is plagued by broken families missing tight-knit social structures, which is causing a cascading failure that is having devastating effects emotionally and financially that reverberate throughout the entire country. It's largely due to single mothers, many of which were raised by single mothers themselves, compounding the problem. Working mothers, who turn their children over to strangers at day care centers so they can go sit in a cubicle behind a computer for eight hours a stretch only contributes to the breakdown, a situation which is impossible to avoid for most families because of the current cost of living. The ideal single income family with a stay at home mom of the 1950s is sadly a bygone era in America.

Parents used to be able to trust leaving their children alone in front of the television when *Sesame Street* or *Barney and Friends* were on to keep them entertained while mom did laundry, cleaned the house, or got dinner ready, but today the major brand name television stations are cultural poison and toddlers are given Internet connected devices to play games and watch cartoons which are being covertly used to indoctrinate them with enemy propaganda before they can even talk.

Political science professor James Kurth wrote, "The great movement of the second half of the nineteenth century was the movement of men from the farm to the factory…The greatest movement of the second half of the twentieth century has been the movement of women from the home to the office…[This] movement separates the parents from the children, as well as enabling the wife to separate herself from her husband. By splitting the nuclear family, it is helping to bring about the replacement of the nuclear family with the non-family."[109]

TikTok stars, teachers, and traditional Hollywood celebrities have mostly replaced parents as the primary influence on children's lives. And now that we're into the third generation of nearly half of all children growing up in broken homes where the parents have separated (or were never married in the first place) perhaps out of spite from being raised in dysfunctional families, many Liberals today are vehemently anti-family and despise what was once the cultural norm—like Edward Norton's character in *Fight Club* who "felt like destroying something beautiful" because of his nihilism.

The official website for the Black Lives Matter movement explained one of their goals was to "disrupt the Western-prescribed nuclear family structure.[110] Not to preserve, protect, or restore it—but to disrupt and *dismantle it.*

---

[109] The National Interest "The American Way of Victory" by James Kurth page 5 (Summer 2000)

[110] The New York Post "BLM site removes page on 'nuclear family structure' amid NFL vet's criticism" by Joshua Rhett Miller (September 24th 2020)

At a TEDx talk, a popular forum for "experts" to present their ideas, feminist Merav Michaeli detailed why she wants marriage to be abolished. "We must cancel marriage," she begins. "Not only religious marriage. Marriage is not an issue of religion. Also civil marriage. I want all secular states to totally eliminate all registration and regulation of marriage. I want to cancel the very concept of marriage."[111] And she certainly isn't alone.

Feminist activist (and lesbian) Masha Gessen once admitted that the Left's goal of legalizing gay "marriage" was to eventually eliminate marriage and monogamous relationships altogether. "Gay marriage is a lie," she said, back in 2012, three years before the Supreme Court mandated it be legalized in all 50 states. "Fighting for gay marriage generally involves lying about what we're going to do with marriage when we get there. It's a no-brainer that the institution of marriage should not exist," she concluded.[112]

She's a contributor for *The New York Times*, *The Washington Post*, *The Los Angeles Times*, and numerous other mainstream publications, so she's not just some fringe queer on TikTok. She is one of the establishment's LGBTQ activists (who now uses they/them pronouns).

There is a relentless assault on intimate and committed relationships (not to mention gender norms and heterosexuality in general), and aside from the moral decay in society, technology is making it easier than ever to shop around for one-night stands and swipe through dating apps to see if the grass appears greener elsewhere.

---

[111] Tedx Talks "Cancel Marriage: Merav Michaeli at TEDxJaffa" (November 10th 2012)

[112] The Blaze "Lesbian Activist's Surprisingly Candid Speech: Gay Marriage Fight Is a 'Lie' to Destroy Marriage" by Mike Opelka (April 29th 2013)

Tradwifes

As a reaction to modern Liberal society, the term "Tradwife" has emerged in some Conservative circles to refer to a traditional wife who chooses to be a stay at home mom and take care of the house and kids instead of turning them over to a daycare center and heading off to be stuck in a cubicle all day in the corporate world. They're not gold diggers who don't want to work—they're traditionalists who seek to restore the kind of family culture that was the norm in previous generations. Often this involves modest living since the families are supported by only one income. But these lifestyles are under attack by the very Liberal Establishment they are trying to avoid.

In response to a story by the BBC about a tradwife named Alena Kate Pettitt who runs a YouTube channel called The Darling Academy with just a few thousand subscribers where she encourages other women to embrace the lifestyle, Becca Lewis (who published the infamous "YouTube Alternative Influence" report in 2018 complaining about how popular many Conservative YouTubers had become), said the tradwife featured in the story was "radicalizing" right-wing extremists.

"Who needs YouTube rabbit holes when you have the BBC broadcasting literal white supremacist propaganda," she said.[113] Yes, a woman who chooses to take care of her kids at home while the husband goes off to work and prefers the traditional gender roles is considered to be "white supremacy" to Liberal lunatics.

---

[113] https://web.archive.org/web/20200122031509/https://twitter.com/beccalew/status/1219820746643406850

The New York Times is also upset over the rise of Tradwives. They published a story titled "The House Wives of White Supremacy" which started, "Over the past few years, dozens of YouTube and social media accounts have sprung up showcasing soft-spoken young white women who extol the virtues of staying at home, submitting to male leadership and bearing lots of children —being 'traditional wives.'" It goes on, "These accounts pepper their messages with scrapbook-style collections of 1950s advertising images showing glamorous mothers in lipstick and heels with happy families and beautiful, opulent homes."[114]

The article focused on one particular woman who goes by *Wife With a Purpose* (Ayla Stewart) on YouTube and attacked her as "the most prominent and certainly most openly white supremacist of the women who call themselves tradwives, but she is not an anomaly."[115] Ayla Stewart caught the eye of the Liberal Media Industrial Complex when she posting a video with the tongue in cheek title "The White Baby Challenge," saying she had made six—and challenged other women to match or beat her number of kids.[116]

But while Black and Latino women can boast about making more brown babies to quicken the demographic decline of White people into a minority group in the U.S., if any White person expresses interest in boosting the White population, they are denounced as a "Nazi."

CNN complained that "Though the numbers of self-identified tradwives are low, social media has allowed

---

[114] New York Times "The Housewives of White Supremacy" by Annie Kelly (June 1st 2018)

[115] Ibid.

[116] Salon.com "Alt-right women and the "white baby challenge"" by Alexandra Minna Stern (July 14th 2019)

THE FAMILY

them to reach sizable audiences. The 10 to 15 largest tradwife accounts have tens of thousands of followers across Instagram and YouTube."[117] CNN also decried that some of them "nod to White nationalist ideas such as Replacement Theory" and don't support LGBTQ people and use phrases like "the natural order" when talking about relationship dynamics and gender roles.

They're especially concerned that, "Some promote homeschooling to avoid exposing their children to progressive ideas about sex education and gender identity."[118]

The New Statesman, a radical Leftist publication founded by the Fabian Society—a British socialist organization whose original symbol was literally a wolf in sheep's clothing, openly supports "abolishing" families, saying, "Family is a terrible way to satisfy our desire for love and care, according to the writer and academic Sophie Lewis. The solution? Abolish it."[119]

The article sung praises of Sophie Lewis's insane ideas which are detailed in her book titled *Abolish the Family: a Manifesto for Care and Liberation,* where she compares families to prisons.[120]

Cooking is "Sexist"

Marxists work to attack and undermine every custom and social norm in order to sow chaos and destabilize the

---

[117] CNN "'Tradwives' promote a lifestyle that evokes the 1950s. But their nostalgia is not without controversy" by Harmeet Kaur (December 27th 2022)

[118] Ibid.

[119] The New Statesman "Red love, for all" by Eric Maglaque (September 23rd 2022)

[120] Ibid.

culture in hopes of being able to push their agenda through as a replacement for the "old" ideas. And aside from trying to stigmatize stay at home moms, they're also trying to portray women who cook for their husbands and families as "oppressed" and embarrassingly "old fashioned."

Every time surveys come out showing how many people still believe all women should know how to cook, feminist bloggers fume. "Good grief. It turns out gender stereotypes are just as bad today as they were 30 years ago," reports *Women's Health* magazine.[121] Saying "women should know how to cook" shouldn't even be a controversial statement. It's like saying all accountants should know how to add. Of course they should! There's something wrong with them if they don't. (And yes, all men should know how to use a variety of basic tools. I'll get to America's masculinity crisis later in this chapter.)

The Today Show in Australia (another hotbed of liberalism, particularly in Melbourne) did an entire segment attacking a stay at home wife after she posted something on Facebook about how she makes her husband breakfast and coffee in the morning, saying it was "sexist" and like living back in the 50s. "Has he hypnotized her or something? Who does this stuff?" asked one of the hosts. "I mean, I like my husband, but make your own bloody breakfast," said another.[122]

Feminists even claim that the standard specifications of kitchens are sexist, because the height of countertops

---

[121] Women's Health "People Still Believe Women Belong in the Kitchen and Men Belong at the Office" by Kristina Marusic (March 10th 2016)

[122] https://twitter.com/TheTodayShow/status/1225146029537931264

THE FAMILY

and sinks were set in order to be an ideal height for the average-sized woman.[123] And why shouldn't they be? A viral video of a girl cooking on a Twitch livestream showed the pan catch fire and she didn't know what to do so she literally started asking her viewers in a panic hoping they would type something in the chat to help her.[124] It was a grease fire, but the first thing she did was take the pan off the stovetop, turn on the sink, and pour running water all over it, so the fire then got even bigger!

If she would have taken HomeEc class in school (like all girls should), or learned how to cook from her mother like she should have ever since she was little, she would have known to smother the fire by putting the lid on the pan (if it was a metal lid, not glass), or pour baking soda all over it (which releases carbon dioxide when heated so it smothers the flames), or take the pan outside and set it on the driveway where nothing else will catch fire.

But Home Economics (or HomeEc) classes have been deemed sexist and mandating that all girls enroll in them is "sexist."[125] For generations while boys were in auto shop or wood shop class learning about how to fix and maintain vehicles and use tools to build things; girls took HomeEc and learned about cooking, sewing, child care, home management, and interior design so when they entered the real world they would know how to take care of sick children and cook healthy meals for their families —things every mom needs to know, but now learning the essential responsibilities that people need in order to have

---

[123] QZ.com "The specifications of American kitchens are actually sexist" by Rachel Z. Arndt (October 13th 2015)

[124] The New York Post "Cook's kitchen goes up in flames during livestream: 'I don't know what to do!'" by Eric Keller (May 12th 2022)

[125] Salon "The history of 'home economics' is both surprisingly radical and conspicuously regressive" by Gail Cornwall (May 9th 2021)

a productive and well balanced life are shunned, thanks to feminism.

Feminist Poison

Feminism isn't about "equal rights" for women anymore, and hasn't been for generations. It's about disrupting the social order, the divisions of labor, and partnerships between the two sexes and is attempting to suppress the natural instincts of women and turn them against men (or *the Patriarchy,* as feminists say) and even against the idea of being mothers.

Feminism has meant different things depending on the time period and has gone through four different phases, or waves as they're called, since the early 1900s when groups of women banded together to demand the right to vote (called women's suffrage), resulting in the 19th amendment passing in 1919.

The 1960s and 70s marked the second wave, where groups of women demanded they be given more political positions and worked to legalize abortion (succeeding in 1973 with Roe v. Wade). But many feminists still weren't happy, so they continued complaining about things which led to the third wave in the 1990s where they demanded even more women be given leadership positions in the government and business—while simultaneously complaining about men "objectifying" them as they boosted their sex appeal through every possible means in order to use their sexuality to their advantage since they know men are innately suckers for any beautiful woman's requests.

Then around 2012 the fourth wave of feminism arose due to the advent of social media which allowed angry and ugly women from across the country to connect with each other online and affirm each other's maladjustments and abnormal ideas, culminating in new "causes" like celebrating abortions, obesity, and their periods.[126]

Stuck in online echo chambers, most fourth wave feminists (who are usually queers with blue hair which is used to signal to others that's who they are), these women usually find themselves trapped in a downward spiral and hating normal women (especially beautiful ones and White women) for existing, and are so spiteful of their happiness, marriages, and motherhood that they are determined to tear down every institution and social norm that embraces such lifestyles.

The "Women's March" held every January isn't about "women's rights," it's a feminist parade. This is where Madonna voiced her fantasies about blowing up the White House after Donald Trump beat Hillary Clinton for the presidency, and where actress Ashley Judd did her famous rant about her period and having to pay sales tax when she buys tampons.[127]

The feminists today who constantly whine about imaginary problems—like men supposedly making more money than women, fail to acknowledge that men often work jobs which involve much higher safety risks and are exposed to greater physical and health hazards. Not to mention they regularly work jobs that involve backbreaking labor (like construction, pouring concrete, laying brick, roofing, etc.) and also jobs that involve getting dirty every day (like a mechanic or garbage man).

---

[126] The New York Post "Gen Z women are ditching pads, tampons and embracing 'free bleeding' in latest trend" by Mary Madigan (September 5th 2023)

[127] USA Today "Ashley Judd slams critics of Women's March speech: I got the P word from Trump" by Cara Kelly (January 22nd 2017)

A *Sex and the City* writer, the famous show that aired on HBO following the exploits of a group of women living in New York City, later said she regrets choosing a career over having children because now she is "truly alone."[128] She's worth nearly twenty million dollars, but now says she regrets where she placed her priorities when she was younger. Most feminists eventually find themselves in the same position (minus the wealth) realizing that once their looks fade and guys stop paying attention to them, they have no purpose in life and nobody loves them.

Not having children has other implications aside from future loneliness for most people. And it doesn't just raise the difficult question of who will help look after you when you become elderly, or who will make sure the nursing home isn't taking advantage of you or abusing you. But also who will visit you in the hospital when you get sick or need surgery? Who will inherit your "stuff" when you die? Who will clean out your house? Who will organize your funeral? Who will even know that you died?

Relationships in Shambles

Online dating was once seen as something only computer geeks did. Even when Match.com first launched in the early 1990s many people thought it was odd, and "online dating" was often ridiculed. But today when most people never leave their phone more than an arm's length away, apps like Tinder have turned online

---

[128] The Daily Mail "Sex and the City writer Candace Bushnell, 60, admits she regrets choosing a career over having children as she is now 'truly alone'" (July 28th 2019)

dating into a game. Swiping through potential matches is like looking for a new shirt or someplace to eat. With the new apps to find dates while sitting on your couch at home instead of having to leave the house to go anywhere like a party or even a bar, people feel if a relationship ends they can just pick up their phone and find another date later that day. And like ordering dinner, they scroll through the menu looking at photos and listed interests until they see something they like. It's almost strange now to ask a girl out on a date in person at school, the gym, or at the store.

These "dating" apps have cheapened relationships, leading to others being treated as if they're disposable.[129] They've caused a hedonistic hookup culture, and virtually ruined dating dynamics. Facebook and other social media sites make it easy for old classmates or just friends of friends to contact people privately. And prior to social media and cellphones, if a married person wanted to cheat on their spouse, they couldn't just have their lover call the home phone which sat in the kitchen because it could be picked up by the husband/wife or the kids and blow their cover.

But now everyone has their own phone, and if you don't have their number you can message them privately on Facebook or Instagram. These endless options combined with the moral decay of the culture has caused long term relationships (and especially marriage) to dramatically decline, which will have disastrous consequences further down the road. Facebook is

---

[129] New York Post "Inside the 'disposable' young American dating curse: 'On to the next one'" by Adriana Diaz (March 3rd 2022)

THE FAMILY

actually cited in one-third of divorces as a major contributing factor.[130] One survey of Tinder users found that two-thirds of them were already in a relationship, and many of them were even married.[131] But not all of them are looking to cheat or find someone else to dump their partner for. Many of them, it turns out, just crave the attention of others like those who obsess over their Instagram "likes." They're seeking validation through matches on Tinder, even though they never intend to actually meet up with anyone.[132]

Normalizing Porn

People once had to go to a seedy adult bookstore or gas station to buy a Playboy or Penthouse magazine, or find where their dad hid his pornos, but now endless porn is just a couple taps away and with few parents using restrictions on their children's tablets or smartphones, it's fully accessible for anyone of any age. For decades since the proliferation of Internet porn the only "safety" mechanism in place is a button users click to "verify" they're at least 18-years old, which is just a self-

---

[130] The Daily Mail "The Facebook divorces: Social network site is cited in 'a THIRD of splits'" by John Stevens (December 30th 2011)

[131] NBC News "Many on dating apps are already in relationships or aren't seeking actual dates, new study finds" by Angela Yang (July 13th 2023)

[132] Elite Daily "Most People Use Dating Apps For Validation — Is That Bad?" by Sarah Ellis (November 6th 2019)

certification with zero actual verification of their identity or age.[133]

Producing porn, whether explicit photos or a sex tape, used to be completely taboo and something that only extremely vulnerable girls from broken families or those with drug problems would succumb to, but slowly the Left has been normalizing that as well. In 2016 a new "social media" platform launched called OnlyFans which is basically Instagram for adult content where girls post sexually explicit photos and videos of themselves behind a paywall for their subscribers.

It's not even an underground or fringe platform. OnlyFans is so huge that it's now part of American pop culture and boasts three million "content creators" (virtual prostitutes).[134] And tabloids like *The New York Post* regularly publish stories about women who quit their respectable jobs as nurses or scientists, and then "get rich" from their OnlyFans accounts.[135]

In 2021 OnlyFans reluctantly announced they would no longer allow sexually explicit content (which is the only reason it exists) due to banks and credit card processors threatening to refuse to do business with them anymore after a letter signed by 100 members of Congress demanded the Department of Justice investigate them because the site "has become a major marketplace for buying and selling Child Sexual Abuse Material

---

[133] Numerous states have recently introduced laws to enforce ID verification in order to view porn sites, and there is an ongoing legal battle between those states and popular porn sites which are working to get courts to strike them down on "first amendment grounds."

[134] Business Insider "OnlyFans now has more than 3 million content creators and is a 'global business', says the CEO" by Jyoti Mann (May 13th 2023)

[135] The New York Post "Boston nurse Allie Rae left job for OnlyFans, now makes $200K a month" by Alex Mitchell (August 18th 2021)

(CSAM) in the United States, as well as soliciting sexual activity with minors."[136] But six days later, the credit card processors changed their mind about severing ties with the "social media" amateur porn giant, so it continues to thrive.[137]

YouPorn and Pornhub are other user generated porn platforms for explicit homemade videos, which have been used to host not just revenge porn (recorded or published without the consent of one of the participants) but also child sexual abuse material as well.[138] These platforms allow turn-key porn production anyone with just a webcam or cellphone can make, all from the comfort of their own bedroom.

In the past, girls would have to respond to postings from porn companies (usually disguised as "model agencies" looking for vulnerable girls to exploit) and travel to their studios because the infrastructure to produce and sell it was expensive and required a degree of technical skills to run a whole website and setup payment systems for credit cards, but OnlyFans and the other "do it yourself" porn platforms have made it just as easy as being an Instagram influencer or YouTuber.

Perhaps equally shocking is that Twitter also allows hard core porn to be posted and shared.[139] Elon Musk didn't ban it after he purchased the platform, and it's the only major social media platform that allows it. Facebook

---

[136] Vice "The Congresswoman Behind FOSTA Is Coming for OnlyFans" by Samantha Cole (August 12th 2021)

[137] The New York Times "OnlyFans Reverses Its Decision to Ban Explicit Content" by Jacob Bernstein (August 25th 2021)

[138] "Breitbart "Pornhub Under Fire for Allegedly Hosting Rape, Child Porn Videos" by John Nolte (February 10th 2020)

[139] Vice "Porn Is Still Allowed On Twitter" by Samantha Cole (November 3rd 2017)

and Instagram have strict policies against just nudity, but Twitter allows hard core porn. That alone should have caused it to be banned from the Apple and Android App Stores, which both have strict policies against sexually explicit content, but they mysteriously allow Twitter to operate as an X-rated app.

And while Democrats whine about "hate speech" on the platform (speech they hate), none of them have a problem with Twitter hosting countless hardcore pornographic videos and allowing accounts by porn stars to promote their explicit content.

Many people who get addicted to porn eventually need more hardcore videos in order to become aroused and get off, so they start watching fetish porn involving all kinds of perverted acts hoping to satisfy their growing sexual appetites. It literally rewires the pleasure sensors in their brain making them less aroused by "normal" porn, and sexual encounters with (actual) women.[140]

Many porn addicts experience what's called porn-induced erectile dysfunction when they try to have sex with a woman because the reward centers of their brain have been desensitized from watching so much porn, and like a drug addict who needs larger doses in order to get high, they have artificially caused a tolerance to build up in terms of sexual arousal.[141]

---

[140] The Telegraph "How porn is rewiring our brains" by Nisha Lilia Diu (November 15th 2013)

[141] Time "Porn and the Threat to Virility" by Belinda Luscomb (March 30th 2016)

Promoting Prostitution

Watching porn, and producing amateur "social media" porn isn't just being normalized in the New World Order through OnlyFans, PornHub, and YouPorn. An increasing number of Liberals are boldly supporting the normalization and legalization of *prostitution*. The slogan for their plan is "sex work is real work."[142] It used to be virtually impossible to find anyone except some odd libertarian eccentrics who would call for the legalization of prostitution, but now the idea is gaining popularity in Democrat circles as the next frontier of "civil rights."[143]

Congresswoman Alexandria Ocasio-Cortez has openly endorsed prostitution as a profession, parroting the mantra that "sex work is real work."[144] Ana Kasparian, cohost of *The Young Turks*—one of YouTube's most popular "news" channels, says, "it's totally fine if someone's working as a sex worker, something that we're supportive of," and equates prostitution "rights" with abortion rights.[145]

Teen Vogue magazine supports it too, with articles like "Why Sex Work is Real Work" which endorse prostitution to their young teen readers and recommends prostitution apps be created in the same vein of hookup apps, and says there shouldn't be any stigma attached to it.[146]

---

[142] The Age "Sex work is real, legitimate work and should be decriminalised" by Fiona Patten (July 1st 2021)

[143] ACLU.org "It's Time to Decriminalize Sex Work" (July 23rd 2023)

[144] Fox News "AOC responds 'Sex work is work,' to report of NYC paramedic posting racy photos for cash" by Dom Calicchio (December 15th 2020)

[145] The Young Turks YouTube channel "BOMBSHELL Lauren Boebert Report Exposes Serious Dirt Hidden In Her Past" (June 14th 2022) original URL here: https://www.youtube.com/watch?v=9OmfFqEqi6M

[146] Teen Vogue "Why Sex Work Is Real Work" by Dr. Tlaleng Mofokeng (April 26th 2019)

George Soros' Open Society Foundation (the largest private donor for Leftist causes) also endorses it, and recommends people call them "sex workers" rather than "prostitutes" because "The term 'sex worker' recognizes that sex work is work. Prostitution, on the other hand, has connotations of criminality and immorality."[147]

Their official stance on the issue is "Sex workers sell sexual services in order to earn a livelihood. The vast majority of sex workers choose to do sex work because it is the best option they have. Many sex workers struggle with poverty and destitution and have few other options for work. Others find that sex work offers better pay and more flexible working conditions than other jobs. And some pursue sex work to explore and express their sexuality."[148]

The TEDx forum also promotes it, giving a platform to a woman for her talk titled "Sex Work is Real Work" in 2022.[149] The ACLU also supports legalizing prostitution, posting their official stance on the issue in an article titled, "Sex Work is Real Work, and it's Time to Treat it That Way."[150]

The Democrat Supervisor of the City of San Francisco, Hillary Ronen, introduced a resolution in early 2023 urging state legislatures to decriminalize prostitution in California.[151] And it likely won't be long before this is

---

[147] OpenSocietyFoundations.org "Understanding Sex Work in an Open Society" (April 2019)

[148] Ibid.

[149] Tedx Talks YouTube channel "Sex work is real work, and it's here to stay | Samantha Sun | TEDxLSE" (August 19th 2022)

[150] ACLU.org "Sex Work is Real Work, and it's Time to Treat it That Way" (LaLa B Holston-Zannell (June 10th 2020)

[151] ABC 7 News "Resolution pushing to legalize sex work in CA introduced by SF supervisor" by Stephanie Sierra (February 14th 2023)

a major Democrat Party platform for future congressional or presidential candidates.

Abortion

The messaging behind supporting abortion went from "safe, legal, and rare" to women wearing t-shirts that read "I Had An Abortion" (sold by Planned Parenthood), and Hollywood actresses proudly proclaiming that without getting abortions when they were younger, they wouldn't have been able to become "stars."[152]

An organization calling itself "The Satanic Temple," which exists solely to hate and troll Christians, has wealthy financial backers and lawyers who help them file lawsuits against Christians—including challenging states which have restricted abortions, claiming that banning or restricting abortions violates their "right to practice their religion," and literally refers to the practice as a "Satanic abortion ritual."[153]

After the Supreme Court overturned Roe v. Wade in 2022, the ADL [Anti-Defamation League, a Leftist Jewish secular organization] issued a statement denouncing the decision and called abortion a "Jewish value."[154]

In my previous book, *Hollywood Propaganda: How TV, Movies, and Music Shape Our Culture*, I detail how Planned Parenthood has a special department dedicated to lobbying Hollywood studios and writers to encourage

---

[152] The Blaze "Hollywood actress Michelle Williams credits abortion for her success in Golden Globes speech" by Aaron Colen (January 6th 2020)

[153] The Washington Times "The Satanic Temple challenges Idaho, Indiana abortion bans" via Associated Press by Rebecca Boon (October 5th 2022)

[154] https://web.archive.org/web/20230122023959/https://twitter.com/ADL/status/1616514095892598812

them to insert pro-abortion messages in their projects.[155] For the last decade now they even host a special reception with hundreds of producers, directors, and writers to celebrate films and TV shows that promote abortion.[156]

In 2017, the dating app OkCupid partnered with Planned Parenthood to integrate a special profile badge on users' accounts to show if they "Stand with Planned Parenthood" as a way to signal to potential matches that if those women get pregnant, guys could be at ease knowing they would kill the baby so they wouldn't have to become fathers.[157]

When the new Roe v. Wade draft decision was leaked showing the Supreme Court had overruled the previous 1973 decision, a move that would now allow each state to decide whether they want to ban or restrict abortions, Democrats had an even bigger meltdown than usual. Congressman Eric Swalwell warned "The Republicans won't stop with banning abortion. They want to ban interracial marriage. Do you want to save that? Well, then you should probably vote."[158]

Chelsea Manning, (born Bradley Manning before "transitioning" into a "woman" who had been convicted of espionage after leaking classified documents to Wikileaks during the Obama administration), encouraged

---

[155] National Catholic Register "Planned Parenthood 'Secret Weapon' Script Doctor Feeds Abortion Line to Hollywood" by Lauretta Brown (September 23rd 2019)

[156] PlannedParenthood.org "Planned Parenthood Hosts 8th Annual Sex, Politics, Film, & TV Reception at Sundance Film Festival" Press Release (January 27th 2020)

[157] The New York Times "OkCupid Introduces Feature in Support of Abortion Rights" by Valeriya Safronova (September 20th 2021)

[158] https://twitter.com/RepSwalwell/status/1521340822989402113

"her" Twitter followers to buy guns and start training in teams to "protest" the court's decision.[159]

Chicago mayor Lori Lightfoot echoed this sentiment, saying, "To my friends in the LGBTQ+ community—the Supreme Court is coming for us next. This moment has to be a call to arms."[160] She and others were concerned the Supreme Court may also reverse their decision on gay "marriage," which hopefully they will someday, which is what she meant by they're "coming for us next."

After the stunning overturning of Reo v. Way *Vice News* published a story about how people can make "DIY abortion pills" from horse medication, saying "Misoprostol is relatively easy to acquire from veterinary sources, since in addition to medically inducing abortions, it's also used to treat ulcers in horses."[161] The fury unleashed by the Democrats over them not being able to kill babies at will, even up until just before the moment of birth makes them look no different than the ancient Canaanites who used to sacrifice their infants to Molech.

To add some perspective, it's a crime to damage or destroy the eggs of a Bald Eagle, and many other animals that are considered endangered species. It's a felony, in fact.[162] It's even a crime to harm various *plants* if they're located on designated Wetlands.[163] So quite literally,

---

[159] https://web.archive.org/web/20230906205340/https://twitter.com/xychelsea/status/1521567314373664768

[160] https://twitter.com/LoriLightfoot/status/1523844510735908864

[161] https://twitter.com/motherboard/status/1521511916912488448

[162] Under the Bald and Golden Eagle Protection Act of 1940 (16 U.S.C. 668-668d)

[163] Office of Legislative Research "Penalties for Disturbing Inland Wetlands" by Janet L. Kaminski Leduc, Senior Legislative Attorney (December 10th 2010)

plants and bird eggs are considered more precious to Liberals than unborn human babies.

The Masculinity Crisis In America

Aside from most women not knowing how to cook anymore (or sew, or properly keep a house clean), the majority of men are also failing in their social responsibilities. They don't know how to check or change the oil in their cars, or even know when it should be done. Lucky for them, newer cars have oil change monitors which notify drivers when it's time, but that's beside the point.

Many don't know how to use basic tools (and don't even own any). They wouldn't even know how to stop a squeaky kitchen cabinet (hint: you lubricate the hinge). This is because they're raised without fathers, so they never learn the basic knowledge or skills that have been a standard part of boy's lives since the beginning of time.

So many turn to online role models in hopes of learning what being a man is all about, but unfortunately many of those men are preying on the vulnerable and lost in order to take advantage of them financially and use them to boost their own out of control egos. Countless young men came to look up to Andrew Tate, a former kickboxer turned camgirl kingpin who made his fortune as a pornographer exploiting women (and the lonely gullible men who paid to interact with them online).[164]

He later hired a team of social media managers to promote his new scheme of teaching men "how to be men" through his "Hustlers University" online course—

---

[164] Mirror "Andrew Tate's webcam business employed 75 women and made him first million" by Harry Davies (December 30th 2022)

which also offers an affiliate program to entice his fans to promote it to others in hopes of making a commission and make some "easy money" themselves.[165]

He is an entertaining guy, like a heel in professional wrestling (the bad guy) playing the part to a T, always wearing sunglasses indoors like some rock star and posting pictures of himself standing in front of fancy cars or seated in a private jet with his shirt halfway unbuttoned, but Andrew Tate is a complete failure of a man. He is a misogynist in the truest sense, but a broken clock is right twice a day.

Sure, some of the cliché truisms he says are valid critiques of society, but the guy is a complete scumbag which was clear from the moment he first started going viral (due in large part to financially incentivising his young teenage fans to spam video clips of him across social media through an affiliate marketing scheme).[166]

It's amazing how so many Conservatives came to see him as some kind of inspiration and sage especially when there are so many clips of him and his brother in their past openly bragging about their camgirls cashing in on suckers.[167]

He'll never know what love is or be in a healthy relationship, let alone a marriage, because he has no conscience and his entire schtick is a money-making charade that compensates for the deep insecurities he is desperately trying to hide.

The so-called *manosphere,* which is the online community of pickup artists, men's rights activists, and

---

[165] Vice "The Dangerous Rise of Andrew Tate" documentary (January 13th 2023)

[166] Ibid.

[167] Mirror "Brothers make millions using webcam girls to sell 'sob' stories to desperate men" by Emer Scully (March 19th 2022)

hyper anti-feminists is full of phonies and frauds. A prime example being "Jack Murphy" (whose real name is John Goldman) who became a popular "guru" selling online courses claiming he'll teach guys how to be "real men" through his "Liminal Order." He was exposed as a literal cuck (who enjoyed having his wife getting screwed by other men) and sticking dildos up his butt (and talking about having sex with other men) while he was working as the male equivalent of a camgirl.[168]

Other desperate young men look to psychologist Jordan Peterson as a parasocial father figure who is best known for his advice to "clean up your room" which is a metaphor he uses to encourage people to take control of their own lives instead of allowing their environment to dictate their behavior. But despite him building his reputation as a self-help guru with all the answers to life's questions, he had a mental breakdown, becoming suicidal and addicted to benzodiazepines, an anti-anxiety drug, after he couldn't handle the pressures of his wife's kidney cancer diagnosis.[169] A psychologist who couldn't even handle his own problems and emotions, yet became a social media celebrity by dispensing what is seen as profound wisdom to everyone else on how to manage theirs.

Former Rolling Stone music critic Neil Strauss wrote an interesting book called *The Game: Penetrating the Secret Society of Pickup Artists* in 2005, back when online dating was still seen as something only for nerds and

---

[168] JackMurphyLive.com "Cultivating Erotic Energy from a Surprising Source" by Jack Murphy (October 9th 2015) archived here: https://archive.ph/2016.01.18-005825/http://jackmurphylive.com/cultivating-erotic-energy/

[169] New York Post "Jordan Peterson says he was suicidal, addicted to benzos" by Jesse O'Neill (January 31st 2021)

before dating apps, which detailed his experiences learning how to develop the courage (and strategies) to actually walk up to women in person and talk to them and get their numbers and schedule dates. Aside from being an autobiographical story about his own journey and personal transformation, the book also conveys how anyone can use the same techniques as he did to dramatically improve their dating life.

His sidekick "Mystery" (Eric Von Markovic) later published his own how-to guide titled *The Mystery Method*, which despite occasionally recommending using some unethical tactics (like lying or stretching the truth) actually does have the social science down pretty solid regarding early stage relationship dynamics, and contains proven strategies to start conversations with girls and get dates the old fashion way—in the real world—face to face, not through some app.

The biggest problem most single and lonely guys face is illustrated by NHL star Wayne Gretsky who used to say you miss 100% of the shots you don't take, and all strategies and tactics aside, if books like Neil Strauss's or Mystery's just convince young men to take action and actually ask out women they're interested in instead of being afraid of rejection, that alone would make a world of difference.

Learning the art of the pickup shouldn't be about bringing girls home from the bar and getting laid (which is actually a terrible idea). It's about developing the skills and confidence to ask the cute bank teller or receptionist at the dentist office for her number if you feel a connection instead of walking away and thinking "what if" on your way home.

While feminism (and all other forms of Liberalism) have thrown relationship dynamics out of balance, and created monsters, there are still plenty of girls who haven't fallen victim to the new culture, and will feel as though they've been rescued by Prince Charming from it once they find a guy whose interests, values, and goals align with their own.

American Symbols and Holidays

The enemy hates America, our past, our present, and everything we stand for—including symbols of our country like the Founding Fathers, the American flag, and even our national holidays. They're trying to change the meaning of America from a place of freedom, prosperity, and ingenuity, to one of exploitation, racism, and oppression in order to weaken the foundation of our society so it will collapse into a socialist / communist revolution.

This is the same strategy China's dictator Mao Zedong used by directing his student-led paramilitary group of faithful followers called the Red Guards to target the "Four Olds"—old customs, old culture, old habits, and old ideas; to have them eradicated so the "new" China could emerge with a bureaucratic superstructure controlling all education, art, and entertainment to facilitate the communist society he had envisioned.[170]

A country's holidays not only preserve its culture, but help each new generation carry on traditions, reflect back on important events, and enjoy the benefits a country has to offer. But now nearly every American holiday from fairly small ones that don't cause much of a celebration like Columbus Day, to big ones like Mother's Day, Father's Day, Easter, and Christmas are attacked every year by the ungrateful and spiteful rejects in our society—

---

[170] The Guardian "The Cultural Revolution: all you need to know about China's political convulsion" by Tom Phillips (May 10th 2016)

just like Mao Zedong's Red Guard did in China, hoping to eliminate patriotism in America and pride in our culture.

Many of them can't even enjoy Martin Luther King Day because it just reminds them of what White people did to the poor Blacks generations ago. I'll detail the attacks on Christmas and Easter in the next chapter because those are the two main targets of the American Marxists, but their list is long, so here's just a brief overview:

Independence Day

Every year when the 4th of July comes around now countless Black people and self-hating Whites cry about how Blacks weren't free when the Declaration of Independence was signed in 1776, so they can't be grateful for the freedoms they enjoy *today* as a result of living in this country. Their opposition to the holiday is like clockwork, and every year there are columns published in mainstream Liberal outlets about how the 4th of July makes Black people feel bad, and lists their grievances about why they shouldn't celebrate it.[171]

The holiday causes disgruntled "African" Americans to blame "the White man" for their own personal failures because of what happened to ancestors of theirs whose names they don't even know. Many dream of one day getting reparations, and think they're entitled to millions of dollars each.[172] Marxist Democrat Congresswoman Cori Bush from Missouri says "When they say that the

---

[171] Pennsylvania Capital-Star "Ten reasons why Black people shouldn't celebrate Independence Day" by Michael Coard (July 4th 2023)

[172] Associated Press "San Francisco board open to reparations with $5M payouts" by Jaine Har (March 15th 2023)

4th of July is about American Freedom, remember this: the freedom they're referring to is for white people. This land is stolen land and Black people still aren't free."[173]

Vox, a well-funded Leftist "news" website published an article titled "3 Reasons the American Revolution Was a Mistake," which argues that declaring independence from England was "a monumental mistake" and "We should be mourning the fact that we left the United Kingdom, not cheering it."[174]

It goes on to say that the United States should have remained a British colony because fewer Native Americans would have been oppressed and slavery would have supposedly ended sooner! They even claim our form of government would be better since Britain has a parliamentary system instead of our three branch separation of powers system. (Britain doesn't have a free speech amendment in their constitution, by the way, and instead have strict laws that criminalize "hate speech.")

Of course *Vox* couldn't conclude their screed without distain for White people, saying, "The main benefit of the revolution to colonists was that it gave more political power to America's white male minority."[175] It's always the White man's fault!

On the eve of Independence Day a few years ago, *The Washington Post* declared, "It's time to reconsider the global legacy of July 4th 1776," and denounced American independence saying it "helped further colonialism and

---

[173] Newsweek "Progressive Lawmakers Call Fourth of July Freedom for Whites: Blacks 'Still Aren't Free'" by Christina Zhao (July 4th 2021)

[174] Vox "3 Reasons the American Revolution Was a Mistake" by Dylan Matthews (July 3rd 2019)

[175] Ibid.

white supremacy."¹⁷⁶ The article goes on to lament how after freeing ourselves from the British empire we went on to build an empire of our own, acquiring Hawaii, Puerto Rico, the Philippines, and Guam—and that America reinforced "black and indigenous lives did not matter."¹⁷⁷

The Associated Press published a story on Independence Day in 2023 about how the word "patriot" is now often seen as a negative word because "Today, the word and its variants have morphed beyond the original meaning. It has become infused in political rhetoric and school curriculums, with varying definitions, while being appropriated by white nationalist groups."¹⁷⁸

That same year Ben and Jerry's, the over-priced "super premium" ice cream tweeted, "This 4th of July, it's high time we recognize that the US exists on stolen Indigenous land and commit to returning it," and linked to a petition demanding South Dakota give the land where Mount Rushmore stands back to the Sioux Indian tribes as part of the Land Back movement, which demands that "traditional territories" of Native American tribes be given back to them.¹⁷⁹

But it turns out that the Ben and Jerry's factory in South Burlington, Vermont sits on land that used to belong to the Abenaki tribe until British colonists arrived

---

[176] Washington Post "It is time to reconsider the global legacy of July 4, 1776" by Elizabeth Kolsky (July 3rd 2020)

[177] Ibid.

[178] Associated Press "In a polarized US, how to define a patriot increasingly depends on who's being asked" by Gary Fields, Margery Beck and Rebecca Boon (July 3rd 2023)

[179] Newsweek "Ben & Jerry's Suggests Returning 'Stolen Indigenous Land' in July 4 Message" by Maura Zurick (July 5th 2023)

in North America and forced them out.[180] They probably didn't even know that, and surely don't care, because if they meant what they said about supporting the Land Back movement they would turn the deed to their property over to the tribe.

Thanksgiving

Thanksgiving offends Liberals too because it reminds them of how the pilgrims "stole the land from Native Americans." But if someone is dumb enough to trade Manhattan for $24 worth of beads and trinkets (which is purportedly what the Native Americans did with the early settlers), then that's their loss. Many Liberals go so far as to say Thanksgiving is a celebration of "White imperialists" and the supposed "genocide" early settlers committed against the natives.[181]

But it's not just a few thousand crazies on Twitter. Such insane ideas have institutional support, and as usual, that of Hollywood celebrities.[182] Marxist media outlets now publish editorials from Native Americans every year about how Thanksgiving hurts their feelings because it reminds them of their ancestors' failings. The official YouTube Twitter account even posted an animated GIF showing a group of Native American girls tipping over a

---

[180] Newsweek "Abenaki Tribe Demand Ben & Jerry's Pay Reparations for 'Stolen' Land" by Aleks PLhillips (July 14th 2023)

[181] Pennsylvania Capital-Star "A reminder for your holiday table: Thanksgiving celebrates a racist genocide" by Michael Coard (November 22nd 2022)

[182] The Washington Times "'Big Bang Theory' star: Thanksgiving 'one of the grossest examples of genocide'" by Douglas Ernst (November 21st 2017)

dinner table filled with the traditional food in protest of the holiday.[183]

They also tweeted a link to a video by Francesca Ramsey (best known for complaining about White kids wearing certain Halloween costumes) titled "5 Comebacks For Your Racist Relative During The Holidays," because Leftists obsess over non-White people who suffer from inferiority complexes.[184] Previous years' tweets had been about helping non-profit organizations feed homeless and needy people on Thanksgiving, or "Thanksgiving Fun Facts," but that was before YouTube went full libtard.[185]

When the NFL's Washington Redskins were scheduled to play Thanksgiving once year, it added extra "insult" according to those triggered by holiday because they considered the team's very name to be a "racist slur."[186] A few years later the team's name was changed to the "Washington Football Team" (after 87-years as the Redskins) as an interim name, and then later to the Washington Commanders in order to appease critics who kept harping about how the team's name was "racist."

Marxist media outlets now even ring the alarm about the supposed "environment impact" of Thanksgiving, claiming that it increases greenhouse gas emissions and is

---

[183] Daily Caller "YouTube Wants To Make You Feel Bad for Celebrating Thanksgiving" by Scott Greer (November 23rd 2017) Original tweet located here: https://twitter.com/YouTube/status/933757068661665793

[184] https://twitter.com/YouTube/status/933787264131436551

[185] https://twitter.com/YouTube/status/6103267103

[186] Newsweek "Washington Redskins Use Thanksgiving Game To Promote Racial Slur, Native American Leaders Say" by Beatrice Dupuy (November 21st 2017)

contributing to climate change.[187] Vice "News" calculated what they claimed to be the CO2 emissions for preparing a turkey, writing, "cooking a typical Thanksgiving dinner contributes 80 pounds of CO2 to the planet's decline. That's equivalent to the carbon emissions of driving about 100 miles in your average American car."[188]

Others echo these concerns, including *The Huffington Post,* which published an article titled "The Environmental Impact Of Your Thanksgiving Dinner," and suggested "alternative ingredients that cause less environmental damage," going so far as to say people should consider *not serving turkey at all*, and use plant-based foods instead.[189]

Many of the White people who hate Thanksgiving are just spiteful since they grew up in dysfunctional families that probably don't even get together for the holiday, or if they did when they were growing up, it was an utter disaster and regretful. But instead of trying to break the cycle by starting their own family to restore the tradition, they just invent reasons to complain about the holiday and try to spoil everyone else's fun.

A new form of virtue signaling has arose in recent years called a "land acknowledgement," where people openly apologize to ancient Native American tribes which used to live in the region where an event is occurring. For example, at the Oscars in 2020 just before actor Taika Waititi presented the nominees for an award, he did a "land acknowledgement" by saying that the Tongva, the

---

[187] Vice "How Much Environmental Damage Did Your Thanksgiving Dinner Do?" by Ashley P. Taylor (November 8th 2017)

[188] Ibid.

[189] Huffington Post "The Environmental Impact Of Your Thanksgiving Dinner" by Alexandra Emanuelli (November 5th 2019)

Tataviam, and the Chumash used to live in the vicinity where the Oscars ceremony was being held.[190] It's a way of apologizing for White people modernizing the region, or as the Leftists say, "colonizing" it.

Such a ridiculous practice isn't just done by Hollywood actors who often embrace fringe causes hoping to look like they're helping ordinary people. To kick off an online Microsoft training seminar in 2021, the hosts began by saying, "We need to acknowledge that the land where the Microsoft campus is situated was traditionally occupied by the Sammamish, Duwamish, Snoqualmie, Suquamish, Muckleshoot, Snohomish, Tulalip, and other coast-Salish peoples since time immemorial. A people who are still continuing to honor and bring to light their amazing heritage."[191]

These ridiculous land acknowledgements even occur before some city council meetings and board of supervisors meetings.[192] A growing number of schools even hold land acknowledgment ceremonies, and some have put up plaques inside of schools as a form of their "acknowledgement" as well.[193]

The idiots who engage in such a ridiculous practice never mention that Native American tribes were at war with each other, long before the European settlers arrived in North America (not to mention they committed genocide against each other as well, and enslaved those

---

[190] The Hill "The Oscars acknowledged the indigenous land Hollywood sits on" by Anagha Srikanth (February 10th 2020)

[191] ABC 4 News "Annual Microsoft Ignite conference entices criticism over 'woke' introductions" by Ann Dailey Moreno (November 5th 2021)

[192] SCV News "Supervisors Make History with Their First Native American Land Acknowledgement" (December 7th 2022)

[193] NBC 15 WMTV "Madison School District holds land acknowledgement ceremony for Ho-Chunk tribe" by Kylie Jacobs (April 25th 2022)

from other tribes who survived).[194] But as usual, all the problems other ethnic groups have experienced throughout all of history, are blamed on White people.

Halloween

"Progressives" can barely enjoy Halloween anymore either because some stores might sell costumes the snowflakes think are "cultural appropriation." These same people don't have a problem letting kids dress up as psychotic mass murderers for Halloween, but if they happen to wear a rasta wig or sombrero, then it's the end of the world.

Megyn Kelly was famously fired from hosting NBC's flagship show *Today* after saying she didn't see a problem with White kids dressing up as characters that happen to be of another race.[195] The following day she even issued a dramatic apology on air, starting the show by saying how sorry she was—how she was "wrong," and it's "not okay." But that was the last time she would appear on the show.[196] From the media outrage over her comments, you would have thought she shouted out the n-word on air, but she just dismissed the insane controversy over White kids wearing certain Halloween costumes.

Disney pulled a costume for their animated film *Moana* after morons complained that it was "brownface"

---

[194] Smithsonian Magazine "How Native American Slaveholders Complicate the Trail of Tears Narrative" by Ryan P. Smith (March 6th 2018)

[195] CNN "Megyn Kelly apologizes for defending blackface Halloween costumes" by Tom Kludt (October 25th 2018)

[196] USA Today "Megyn Kelly will not return to NBC's 'Today' show following blackface controversy" by Jayme Deerwester (October 26th 2018)

and "cultural appropriation," thus offensive.[197] In the film, a demigod named Maui (voiced by Dwayne "The Rock" Johnson) is a Pacific Islander, with his arms covered in tattoos and he wears a grass skirt. But if that style of clothing is worn by a White kid who loves the movie, then that's "offensive" to Pacific Islanders. So the costume was recalled and banned.[198]

There were even complaints about White kids wearing the Black Panther costume in some promotional pictures advertising the sale of the costume on Walmart and Target's websites.[199] Their grievances are obviously absurd, but imagine the backlash if White people complained that a Black kid was pictured modeling a Superman costume! The Democrats in Congress would pass a resolution denouncing the complaints and the Justice Department would launch a Civil Rights investigation!

Mother's Day

Mother's Day is offensive to many Liberals too now since gay men who are raising children are confronted with the reality of the horrifying and unnatural environment they're forcing "their" children to grow up in, so there's a push to make Mother's Day "more inclusive" for LGBTQ people.[200]

---

[197] USA Today "Disney pulls offensive 'Moana' Halloween costume" via Associated Press (September 21st 2016)

[198] Time "Disney Stops Selling Controversial *Moana* Halloween Costume" by Melissa Chan (September 22nd 2016)

[199] All of the pictures featuring White kids wearing the costume on Target's website were then removed, and replaced by black boys for Halloween 2018

[200] Fortune "Making Mother's Day More Inclusive" by Ellen McGirt (May 10th 2018)

For Mother's Day 2022, clothing company Calvin Klein released an ad featuring a pregnant transgender "man" wearing only underwear with "his" belly sticking out where the poor unfortunate baby is growing.[201] The person's breasts were surgically removed, so the mother won't be able to properly feed the baby once it's born and will have to resort to formula instead of breastmilk.

Some transgender "women" are even posting photos online showing them "breastfeeding" babies, who they abuse by having the babies suck on their fake "breasts" despite not being able to produce any milk.[202]

There are now even transgender "women" who post TikTok videos about how they're deciding to celebrate Mother's Day despite actually having *fathered* children because now they identify as "women."[203]

The "Human Rights Campaign," a Leftist queer lobbying organization, has a guide for teachers called "Welcoming Schools" which encourages them to "develop more inclusive practices around celebrating Mother's and Father's Days" and recommends a book called *Stella Brings the Family* which is about a girl whose school is having a Mother's Day celebration but Stella has "two daddies" and doesn't have a mom to invite to the party so the book is designed to "help" kids

---

[201] KATV ABC 7 "Calvin Klein slammed for 'pregnant man' in Mother's Day commercial" by Zachary Rodgers (May 13th 2022)

[202] The Daily Mail "Gender-critical campaigners slam trans woman activist for using a child as an 'identity prop' after she posted image of her breastfeeding on a bus" (July 7th 2023)

[203] Toronto Star "How these transgender moms are celebrating Mother's Day" by Tessa Vikander (May 10th 2018)

"acquire the vocabulary to talk about LGBTQ families."[204]

An increasing number of schools are just canceling Mother's Day celebrations altogether. The madness seems to have started in 2017 and has since spread.[205] *The Washington Post* complains, "For some gay parents, Mother's Day (or Father's Day) is awkward" and features numerous gay couples who call them "Hallmark holidays" that "don't merit a celebration."[206]

GLAAD—the Gay and Lesbian Alliance Against Defamation lobbying organization, has a "Mother's Day Resource Kit" that provides "potential story ideas and suggestions on how to make coverage of Mother's Day more inclusive." Some of their recommendations are to, "Include a lesbian or transgender mother as part of a composite profile of how mothers in the region enjoy the holiday. Profile a lesbian couple's journey to adopt (either locally or abroad). Report on the legal difficulties faced by lesbian couples as they try to become parents. Profile a mother who has come out as lesbian, bisexual or transgender to her children, spouse/partner or extended family. Profile a child who has come out to his or her mother or grandmother."[207]

---

[204] Welcoming Schools: a Project of the Human Rights Campaign Foundation "Diverse Families on Mother's & Father's Day" document posted on their website here: https://hrc-prod-requests.s3-us-west-2.amazonaws.com/welcoming-schools/documents/WS_Lesson_Diverse_Families_on_Mothers_and_Fathers_Days.pdf

[205] KREM CBS 2 "School cancels Mother's Day in effort to celebrate diversity" by Joshua Staab (May 8th 2017)

[206] Washington Post "For some gay parents, Mother's Day (or Father's Day) is awkward" by Gail Cornwall (May 8th 2017)

[207] Glaad.org "Mother's Day Resource Kid" posted here https://glaad.org/publications/mothersdaykit

In 2018 *Fortune* magazine published an article titled "Making Mother's Day More Inclusive" and shows two gay Black men with a baby. It starts off saying "Mother's Day can be fraught for many reasons for many people," and repeats the same Leftist complaints about how gay men raising children together are uncomfortable with the holiday.[208] Some lunatics are even upset that Mother's Day leaves out women who don't have children and say it should be a day "for all women" and "there's no need to feel left out" if a woman never had children![209]

The British Medical Association, the equivalent of the American Medical Association in the United States, issued new "guidance" in 2017 recommending doctors and other health care providers not refer to pregnant women as pregnant *women*, and instead call them *pregnant people*.[210] While laughable at the time, the insane trend has caught on and now the Center for Disease Control in the United States,[211] Planned Parenthood, and other organizations recommend using the same term.[212] That or *birthing person*.[213]

---

[208] Fortune "Making Mother's Day More Inclusive" by Ellen McGirt (May 10th 2018)

[209] Daily Mail "Mother's Day is for all women" by Elizabeth Wilson (March 16th 2007)

[210] The Telegraph "Don't call pregnant women 'expectant mothers' as it might offend transgender people, BMA says" by Laura Donnelly (January 29th 2017)

[211] Media Research Center "Gender Scrub: CDC Changes Flu Guidance Terms From 'Pregnant Women' To 'Pregnant People'" by Tierin-Rose Mandelburg (November 1st 2022)

[212] CNN "The language we use to talk about pregnancy and abortion is changing. But not everyone welcomes the shift" by Harmeet Kaur (September 4th 2022)

[213] Newsweek "Biden Admin Replaces 'Mothers' With 'Birthing People' in Maternal Health Guidance" by Benjamin Fearnow (June 7th 2021)

During her confirmation hearing after being appointed as Supreme Court nominee, Ketanji Brown Jackson (who was chosen by Joe Biden simply because she's a Black woman) couldn't even provide a definition for the word *woman* when asked by Republican Senator Marsha Blackburn. "I'm not a biologist," she responded, which proved the point the senator was trying to raise by asking it.[214]

Liberals are afraid to say what a woman is now, because they don't want to ostracize transgender people who "identify" as women. And admitting that trans "women" aren't real women would derail the Marxists' gender bending agenda, so when asked the basic question "what is a woman?" they freeze up, and avoid answering the question, or provide a nonsense response like "a woman is whoever identifies as a woman."

Father's Day

Father's Day reinforces *cisgender heteronormative patriarch stereotypes* of men controlling the grill and so Liberals are upset about that, and they also feel it's offensive to single mothers whose children don't have fathers in their lives—and lesbian couples who have adopted children or purchased sperm from a sperm bank and had themselves artificially inseminated since their poor children don't have a dad.

And since most Black kids don't have fathers in their homes and Father's Day is an uncomfortable reminder of

---

[214] The New York Times "A demand to define 'woman' injects gender politics into Jackson's confirmation hearings." by Jonathan Weisman (March 23rd 2022)

that fact, the holiday is also deemed racially insensitive.[215] The average Black woman has children by two or three different fathers (*baby daddies* as they call them), none of whom they've ever married and on average none of them even live in the home with her and the children.[216] Another uncomfortable fact about the Black community you're not supposed to mention, which has also been the inspiration for some very politically incorrect jokes you're not supposed to tell either.

The Huffington Post published an article titled "Three Reasons Why Father's Day Should Be Abolished," and complains that dads are often the "secondary parent" because the mother is usually the primary caregiver since men typically work longer hours while moms are in charge of childcare and housework, and even calls the holiday a waste of money.[217]

Others who have no children, along with those whose fathers were abusive or absent, are also upset about Father's Day, prompting *The Chicago Tribune* to ask "Is Father's Day Outdated?" They say since the holiday triggers bad memories for some it should be abolished. Others have been calling for it be renamed "Special Person's Day" instead.[218] For these same reasons some

---

[215] Reuters "Father absence "decimates" black community in U.S" by Joyce Kelly (June 14th 2007)

[216] Forbes "Multiple Baby Daddies Can Make You Poor" by Kiri Blakeley (April 1st 2011)

[217] Huffington Post "Three Reasons Why Father's Day Should Be Abolished" by Jeremy Davies (June 14th 2017)

[218] The Independant "'Special Person's Day': Campaign to change Father's Day sparks outrage" by Sarah Young (August 29th 2017)

schools are now doing away with acknowledging the holiday at all.[219]

LGBTQ groups are upset that Father's Day is about normal men (straight men) and not homosexuals or transgenders, so GLAAD published a "Father's Day Resource Kit" (just like they did for Mother's Day) to encourage their allies in the media to make sure they include queers in their Father's Day news coverage and television show plots.[220]

"The lives of gay, bisexual and transgender parents and their families are often absent in Father's Day coverage since print and electronic press reports often focus solely on straight parents," they complain. Their "resource kit" even provides story ideas and other suggestions on how to make Father's Day more "inclusive" which are just as ridiculous as you could imagine.[221]

Valentine's Day

Valentine's Day upsets these same crazies too because it "perpetuates heteronormativity," a Leftist buzzword meaning that heterosexual couples are the norm (which of course they are) but that upsets them because all the commercials throughout the entire history of the holiday (until the queer Pride pandemic) featured couples consisting of a man and a woman celebrating the holiday and that reminds LGBTQ people that they are a fringe

---

[219] Good Housekeeping "School Cancels Mother's and Father's Day Activities and Some Parents Are Furious" by Sarah Schreiber (May 9th 2017)

[220] Glaad.org "Father's Day Resource Kit" posted on their website here: https://glaad.org/publications/fathersdaykit/

[221] Ibid.

minority (despite efforts to artificially amplify their representation in media).

It used to be just feminists who get upset about Valentine's Day because they're perpetually single and have nobody special in their lives to celebrate it with, so they lash out every February 14th when it comes around, publishing a slew of blogs, YouTube videos and TikToks complaining about it. But now with the Marxist's cultural insurrection underway, Valentine's Day is under attack for not being gay.

The ADL complains, "Be aware of how some holidays can reinforce restrictive social norms around gender identity and sexual orientation. For example, as students get older and Valentine's Day becomes more focused on romantic relationships and not friendships, celebrations may reinforce heterosexist notions that all relationships are between a boy and a girl and marginalize LGBTQ youth, or youth who simply are not interested in romantic relationships."[222]

University student newspapers are usually the most upset about Valentine's Day being about normal (heterosexual) couples, and every year publish articles spewing their heterophobia. The University of Utah's paper complains, "For individuals that identify outside of the gender binary, this heteronormative depiction of Valentine's Day presents other problems—not only does it exclude any potential relationships they might be involved in, it also dismisses the existence of their gender identity altogether."[223]

---

[222] ADL.org "Considerations for Inclusive Holidays and Observance" (May 21st 2014) posted here https://www.adl.org/resources/tools-and-strategies/considerations-inclusive-holidays-and-observances

[223] The Daily Utah Chronicle "Heteronormative Valentine's Day and its Effects on Students at the U" by Emily Anderson (February 13th 2017)

One student interviewed for the article said, "I perceive Valentine's Day as a huge piece of heteronormativity. While having good intentions, it really pushes the norm of cis[gender] male and cis[gender] female romance. For instance, pretty much every movie and TV show's portrayal of this day is between a cis[gender] man and cis[gender] woman. It makes me a little upset, especially because I feel like my ideal relationship is never shown onscreen."[224]

"Cisgender" if you don't know, is a cultural marxist term meaning someone whose genitalia matches their gender identity, or as they say, whose gender identity "corresponds" to the sex they were "assigned at birth." *Cis* is Latin for "on this side of," which is the opposite of *trans* which means "across from" or "on the other side of." Or as comedian Norm MacDonald used to say, "It's a way of marginalizing a normal person."

The student newspaper at California State University, San Marcos whines that, "The holiday perpetuates a fixed depiction of couples and romance as primarily held between a man and a woman," and blames "the media" for heterosexual relationships being viewed as the norm.[225]

Some elementary schools are canceling Valentine's Day celebrations which involve arts and crafts and forbid students from handing out Valentine's cards to their classmates. One such school sent out a notice to parents saying, "While we acknowledge the celebration of Valentine's, and are mindful of the popularity of that day, it is not celebrated by all students/families in our

---

[224] Ibid.

[225] The Cougar Chronicle "Heteronormative Valentine's depictions marginalize LGBTQIA+ community" by Samantha Carrillo (February 7th 2018)

community. It is essential that all students feel welcomed and reflected at school, and that our celebrations do not negatively impact our families and students."[226] It also explicitly told parents not to let their children bring any Valentine's cards or candy.

The principal of an elementary school in Saint Paul, Minnesota who canceled Valentine's Day celebrations said he was concerned that kids doing arts and crafts or exchanging Valentine's Day cards may "suppress" some students![227] Elementary schools in an East Lansing, Michigan district also canceled Valentine's Day celebrations, saying they can cause "unintended consequences" such as "drama and teasing."[228]

A Rutgers University psychology professor is urging *all schools* to cancel Valentine's Day celebrations because it's about "romantic love" and so it "does not have a place in school."[229]

It Never Ends

Columbus Day is another annual reminder of how the early European settlers treated the natives which sparks the usual rounds of complaints, so progressives have been pushing to not just cancel Columbus Day, but to replace it

---

[226] CTV News "Kitchener school cancels Valentine's Day in the classroom" by Carmen Wong (January 31st 2023)

[227] Star Tribune "St. Paul school kisses Valentine's Day, other 'dominant holidays,' goodbye" by Paul Walsh (January 29th 2016)

[228] Lansing State Journal "East Lansing schools call off Halloween, Valentine's Day celebrations over equity concerns" by Mark Johnson (October 14th 2021)

[229] SheKnows.com "Is It Time for Elementary Schools to Stop Celebrating Valentine's Day?" by Randi Mazzella (February 6th 2018)

with a new holiday they call Indigenous Peoples' Day to honor and commemorate Native Americans.

In 1992 the city of Berkeley, California symbolically renamed Columbus Day to Indigenous Peoples' Day and nobody really noticed or took the move seriously and just wrote off the idea as coming from a bunch of hippies, but as the years went on more and more cities began officially replacing Columbus Day with Indigenous Peoples' Day.[230] In 2017 the Los Angeles city council voted to do so, becoming the largest city to make the change.[231]

Two years later Washington D.C.'s city council did the same thing.[232] And as president, Joe Biden issued a presidential proclamation in 2021 declaring October 10th (Columbus Day) to be "Indigenous Peoples' Day."[233] Now on the iPhone calendar it marks the "holiday" automatically as such, and the notification cannot be removed.[234]

At some point they'll probably fully cancel Columbus Day, purging it from all calendars like the toppled confederate monuments were removed from public display and the confederate flag banned, claiming it's disgraceful to commemorate the "violent colonization in the Western hemisphere."

---

[230] The Daily Californian "Berkeley celebrates 25 years of Indigenous Peoples' Day" (October 8th 2017)

[231] CBC Los Angeles "Los Angeles Marks Third Official Celebration Of Indigenous Peoples Day" (October 12th 2020)

[232] CNN "DC Council votes to replace Columbus Day with Indigenous Peoples' Day " by Alaa Elassar (October 9th 2019)

[233] Associated Press "Biden is first president to mark Indigenous Peoples' Day" by Zeke Miller and Ellen Knickmeyer (October 8th 2021)

[234] Media Research Center "Latest Apple Update Deletes Easter From iPhone Calendar, But Leaves 'Indigenous Peoples Day'" by Brittany M Hughes (February 19th 2018)

But if the European settlers hadn't colonized North America, instituted our form of government—bringing with it law and order, and designed and built the infrastructure of modern society; then the Native American tribes may still be living in tepees, warring with each other, and doing rain dances hoping to get their crops to grow so they wouldn't starve instead of having the luxuries of grocery stores and other modern conveniences.

And without the Europeans establishing colonies here, the African Americans wouldn't be Americans at all, because if their ancestors weren't brought here as slaves then they would have been born and raised in any number of the third world countries in Africa, many living in dirt huts and walking around barefoot not owning any shoes. But because of what their ancestors went through, they get to enjoy everything that the United States has to offer.

American Monuments

When there's a revolution in a country, the old flag and monuments are torn down and replaced by symbols of the new regime. There is a famous video of a gigantic Saddam Hussein statue being toppled during the War in Iraq showing Iraqis celebrating and hitting it with their shoes once it fell to the ground (a sign of disrespect in their culture).[235] And in the 21st century United States, countless monuments were toppled in a similar fashion as the attempted Marxist revolution began heating up.[236]

---

[235] Los Angeles Times "Army Stage-Managed Fall of Hussein Statue" by David Zucchino (July 3rd 2004)

[236] CNN "Protesters tear down statues from Confederate monuments in DC and North Carolina" by Jennifer Henderson (June 20th 2020)

Since Leftists hate America's history, culture, and customs, it only makes sense that they would focus that hatred on American monuments. But not just the old "racist" Confederate monuments, which have stood in the South for a hundred and fifty years. They also want statues of the Founding Fathers torn down, and ultimately the American flag that flies on top of the U.S. Capitol building.

During a discussion about numerous Confederate monuments being torn down across the South on CNN, one of their contributors named Angela Rye called for statues of George Washington to be torn down too because he owned slaves, saying, "To me, I don't care if it's a George Washington statue or Thomas Jefferson, they all need to come down."[237] Race-baiting grifter extraordinaire Al Sharpton agrees.[238] And so did the city council of New York, which had a statue of Thomas Jefferson removed from City Hall which had stood there for over 100 years.[239] Later they considered removing more statues and artwork of Jefferson, and those honoring George Washington too.[240]

A few years before the height of the anti-Confederate monument hysteria (which succeeded in removing nearly 100 monuments across the South in the year 2020 alone), protesters in Atlanta vandalized a Peace Monument that

---

[237] RealClear Politics "CNN's Angela Rye: Washington, Jefferson Statues 'Need To Come Down'" by Ian Schwartz (August 18th 2017)

[238] National Review "Al Sharpton Puts Jefferson Memorial on Notice" by Kyle Smith (August 16th 2017)

[239] CNN "A statue of Thomas Jefferson is removed from New York City Hall after 187 year" by Sara Smart (November 24th 2021)

[240] New York Post "NYC Council advances bid that could yank monuments honoring Washington, Jefferson, Columbus" by Carl Campanile (September 18th 2023)

was set up in 1911 to symbolize reconciliation between the North and the South after the Civil War, thinking it was a Confederate statue of some kind.[241] A statue of Abraham Lincoln (who freed the slaves) was vandalized in Chicago with graffiti saying "colonizer."[242]

Mount Rushmore is also a target of frequent protesters and even threats to blow it up.[243] *Vice News* wrote an article originally titled "It's Time To Blow Up Mount Rushmore" and then quietly changed it to "Let's Get Rid of Mount Rushmore" after controversy grew about them trying to incite violence.[244]

Speaker of the House Nancy Pelosi responded to the rash of vandalism and angry mobs toppling confederate monuments in the wake of the George Floyd riots by saying, "If the community doesn't want the statue there, the statue shouldn't be there," adding, "I don't care that much about statues."[245] One reporter pressed her, asking "Respectfully, shouldn't that be done by a commission, or the city council—not a mob, in the middle of the night throwing it into the harbor?" to which she responded, "People will do what they do," and shrugged off the mobs as if what they were doing was no big deal.[246]

---

[241] Breitbart "Protesters in Atlanta Vandalize 'Peace Monument' After Mistaking It for Confederate Symbol" by Penny Starr (August 16th 2017)

[242] Chicago Tribune "Lincoln statue in Chicago's Edgewater park defaced" by Robert McCoppin (November 25th 2022)

[243] WKYC "'Not on my watch.' South Dakota Governor vows to protect Mount Rushmore as statues, monuments across US are torn down" by Erin McHugh (June 24th 2020)

[244] Newsbusters "Vice: Let's Blow Up Mount Rushmore" by Corinne Weaver (August 17th 2017)

[245] Newsweek "Pelosi Draws Republican Fire Over Dismissive Columbus Statue Comments" by Jacob Jarvis (July 10th 2020)

[246] Ibid.

Interestingly, George Orwell foresaw this kind of cultural erasure in his novel *Nineteen Eighty-Four*, writing, "One could not learn history from architecture any more than one could learn it from books. Statues, inscriptions, memorial stones, the names of streets—anything that might throw light upon the past had been systematically altered."[247]

They're engaged in a cultural genocide (not to be confused with an ethnic genocide, which is the deliberate killing of a large group of *people* from a particular nation or ethnic group with the purpose of eradicating it). *Cultural* genocide is defined as "acts and measures undertaken to destroy nations' or ethnic groups' culture through spiritual, national, and cultural destruction."[248] This is done through destroying cultural artifacts like books, artwork, and monuments (or even buildings).

Destruction of such artifacts is actually a violation of numerous international treaties which aim to protect such objects even in times of war. The Treaty on the Protection of Artistic and Scientific Institutions and Historic Monuments (also known as the Roerich Pact), which was signed by 21 different countries reads, "The historic monuments, museums, scientific, artistic, educational and cultural institutions shall be considered as neutral and as such respected and protected by belligerents. The same respect and protection shall be due to the personnel of the institutions mentioned above. The same respect and protection shall be accorded to the historic monuments,

---

[247] Goodreads.com "George Orwell Quotes"

[248] The Armenian Genocide Museum-Institute listed on their website home page here: http://www.genocide-museum.am/eng/cultural_genocide.php

museums, scientific, artistic, educational and cultural institutions in time of peace as well as in war."[249]

The National Anthem

For generations the National Anthem had been proudly played before nationally televised sporting events to signify how fortunate we are to live in the United States where citizens can enjoy such entertainment at their leisure, but that tradition too came under attack by anti-American forces within our own country.

That battle became part of pop culture in 2016 when the San Francisco 49ers quarterback Colin Kaepernick (who was adopted as a child by a nice White family since his Black biological mother and father abandoned him) started kneeling (or sitting) during the song instead of proudly standing with his hand over his heart in order to "protest" against supposed "police brutality" and to show solidarity with the Marxist Black Lives Matter movement.[250]

It sparked a national debate with the usual leaders of cultural decay—Hollywood celebrities and Liberal "journalists," siding with Kaepernick and painting him as some kind of civil rights hero. Then the tradition itself was attacked, with many calling for the song to stop being performed at sporting events all together.[251]

---

[249] Treaty on the Protection of Artistic and Scientific Institutions and Historic Monuments (Roerich Pact), 167 L.N.T.S. 289, entered into force August 26, 1935

[250] NFL.com "Colin Kaepernick explains why he sat during national anthem" by Steve Wyche (August 27th 2016).

[251] The Daily Caller "Jon Stewart Says Playing The National Anthem At Sporting Events Is A 'Weird Ritual'" by Katie Jerkovich (January 14th 2022)

Mark Cuban, owner of the Dallas Mavericks NBA team, quietly stopped playing the national anthem before games at his stadium in November 2020, but then resumed the tradition after pushback from the NBA three months later.[252]

New Orleans Saints quarterback Drew Brees *apologized* for saying that he would still stand during the National Anthem and thought people kneeling were disrespecting the flag.[253] The following day after his initial comments he posted a video on Instagram saying, "It breaks my heart to know the pain I have caused. I would like to apologize to my friends, teammates, the City of New Orleans, the Black community, NFL community and anyone I hurt with my comments yesterday. In speaking with some of you, it breaks my heart to know the pain I have caused."[254]

All that for just disagreeing with those who refused to respect the National Anthem at the games! To appease the crazies, the NFL started having a singer perform the "Black National Anthem" before games in the 2021 season, which is a song that some Black people feel "better represents" them.[255] Many disgruntled Black people think the National Anthem itself is racist, and it's a celebration of "White supremacy."[256]

---

[252] NPR "Dallas Mavericks To Resume Playing National Anthem Following Pushback From The NBA" by Bill Chappell (February 10th 2021)

[253] NFL.com "Drew Brees apologizes for comments on flag disrespect" (June 4th 2020)

[254] USA Today "Drew Brees apologizes for his comments on protesting during national anthem after backlash" by Scott Gleeson (June 4th 2020)

[255] New York Times "The N.F.L. will keep playing the Black national anthem before games." by Alanis Thames (September 12th 2021)

[256] The Root "Star-Spangled Bigotry: The Hidden Racist History of the National Anthem" by Jason Johnson (July 4th 2016)

The NAACP, the National Association for the Advance of Colored People, says it's one of the most racist songs in America, and have lobbied legislatures to remove it as a our national anthem.[257]

Democrat Congressman Cedric Richmond of Louisiana, who is the head of the "Congressional Black Caucus" (a group of Black congressmen who work to promote the interests of Black people over other Americans), supported a petition posted on Change.org calling for it to be abolished, saying it contains "racism, elitism, and even sexism."[258]

The American Flag

The American flag obviously symbolizes our great nation (or at least what a great nation we *used* to be), and since the Marxists hate everything about the United States —from our Founding Fathers, to the Bill of Rights, and every aspect of our culture, it should come as no surprise that the very sight of Old Glory sends them into a hissy fit as well.

A survey conducted in 2018 by the non-profit Foundation for Liberty and American Greatness found that 1 out of 5 millennials see the American flag as "a sign of intolerance and hatred."[259] In 2015, I posted a YouTube video showing me asking random people walking along a boardwalk by the beach in southern California if they would sign a petition to "ban" the

---

[257] ABC 7 Chicago "'Star-Spangled Banner' is racist, must be replaced, California NAACP says" by Jory Rand (November 8th 2017)

[258] Local 12 KUTV "Petition to remove 'Star-Spangled Banner' as anthem calls it 'racist, elitist, sexist'" by Adam Forgie (July 4th 2021)

[259] CNS News "Survey Shows 1 in 5 Millennials Sees U.S. Flag as 'Sign of Intolerance and Hatred'" by Emily Ward (December 3rd 2018)

American flag and issue a new flag featuring rainbow stripes for "diversity," and many people gladly supported the cause.[260] While it was slightly funny at the time, it was an early indicator of the declining patriotism in America and the growing hostility from within.

Nike canceled the rollout of a limited edition shoe that was scheduled to be released in 2019 to commemorate Independence Day because it featured the Betsy Ross flag, a flag that represents the original 13 colonies.[261] The cancellation came after complains by Colin Kaepernick who had become the face of Nike, landing a multi-million dollar contract with them the previous year.[262]

In the past, athletes like Michael Jordan and Andre Agassi were the face of the sneaker giant, and they never engaged in divisive political rhetoric or got involved in political causes. Instead, they strictly stuck to sports, knowing it would be bad for business to ostracize half of their fans by publicly aligning with either political party or anything having to do with politics at all. But today, promoting Liberal political causes is put before profits and most of corporate America is now in a competition with each other over who can best use their resources to promote "social justice."[263]

A group of students at a California high school were sent home after they came to class on Cinco de Mayo (the

---

[260] Mark Dice YouTube Channel "Liberals Sign Petition to Ban the American Flag" (June 29th 2015)

[261] New York Times "Nike Drops 'Betsy Ross Flag' Sneaker After Kaepernick Criticizes It" by Tiffany Hsu, Kevin Draper, Sandra E. Garcia, and Niraj Chokshi (July 2nd 2019)

[262] CNN "Here's How Much Colin Kaepernick Will Make in His Controversial New Ad Deal With Nike, According to Sports Experts" by Jennifer Calfas (September 4th 2018)

[263] Harvard Business Review "We're Entering the Age of Corporate Social Justice" by Lily Zheng (June 15th 2020)

Mexican holiday, meaning May 5th) wearing shirts with the American flag on them. The school considered their shirts to be "cultural disrespect" and forbid the students from wearing them.[264] They sued the school for violating their first amendment rights, but the Ninth Circuit court ruled *against* the students![265] Their lawyers wanted to take the case to the Supreme Court, but in 2015 (when it was still dominated by Liberals) they rejected even hearing the case![266]

The Sigma Chi fraternity at Stanford University was told by a school administrator that the American flag flying on their frat house could be seen as "offensive, intimidating, aggressive or alienating" to others.[267] In response, the frat bought an even larger flag the very next day and hung that one outside as a "silent but visible protest."[268] They didn't get a letter from the school because they were flying a Confederate flag or one with an expletive or offensive imagery. They were just flying an *American* flag!

Comedian Sarah Silverman, best known for being Jimmy Kimmel's ex-girlfriend from many years ago, said in her now defunct Hulu show that the American flag makes her "scared" and "shaken" because she's a Jew, and "nationalism is innately terrifying for Jews" because

---

[264] NBC Bay Area "Students Kicked Off Campus for Wearing American Flag Tees" by George Kiriyama (May 6th 2010)

[265] The Washington Post "Not safe to display American flag in American high school" by Eugene Volokh (February 24th 2014)

[266] Reuters "Supreme Court rejects free speech appeal over Cinco de Mayo school dispute" by Lawrence Hurley (March 30th 2015)

[267] The Stanford Review "Does the American Flag Offend You? Stanford Thinks It Might" by Antigone Xenopoulos (November 27th 2018)

[268] The Daily Caller "Stanford Frat Told Their American Flag Was 'Offensive' By Admin, Hangs Much Bigger Flag" by Benny Johnson (December 4th 2018)

the Nazis were nationalists, meaning they were highly dedicated to their own nation and it formed a central part of their identity.

And so Americans saying "We're number one" and posting a flag outside their home is too nationalistic for her, because it's "really like an old bed buddy of racism and xenophobia."[269] So, she's worried that some Americans (the patriotic ones) like America too much, and they remind her of Nazis because of their national pride.

MSNBC contributor and *New York Times* board member Mara Gay says she thinks it's "disturbing" that so many Donald Trump supporters fly the American flag because it sends the message that this is "their" country.[270] And now every year around the 4th of July numerous TikTok videos go viral of Black people complaining about seeing all the American flags everywhere, and insisting that anyone who has one flying outside their house must be "some racist ass White mother fuckers."[271]

The Coming Collapse of the United States?

The polarization between Red states and Blue states has never been more intense, aside from the Civil War era. The coronavirus lockdowns in 2020 and 2021 clearly showed the vast disagreement between different states regarding mandates for masks, vaccines, and forced school and business closures. And with such dramatically

---

[269] The Daily Caller "Sarah Silverman 'Scared' And 'Shaken' At Sight of American Flag" by Amber Athey (December 8th 2017)

[270] Fox News "NYT, MSNBC's Mara Gay: 'Disturbing' to see 'dozens of American flags' on trucks in Long Island" by Brandon Gillespie (June 8th 2021)

[271] https://twitter.com/libsoftiktok/status/1676385840866422790

different views regarding abortion, school curriculums, transgenderism, reparations, and other irreconcilable divides, many wonder at what point do we have a "national divorce" and split the country in two, or numerous different Republics.

When the Soviet Union collapsed in 1991, various regions broke off into independent republics. And the borders of many countries have changed throughout history as they rose and fell. So it's not unforeseeable that at some point in the future the United States could break apart into various regional republics. Nearly a dozen Conservative counties in Oregon have been trying to secede and be annexed into Idaho, in what's called the Greater Idaho Movement.[272]

For decades fringe voices have been calling for Texas to secede, but nobody took such people seriously; although now many have been wondering what possible solution is there to America's growing cultural divide other than a *national divorce?*

If the Supreme Court gets stacked with a Liberal majority and keeps passing draconian laws that businesses and teachers would have to legally follow or get sued into bankruptcy—like the "Equality Act" that Democrats keep hoping to cram through, which would force everyone to recognize dozens of different "genders" and allow anyone to declare themselves a man or a woman (or neither), and let them to participate in any activities which had been exclusive to that sex—including giving them access to locker rooms and showers (and competing on girls sports teams if someone self identifies as a "girl")—then what recourse would normal people have at that point?

---

[272] KGW8 "Bill to adjust Oregon and Idaho border introduced in Oregon Senate" by KGW Staff (January 11th 2023)

Businesses would lose their license and be shut down and sued by left-wing activists or the Justice Department for violating the "civil rights" of the gender benders. Employees would be fired if they refused to play along with a transgender customer's "identity," or if they referred to a co-worker as a he/him or a she/her if that person "identifies" as "gender non-binary."

What do we have in common with today's Democrats? Our moral values, political interests, and economic models are completely polar opposites. The old days of trying to find common ground on various issues or compromise on certain things in order to win other concessions are over.

The debates about what to do politically with the country are no longer about which group of people should get tax cuts or which communities should get federal funding for infrastructure or social welfare programs. They're much more personal, and the differences are so much more extreme than anyone in previous generations could have ever imagined.

Every day more Conservatives want nothing to do with Democrat policies (and vice versa). And not just economic policies, but policies in schools and the workplace. We even have drastically different views about what entertainment we want to watch since many long-established shows, sporting events, and even television commercials now bombard audiences with divisive political propaganda using once-great brand name products like Bud Light, Gillette, and Hershey's to normalize drag queens, celebrate gay "marriage," and promote transgenderism to children.

Our national debt is economically unsustainable, the lack of patriotism and open resentment and hatred for the United States from many of our own citizens is unprecedented. The floods of countless *millions* of illegal aliens who will never assimilate into American culture and instead are only diluting it by importing their own are forever changing the social landscape. Many historians (and ordinary Americans) see the warning signs flashing that we may be in the late stages of an empire—one that appears to be approaching a complete collapse.

Christianity and Churches

People who love sin always hate God because His existence and moral code is offensive to their debauchery, deception, and destructive lifestyles. And while many Liberals hate God, they specifically hate Christians because Christianity is very clear about God's principles. Instead of some generic and nebulous "god," Christians believe in a very specific Deity who has laid out very clear codes of conduct in the Bible. And this conduct is often directly opposed to the way Liberals live their lives.

Muslims mostly avoid scorn from the Left because they're seen as a non-White minority group and thus "oppressed." Liberals rarely if ever criticize Islam or Muslims, but love to espouse their hatred of Christians. Even fewer people criticize Judaism or Jews because they know they'll instantly be branded an "antisemite" and have their career destroyed.

You hear about how terrible "Islamophobia" and "antisemitism" is all the time, but never about *Christianphobia*. It's not even seen as a real word. But Christians are the most hated group of people in America, and contrary to popular belief, the most persecuted religious group in the world.[273] And not just in the Middle East or 3rd world countries in Africa, but also in Europe and even the United States.[274]

When Evangelist Franklin Graham, Billy Graham's son, planned to give a series of sermons around the UK,

---

[273] The Cato Institute "Christianity Is the World's Most Persecuted Religion, Confirms New Report" by Doug Bandow (March 7th 2022)

[274] Catholic News Agency "Nearly 1,000 hate crimes against Europe's Christians recorded in 2020" by Courtney Mares (November 16th 2021)

every venue he had booked (including in Birmingham, Liverpool, and Sheffield) canceled on him over what they said was his past "homophobic and Islamophobic" comments for preaching that homosexuality is "something to be repentant of, not something to be flaunted, praised or politicized," and for calling Islam a "wicked and evil" religion.[275]

The city council in San Antonio, Texas voted to ban Chick-fil-A from their new airport, claiming the restaurant has a "legacy of anti-LGBTQ behavior" because it's a Christian owned company and famously stays closed on Sundays, the Lord's Day.[276] Shortly after, another airport in Buffalo, New York did the same thing for the same reason.[277] *New York Magazine* then published an article celebrating the ban and listing a bunch of other restaurants that sell chicken sandwiches, recommending people eat there instead, so they're not "supporting our nation's hate mongers."[278]

The New Yorker (different from *New York Magazine*) complained that Chick-Fil-A was "infiltrating New York City" when they expanded there, and called it "creepy" that their corporate mission statement mentions God.[279]

---

[275] CNN "Evangelist preacher Franklin Graham planned a seven-city UK tour. All seven venues have dropped him" by Rob Picheta (February 6th 2020)

[276] WPTV "Chick-Fil-A banned at San Antonio airport due to alleged "legacy of anti-LGBTQ behavior'" (March 23rd 2019)

[277] USA Today "Chick-Fil-A won't be landing at Buffalo airport" by Jefferson Graham (April 2nd 2019)

[278] New York Magazine via Grub Street, their food and restaurant blog "The Great New York Chicken Sandwiches That Aren't From Chick-fil-A" by Chris Crowley (March 21st 2019)

[279] The New Yorker "Chick-fil-A's Creepy Infiltration of New York City" by Dan Piepenbring (April 13th 2018)

The Left hates Hobby Lobby, the mega arts and crafts store for the same reason. They've donated to various Christian causes supporting pro-life legislation and opposing gay "marriage."[280] And they're also closed on Sundays, an old tradition many businesses followed until around the 1980s. So Hobby Lobby is often the target of rabid Leftists online who would never even shop there anyway because they don't have an ounce of creativity in their brains so they would never even think of going to an arts and crafts store.

One of America's largest Christian legal defense groups, Alliance Defending Freedom, was banned from Amazon.com's charity fundraising program *Amazon Smile* after the Southern Poverty Law Center branded them a "hate group" because they defend businesses in court which are bullied by LGBTQ extremists trying to force them to engage in practices that violate their religious beliefs—like baking gay "wedding" cakes and catering gay "weddings."[281]

At the Jersey Shore, a large pier in the Ocean Grove community that has two sections, one which extends perpendicular to the main walkway near the end, has been interpreted to look like a Christian cross from the air, so it came under attack by LGBTQ extremists who complained it was a religious symbol.[282]

In one of Project Veritas' undercover investigations they caught an assistant principal in Connecticut on tape

---

[280] The Atlantic "How *Hobby Lobby* Split the Left and Set Back Gay Rights" by Molly Ball (July 20th 2014)

[281] The Daily Caller "Prominent Christian Legal Group Barred From Amazon Program While Openly Anti-Semitic Groups Remain" by Peter Hasson (May 5th 2018)

[282] New York Post "Holy war at Jersey Shore: Critics, supporters argue over cross-shaped Ocean Grove pier" by Dean Balsamini (August 27th 2022)

saying that he wouldn't hire Conservatives or Christians.[283] If someone said the same thing about not hiring Jews or Muslims it would have caused a national scandal with Democrats in Congress and the Justice Department launching an investigation, but this story went virtually unnoticed in the media.[284]

When a group of Christians were spotted hanging out in a coffee shop in Seattle by the owner (who is a queer) he started yelling at them to leave and said he would "fuck Christ in the ass," and then sexually harassed them by talking about how he has sex with his boyfriend.[285] As the group left he told them to tell their friends (other Christians) not to come there.[286]

The entire incident was captured on video and posted online but the business owner faced no consequences. If he went on a rant about Jews or Muslims and kicked them out, it would have been one of the top stories in the country and Jewish groups like the ADL would have ran him out of business by suing him for discrimination. But discriminating against a group of Christians is accepted. And sadly this isn't an isolated incident. It's a growing trend.

A man wearing a "Jesus Saves" shirt in the Mall of America in Minnesota was told by a security guard that he needed to take it off or leave because it was considered to

---

[283] WTNH "Tong opens civil rights investigation into Greenwich schools' hiring practices" by Olivia Lank and Jenn Brink (August 31st 2022)

[284] He was placed on leave and later resigned due to pressure from the local community. But a search on Google News shows zero articles from national news outlets, and only local ones like the Greenwich Free Press, the CT Examiner and Fox 61 WTIC-TV.

[285] The Daily Caller "Angry Gay Owner Unleashes on Christians Drinking Coffee in His Shop" by Amber Randall (October 6th 2017)

[286] Ibid.

be "soliciting," which is a violation of the mall's rules.[287] Just wearing a shirt promoting Jesus was deemed the same as if he was handing out flyers, which is what the ban on soliciting is actually in place to prevent—which is a reasonable policy and one that nearly every business has, but now just seeing the name Jesus on a t-shirt is offensive.

A Christian group in Virginia called the Family Foundation had their dinner reservations canceled after the owner learned that they oppose abortion and gay "marriage."[288] The owner proudly posted on his Instagram about it, and this sort of thing likely happens a lot more than people know because most of the time such discrimination isn't going to make the news since the business owners aren't going to brag about what they've done on social media.

Leftists tried to get the husband and wife team Chip and Joanna Gaines fired from their HGTV home renovation show in 2016 because they go to church and their church—like any real church that believes in the Bible—doesn't support gay "marriage."[289] But despite the controversy they kept their show and they'll be safe as long as they don't voice their opinions about gay "marriage" themselves.

Other Christian HGTV hosts, the Benham brothers (not to be confused with the "Property Brothers," a different pair of twin brothers on the network), were going to help people renovate their shabby homes in a

---

[287] The New York Post "Man ordered to remove 'Jesus is the only way' T-shirt at Mall of America" by Allie Griffin (January 16th 2023)

[288] CBS News "Restaurant denies Christian group service over its anti-abortion and LGBTQ stances" by Megan Cerullo (December 9th 2022)

[289] BuzzFeed "Chip And Joanna Gaines' Church Is Firmly Against Same-Sex Marriage" by Kate Aurthur (November 29th 2016)

new series until they got caught up in a news cycle that smeared them as "anti-gay" and "anti-choice extremists" because unlike Chip and Joanna Gaines who remain silent on the issue, the Benham Brothers denounced gay "marriage," so HGTV dropped them.[290]

After Donald Sterling, the owner of the Los Angeles Clippers NBA basketball team was caught on tape making "racist" remarks about his "girlfriend" (nearly *fifty* years his junior) having sex with Black guys, the league forced him to sell his team—and then some people began arguing that "homophobes" (i.e. Christians who don't support gay "marriage") shouldn't be allowed to own an NBA team either, and wanted to start a witch hunt to force them to sell their teams as well.[291]

Christian schools are even under attack by Liberal attorney generals who claim they're "discriminating" against LGBTQ people if they don't hire them.[292] Similar lawsuits and threats have been made against churches and pastors who refused to host same sex "weddings."[293]

CNN host John King insinuated that Mike Pence's wife should have her Secret Service protection revoked after she decided to volunteer as an art teacher a few days a week at a Christian school that doesn't allow gays or lesbians to be teachers, saying taxpayers were "subsidizing her life" even though every vice president

---

[290] CNN "Benham brothers lose HGTV show after 'anti-gay' remarks" by Lisa Respers (May 9th 2014)

[291] Newsbusters "Esquire's Pierce Asks: Why Doesn't NBA Punish Owners Who Oppose Gay Marriage?" by Paul Bremmer (April 30th 2014)

[292] The Washington Times "Washington state AG targets Christian university in LGBTQ employment probe" by Mark A. Kellner (August 3rd 2022)

[293] The Christian Institute "Gay couple to sue church over gay marriage opt-out" (August 1st 2013)

CHRISTIANITY AND CHURCHES

(and their wives) receive secret service protection.[294] After word first broke that Karen Pence would be teaching at the school, which like all (real) Christian schools, doesn't celebrate homosexuality like most government run public schools do, the hashtag #ExposeChristianSchools trended on Twitter from so many Liberals venting their hatred and Christianphobia.[295]

Singer Lady Gaga even chimed in on the issue, attacking Mike Pence during a concert—calling him the "Worst representation of what it means to be a Christian."[296] CNN then declared that "Christianity's future looks more like Lady Gaga than Mike Pence."[297] It's amazing that a bunch of people who hate Jesus are always telling Christians what Jesus would do. Because of the publicity over the controversy, another school in the district announced that they were now refusing to play any sports against the teams at the one Mrs. Pence taught at.[298]

A Catholic club at Georgetown University— America's oldest Catholic college, was labeled a "hate group" by LGBTQ activists on campus because they believe (correctly) that marriage is between a man and a

---

[294] Fox News "CNN's John King criticized for question about Karen Pence's Secret Service protection" by Brian Flood (January 18th 2019)

[295] The Daily Caller "CONSERVATIVE PUNDITS HIT BACK AGAINST TRENDING '#EXPOSECHRISTIANSCHOOLS'" by Jon Brown (January 20th 2019)

[296] Fox News "Lady Gaga calls Mike Pence the 'worst Christian' during concert over wife's job at anti-LGBTQ school" by Tyler McCarthy (January 21st 2019)

[297] CNN "Christianity's future looks more like Lady Gaga than Mike Pence" by Guthrie Graves-Fitzsimmons (January 24th 2019)

[298] Newsweek "School Refuses to Play Sports at Karen Pence's School Due to Its Anti-LGBTQ Policy" by Marie Perez (January 31st 2019)

woman, so a student senator filed a complaint with the school claiming the Catholic club's beliefs violated the school policy against "fostering hatred or intolerance."[299] Why a Catholic school would even allow LGBTQ students to attend is another question—one you're not supposed to ask. Shouldn't Catholic and Christian schools be allowed to expel students who openly celebrate what the Bible condemns?

Texas Christian University added a course called "Queer Art of Drag" to their curriculum in 2021 as an elective, where students create a "drag persona" and a "lip-sync portfolio" consisting of videos of them singing and dancing in drag. They also have to perform at the school's annual Night of Drag.[300] The fact that a supposed "Christian" college would allow and encourage drag shows is ridiculous, and having a course dedicated to it which gives students credit for it is blasphemous and the school should be forced to remove the word Christian from its name.

Angry queers tried to get the St. Louis Cardinals baseball team to cancel their annual Christian Day, which is a post-game event that has been held for over 30 years where fans who wish to remain in their seats after the game can enjoy speakers (often current or former Cardinals players) who talk about Jesus and the Christian life.[301]

A Marxist LGBTQ extremist group called Stonewall Militant Front organized hoping to shut down a mega

---

[299] Fox News "Georgetown student group targeted as 'hate group' for Catholic beliefs, could be sanctioned" by Caleb Parke (October 24th 2017)

[300] The Washington Times "Texas Christian University slammed for course on 'queer art of drag'" by Valerie Richardson (June 24th 2023)

[301] The Daily Caller "St. Louis Cardinals Resist LGBTQ Outcry Over 'Christian Day'" by Joshua Gill (June 16th 2017)

CHRISTIANITY AND CHURCHES

church in Austin, Texas and doxxed the pastor and his son causing them to be flooded with death threats because the church doesn't support gay "marriage."[302]

Conservative social media personality and former Congressional candidate Laura Loomer was banned from Twitter (under the leadership of Jack Dorsey) for "Islamophobic" comments about Democrat Congresswoman Ilhan Omar, where Loomer just pointed out that Islam oppresses homosexuals and women.[303] At the time she had over 250,000 followers.

But a simple search any day of the week brings up countless profanity-filled vicious and hateful anti-Christian tweets, but nobody is suspended or banned from social media for hate speech against Christians. (Loomer's account was restored four years later along with many others after Elon Musk bought the platform.)[304]

If you look at how much the morality of America has been degenerating, it appears as if we're living in the End Times and the prophecy of the Antichrist doesn't seem so far-fetched. We're seeing the open worship of Satan and not just the corny heavy metal band type of satanic antics, but a more sophisticated, organized, and funded form of satanism. It probably won't be much longer until an admitted satanist is elected to Congress (who will be a Democrat, no doubt).

After Democrats took control of the House of Representatives in the 2018 midterm election, they

---

[302] PJ Media "Militant Antifa Group Targets Christian Mega-Church in Austin; Doxes Pastor's Son" by Debra Heine (August 29th 2018)

[303] NBC News "Laura Loomer banned from Twitter after criticizing Ilhan Omar" by Linda Givetash (November 22nd 2018)

[304] Gizmodo "Elon Has Restored Nearly 12,000 Banned Twitter Accounts, Data Shows" by Kyle Barr (December 3rd 2022)

proposed removing the age-old "so help me God" line from the oath taken before key committee hearings.[305] Leftists want the *government* to be God, but our rights come from God, not the government.

In the New World Order, however, identity politics has become a new religion. Queerness and intersectionality is their faith. And it follows most of the same tenets as a religion, including having its own rituals, path to atonement, and excommunication of "heretics" who stray from the dogma.

Christmas Under Attack

The Left often mocks the War on Christmas *while they wage war*. It's a gaslighting tactic. And like most fronts in the culture war, the Left's attacks on Christmas started small and weren't seen as a threat that would have any effect, but they relentlessly persisted and the trickle turned into a flood. Now the "Satanic Temple"—an anti-Christian hate group, desecrates Christmas displays set up on public property by installing their own satanic-themed displays right next to them every December under threats of lawsuits against local and state governments if they're not allowed to, claiming that forbidding *their* "Christmas" displays would be a violation of their First Amendment.[306]

If they targeted Jewish holidays, the ADL would freak out and get them banned from social media, payment processors, and apps like Venmo and PayPal to cut off

---

[305] Fox News "Dems to strike 'so help you God' from oath taken in front of key House committee, draft shows" by Gregg Re (January 29th 2019)

[306] NPR "Satanic Sculpture Installed At Illinois Statehouse, Just In Time For The Holidays" by Laurel Wamsley (December 4th 2018)

their funding for being a "hate group," but it's acceptable to hate Christians and attempt to desecrate *our* holidays.

As part of the Marxist agenda aiming to destroy American culture, Leftists are working to undermine almost every national holiday, but since Christmas is a *Christian* holiday despite it being mostly secularized for generations, they are extremely upset about it because of its origins and underlying meaning. The name itself is derived from Christ's Mass, marking the celebration of the birth of Jesus Christ, but despite the holiday being more about Santa Claus than it is about celebrating the birth of Jesus these days, Leftists still hate the holiday because its Christian roots will never be forgotten.

It's not "inclusive" enough they say, and it's "offensive" to Jews, Muslims, and atheists (although mostly Jewish secularists who are Liberal atheist non-practicing Jews, also known as JINOs—*Jews in name only*, in the same vein as RINOs—Republican in name only, but you're not supposed to notice that, let alone say it out loud).

Many Jews throw around the word "antisemitism" more than Black people call others "racist." But the "antisemitism" label has much more power and often proves to be extremely damaging to people's careers if it's hurled at them.

An anti-Christian screed in *The Washington Post* starts off, "Please don't wish me a Merry Christmas…It's impolite and alienating to assume I follow your religion."[307] She complains "it is everywhere, for over a month…in a way no other holiday is—not even Easter. It is in every ad, in every window and doorway, and on

---

[307] Washington Post "Please don't wish me a Merry Christmas" by Julia Loffe (December 21st 2018)

everyone's lips." As a Jew, she says, it's "uncomfortable," "weird," "exhausting," and "makes me feel like a stranger in my own land."[308]

She goes on, "Despite the movies and the shopping, despite the Germanic decor, Christmas is still, at its core and by design, about the birth of Christ...Whenever I hear the name, I hear the 'Christ' in it," And she doesn't want to be "reminded a thousand times every winter."[309]

Most atheists enjoy Christmas, decorate their homes each year, buy presents for their loved ones and gather for Christmas dinner. They're not the ones complaining about Christmas (except for a few rare militant ones who are actually just satanists in disguise and hate everything about life). Buddhists aren't offended by being told "Merry Christmas." Neither are Hindus, Sikhs, or Zoroastrians.

An *NBC News* op-ed complained that, "December in America is a constant onslaught of Christmas culture: Every store gets decked out in Christmas finery and puts carols on full blast, seemingly believing that it encourages shopping. Television shows that normally avoid any discussion of anything approaching religious observance suddenly get into the spirit, devoting extra-long episodes to stories about the generous spirit inspired by this time of year."[310]

It went on to complain that "Ostensibly secular offices and schools are suddenly awash in Santas and sleighs and reindeer...It would be bad enough if this aggressive Christmas assault were purely the domain of the rabid

---

[308] Ibid.

[309] Ibid.

[310] NBC News "A 'War on Christmas'? Jews who leave the house in December would beg to differ" by Lux Alptraum (December 2nd 2018)

right wing…But the truth is that liberals—even ones who ostensibly embrace religious diversity—can be just as bad as their conservative counterparts when it comes to enforcing the oppressive Christmas climate."[311]

What she means is Christmas is "oppressive" to the Jews (which she herself is one, including the typical JINO preface "as a Jew" in her tirade). The report concluded that we should "take a long hard look at the way Christmas is used to send the message that America is a nation primarily for Christians."[312]

A former producer for Tucker Carlson's show on Fox News sued him and the network for what she claimed was a "hostile work environment" and said in her lawsuit she faced "antisemitism" because there were "noisy" Christmas decorations in the office, and when she complained about them, she was called a "grinch" and a "scrooge" by a coworker.[313] That's "antisemitism" she says!

But the War on Christmas gets much worse than a small but vocal demographic of non-Christians getting offended that the holiday is an intricate part of American culture. Santa is now seen as a symbol of White supremacy and White privilege by many Liberals, who say it makes Black children feel ostracized.[314] So there are increasing calls to depict Santa as a penguin instead of jolly old Saint Nicholas, to be more "inclusive."[315]

---

[311] Ibid.

[312] Ibid.

[313] Yahoo News "Tucker Carlson accused of promoting a hostile work environment" by Dylan Stableford (April 25th 2023)

[314] Huffington Post "I'm Dreaming Of A Less White Christmas For My Child of Color" by Heather Tirado Gilligan (December 14th 2020)

[315] Los Angeles Times "Santa's existential dilemma: To be white, black or a penguin?" by Robin Abcarian (December 12th 2013)

In a webinar put together by the Jewish ADL aimed at public school teachers, they complained about arts and crafts projects where teachers have students draw pictures of Santa Claus! One of the panelists admitted "Santa Claus is not considered to be a religious symbol, for Constitutional purposes, so asking students to draw a picture of something that's not deemed religious is Constitutional," but then he turned the conversation over to another panelist to explain "even though this is technically Constitutional, an assignment like this is none the less—problematic."[316] It's a problem to them that kids draw pictures of Santa in school!

In 2017 a children's book titled *Santa's Husband* was published which depicts Santa as gay and married to a Black man—a book written by a Jew who, of course, doesn't celebrate Christmas.[317] He just wrote it to denigrate the holiday. CNN praised the book when it was first released as a "fresh new twist" on the story of Santa Claus.[318]

After a political activist named Jacob Wohl recommended that Jews should assimilate into American Christian culture by putting up Christmas lights in December, he started trending on Twitter from so many people attacking him, calling him an "antisemite" (not realizing he himself is Jewish) and his comments even made headlines. Publications like *Newsweek* even twisted

---

[316] ADL.org webinar "Creating More Inclusive School Communities: The December Dilemma & Inclusive Calendar Practices" (November 18th 2021)

[317] Esquire "Santa's Husband' Is War-on-Christmas Trolling at Its Finest" by Jack Holmes (November 1st 2017)

[318] Newsbusters "CNN Hypes Children's Book Portraying Santa Claus As a Gay Man" by Brad Wilmouth (December 17th 2017)

CHRISTIANITY AND CHURCHES

his recommendation by reporting that he "demanded" Jews do it.[319]

After *The Santa Clauses* TV mini-series staring Tim Allen came out on the Disney+ streaming service, a Jewish film critic named Scott Weinberg complained that Tim Allen (who plays Santa) has a line where he laments, "Saying 'Merry Christmas to all' has suddenly become problematic," thus proving the character's point. "It just struck me as a truly weird thing to put in a kid's series," Weinberg said. "'Someone wants to stop us from saying Merry Christmas!' is not some random campaign. It's a low-key effort to vilify anyone who doesn't celebrate this holiday," he concluded.[320] After he was widely mocked on Twitter, he then cried that he was the victim of "antisemitism."[321]

Christmas represents everything we're trying to preserve in America: family, tradition, capitalism, and most importantly, Christ—all things the Left vehemently hates. And they deem it a "microagression" to even say *Merry Christmas* to someone.[322] Starting in 2017 the DC Metro (the government agency that oversees public transportation, such as busses and other rapid transit services) banned any Christmas ads on or in Washington DC busses that mention Jesus, God, or Christianity.[323] So

---

[319] Newsweek "Jacob Wohl Says Jews Must Have Christmas Decorations to Assimilate in U.S." by Ewan Palmer (November 5th 2021)

[320] Washington Examiner "SEE IT: Twitter rages against Tim Allen line in *The Santa Clause* reboot" by Jenny Goldsberry (November 17th 2022)

[321] https://twitter.com/scottEmovienerd/status/1593165239235022849

[322] New York Daily News "Is 'Merry Christmas' a microaggression? And more importantly, even if it is, whose business is it?" by Jonathan Zimmerman (December 19th 2016)

[323] Washington Examiner "DC Metro bans religion from Christmas ads, Catholics sue" by Paul Bedard (November 28th 2017)

no more "Jesus is the reason for the season" or "Keep Christ in Christmas" posters allowed.

And now each year numerous Universities across America struggle with allowing faculty and students to hold Christmas parties out of concerns they'll offend non-Christians who think the holiday is "oppressive." They post sections on their websites urging people to be "culturally sensitive" in December, and saying things like, "Displays that feature exclusively single-themed decorations [meaning Christmas] may be well intentioned, but they can marginalize those who celebrate other religious and cultural beliefs during this season."[324]

Many schools suggest not doing a "Secret Santa" gift exchange either.[325] The Universities don't want the faculty to put up any Christmas decorations that have any religious connotations either (so no baby Jesus in a manger), only secular ones like snowmen. They also request faculty not hold celebrations that even "indirectly" celebrates "religious holidays."[326]

Would Indian or Chinese people who emigrated to a predominantly Muslim country like Saudi Arabia or Pakistan send out memos encouraging people not to celebrate Ramadan or Eid al-Fitr because it might not be "inclusive" enough for them? Would British or Irish people who were working in Israel ask colleagues in that country not to celebrate Jewish holidays or avoid using any religious symbols during popular celebrations there because it wouldn't be "inclusive" enough for non-Jews? Never!

---

[324] https://web.archive.org/web/20170410065003/https://brockport.edu/about/diversity/holiday.html

[325] Ibid.

[326] Campus Reform "Universities strive for 'Christmas'-free campuses" by Anthony Gockowski (December 6th 2017)

CHRISTIANITY AND CHURCHES

Would Christians living in India complain about Hindu symbols being displayed for the celebration of Diwali (the Festival of Lights), one of the most popular celebrations in the country every year? Of course not! But those who are hostile to Christmas are aided by brand name Liberal media outlets every year which amplify their attacks on Christian celebrations in America—and it's time people stop giving into the demands of a small minority who don't want to assimilate and enjoy the biggest holiday around the world.

Most people, out of ignorance (or fear), just point to "Liberals" as the ones who oppose and attack Christmas, and very few people will mention that there is usually a very specific group of Liberals who oppose Christmas—Liberal secular Jews—or Liberal *non-practicing Jews* (not to be confused with the conservative *religious Orthodox Jews*, who believe in God and don't just identify as Jews ethnically or culturally).[327] While Orthodox Jews don't celebrate Christmas either, they're not usually hostile about it like many Liberal JINOs and tend to be friendly with (and respectful of) Christians,[328] despite their differences about Jesus, because Orthodox Jews share many of the same values as Christians, whereas JINOs are typically Leftist atheists.[329]

---

[327] Orthodox Jews make up about 10% of Jews in the United States.

[328] In the United States, most Orthodox Jews are tolerant and respectful of Christians. In Israel, however, they tolerate tours of the Holy Land by Christians, but over there factions of Orthodox Jews firmly oppose Christians evangelizing (preaching) to them in their "Jewish country," and numerous viral videos have captured groups of Orthodox Jews harassing Christians in Israel. Lehava is one such group which is considered ultra-Orthodox.

[329] While Orthodox Jews don't subscribe to the New Testament, both Christians and Orthodox Jews believe in the Old Testament and the values it teaches, while JINOs are typically liberal atheists who are even at odds with Orthodox Jews because JINOs prefer secularism and liberalism to traditional (religious) Judaism.

CHRISTIANITY AND CHURCHES

A lot of people get confused when they hear about Jews who don't believe in God because most non-Jews don't understand that "Jewish" is also an ethnicity *aside* from a religion, but because Jewish ethnicity has been historically linked with Judaism (the religion) most non-Jews don't know that ethnic Jews who no longer follow the religion of the ancient Israelites still identify as Jews because the word has dual meanings.[330]

During a speech at Texas A&M University, Ben Shapiro, one of the most famous Orthodox Jews in America, remarked why so many (ethnic) Jews are Leftists, saying, "This is one of the questions I get most often from non-Jewish audiences, is why are Jews so disproportionately to the left. And the answer is the vast majority of Jews don't go to synagogue, don't believe in God, [and] don't believe in the Bible...Jews are the single most anti-religious, quote unquote 'religious' group in the United States."[331]

And to understand why Jews don't celebrate Christmas and why so many of them actively oppose it being an integral part of American culture, one has to understand the history of Christianity and how Jews rejecting Jesus as the son of God and the Messiah has caused an ongoing division between Jews and Gentiles (non-Jews) for over two thousand years.

Few Christians are aware that Muslims actually believe Jesus was a prophet, they just don't believe he was God in the flesh or that his death atoned for mankind's sins. Muslims believe Jesus was born of a virgin though (which Jews do not), and that he performed

---

[330] Pew Research Center "Who is a Jew?" (October 1st 2013)

[331] Young America's Foundation YouTube Channel "Fighting the transgressives | Ben Shapiro LIVE at Texas A&M University." (November 1st 2022)

miracles—including restoring a blind man's vision, healing a leper, and raising the dead.[332] All of this is written in the Koran, which contains some of the same stories as the Christian Bible.[333]

In Judaism on the other hand (and among JINOs—Jews in name only—who no longer follow the Jewish religion or even believe in God but still identify as Jews culturally), Jesus is viewed as a fraud and a false prophet, and because of the events that led to his crucifixion and being rejected by the ancient Israelites as the messiah—many Jews and Christians have had an often tense opposition between each other ever since.[334]

Easter Under Attack

Even though Easter has been covered with a secular veneer similar to Christmas, the Christian roots are far more visible because the resurrection of Christ is at the core of Christianity and it's seen as a far more religious holiday than Christmas. And since most Liberals hate Jesus and Christianity, Easter Sunday causes them to flip out and spew their hatred every year, usually on social media which is where Leftists prefer to live their lives and air their every grievance as soon as they come to mind.

Anti-Christian posts don't violate the terms of service on the Big Tech social media platforms (unlike criticism of Jews or Muslims) and most Leftists wouldn't even think of criticizing Muhammad, the revered prophet of

---

[332] The New Yorker "How Muslims View Easter" by Rollo Romig (April 6th 2012)

[333] AboutIslam.net "Jesus in the Bible and the Quaran" by Aisha Stacey (November 2nd 2022)

[334] Haaretz "Spike in Incidents of Jews Spitting on Christian Worshippers in Jerusalem" by Nir Hasson (October 2nd 2023)

Islam—or any Muslim holidays, beliefs, or practices; but every Easter the Christianphobes vent their hatred of Jesus and Christians online.

A single post criticizing a Jewish holiday or tradition (like the eating of hamantaschen, a pastry which symbolize the cut off ears of Jewish enemies during their holiday of Purim)[335] or mocking their ritual of swinging a chicken around their head while saying a prayer—thinking it transfers their sins to the chicken, which is an atonement ritual many religious Jews engage in for Yom Kippur,[336] would cause a national outrage and make headlines across the country, but attacking Christians is so commonplace it's now central to mainstream American culture.

Recently, every year when Easter comes around, cries of "antisemitism" come from the Liberal media which continuously work to smear the Christian holy day as an attack on Jews for the crucifixion of Jesus. But shockingly these smears aren't just from the usual media outlets, they're also now coming from some heretical "Christian" or "Catholic" ones as well.

America Magazine, a publication put out by the Jesuits of the United States (a Catholic group), published an article titled "The Gospel of John has been used to justify anti-semitism—so we should stop reading it on Good Friday." It starts out saying, "Over the weekend, I saw a number of comments from Jewish Twitter users expressing concern about the week to come. The Christian celebration of Holy Week brings with it

---

[335] The Jerusalem Post "Ears to you, hamentashen" by Gil HOffman (March 9th 2017)

[336] Brandeis University "Kapparot: The Yom Kippur Tradition of Chicken Twirling" by Lawrence Goodman (August 31st 2021)

increased anti-Semitic comments, threats and violence, and it has for over a thousand years."[337]

It continues, "Reading John's Passion [meaning the Book of John from the Bible] on Good Friday causes real harm. And our practice is far more a matter of tradition than any theological necessity."[338] The writer suggests avoiding some of the specifics about the events that led up to the crucifixion of Jesus because certain historical facts have been deemed "antisemitic" by Jews.

The Book of John is seen as more problematic than the other Gospels (Matthew, Mark, and Luke) because of the verse found in John 8:44 which reads, "You [the Jews who want Jesus to be killed] belong to your father, the devil, and you want to carry out your father's desires." It's deemed an "antisemitic" passage because it paints the Jews who wanted Jesus killed as satanic.

Aside from John 8:44, other verses that echo this sentiment such as Revelation 2:9 (and 3:9) which warn about "those who say they are Jews and are not, but are of the synagogue of Satan," are also deemed "antisemitic."[339] Some Jewish leaders have even called for Bibles to come with warning labels on them which highlight and counteract what they deem "antisemitic" passages and themes about "the seemingly stubborn

---

[337] America Magazine: The Jesuit Review "The Gospel of John has been used to justify anti-Semitism—so we should stop reading it on Good Friday" by Jim McDermott (April 14th 2022)

[338] Ibid.

[339] JewsForJudiasm.org "How does the Book of Revelation promote hatred of Jews?"

nature of the Jewish people and their disloyalty to God."[340]

Billy Graham, the most respected Christian evangelist in the 20th and 21st century, deemed "America's pastor," can be heard on the Nixon White House Tapes referencing these verses since President Nixon secretly recorded every conversation in the Oval Office using a voice-activated tape recorder. The last of the tapes, which contain more than 3,000 hours of conversations, were made public in 2002 and include Billy Graham having a very candid discussion with the president back in 1972 where he can be heard telling Nixon, "You see the Bible makes a distinction, Mr. President, between two groups of Jews. One is called the synagogue of Satan—there are two different kinds."[341]

He continues saying the other group is called the remnant of God's people, who are Jews which will become Christians in the End Times. "And then there's the synagogue of Satan," he says again. "And nearly all of your religious deceptions in the latter days, like the Bible speaks, latter days would be a thousand years; [comes from] what they call the synagogue of Satan. In other words, they are energized by a supernatural power called the Devil. This is what the Bible teaches, whether you believe it or don't believe it, this is the Biblical teaching. This is what I believe. And I believe that they have a strange brilliance about them because they're smart. And they are energized in my judgement by a

---

[340] The Daily Mail "Jewish leaders call for new editions of the Bible and the Koran to carry trigger warnings highlighting anti-Semitic passages" by James Wood (November 23rd 2018)

[341] National Archives "White House Tapes of the Nixon Administration, 1971-1973" Conversation No. 662-004 uploaded to the Nixon Presidential Library and Museum here: https://www.nixonlibrary.gov/white-house-tapes/662/conversation-662-004

supernatural power, and you see, and uh, of course Hitler didn't uh—they had a stranglehold on Germany. On the banking of Germany, on everything in Germany—and the media. They had the whole thing, you see. And he [Hitler] went about it wrong, but this stranglehold has got to be broken or this country is going to go down the drain."[342]

Nixon asked, "You believe that?"

Graham: "Yes sir."

Nixon responded, "Good Lord. I can't ever say it, but I believe it."[343]

When the tape was made public 30 years later, Billy Graham was denounced as an "antisemite" but surprisingly it didn't completely destroy his career or legacy. And the fact that he never talked about such things publicly, but instead kept that conversation for what he thought was a private discussion with the president of the United States, speaks volumes about how dangerous it can be to talk about certain parts of the scriptures.

Even the cross itself has been called an "antisemitic symbol." The London *Guardian* says "Christians must understand that for Jews the cross is a symbol of oppression" and that "Christianity bears primary responsibility for historic antisemitism."[344]

---

[342] New York Times "Billy Graham Responds to Lingering Anger Over 1972 Remarks on Jews" by David Firestone (March 17th 2002)

[343] U.S. News & World Report "Billy Graham's Troubling, Nasty Nixon Moment by James Warren (February 28th 2018)

[344] The Guardian "Christians must understand that for Jews the cross is a symbol of oppression" by Giles Fraser (April 25th 2014)

CHRISTIANITY AND CHURCHES

In 2023, Israel's government proposed a ban on Christians proselytizing in their country.[345] "America's greatest ally," as both the Republicans and Democrats in congress always tout, who we give billions of dollars in aid to every year,[346] tried to ban preaching the Gospel.[347] (And this wasn't the first time).[348] After news of the latest proposition made it to the United States, Israeli Prime Minister Benjamin Netanyahu issued a statement saying he wouldn't sign the bill into law and frantically tried to engage in damage control so Christians would continue to support the State of Israel and the Jewish people.[349]

The "fact checkers" online tried to mitigate the damage too, claiming the proposed bill wouldn't ban people from "talking about Jesus," just *proselytizing*, or trying to convert someone to becoming a Christian. People in Israel could still *talk* about him! A senior editor at *The Jerusalem Post* said, "And it wouldn't exist [meaning the proposed ban] if missionaries would just back off—at least in our own country."[350] Few Christian churches and political pundits will admit that while Israel tolerates Christian tourists—preaching to Jews about

---

[345] Newsmax "Bill Would Outlaw Talk About Jesus in Israel" by Daniel Cohen (March 20th 2023)

[346] It's usually 3 to 5 billion per year, and as of 2023 has totaled $158 billion dollars as reported by the Congressional Research Service (March 1st 2023)

[347] Haaretz "Evangelical Christians Urge Netanyahu to Scuttle ultra-Orthodox Bill Banning Christian Proselytizing" by Ben Samuels (March 21st 2023)

[348] CNN "Proposed Israeli law would ban Christian missionaries" (July 8th 1997)

[349] Associated Press Israeli leader halts bill against Christian proselytizing" (March 22nd 2023)

[350] https://mobile.twitter.com/LahavHarkov/status/1638532945953669120

Jesus is highly discouraged and often results in hostility and scorn.[351]

After Mel Gibson's blockbuster *Passion of the Christ* film was released in 2004, it was widely denounced as "antisemitic" because it was the most popular film about Jesus in generations. A Jewish critic for *The New York Daily News* named Jamie Bernard called it "the most virulently anti-Semitic movie made since the German propaganda films of the Second World War."[352]

The Jewish Anti-Defamation League (ADL) said it "continues its unambiguous portrayal of Jews as being responsible for the death of Jesus. There is no question in this film about who is responsible. At every single opportunity, Mr. Gibson's film reinforces the notion that the Jewish authorities and the Jewish mob are the ones ultimately responsible for the Crucifixion."[353]

Well, Christians who have actually read the Bible would know that's actually how it happened. Groups like the ADL try to split hairs and claim that technically the Romans killed Jesus, but the Bible makes it very clear that the Jewish leadership in Jerusalem at the time were the ones pushing for it.

In Matthew 27:24 the Bible quotes Pontius Pilate (the Roman governor of Judea at the time) saying, "I am innocent of this man's blood...It is your responsibility!" meaning the Jewish Pharisees who had conspired to have Jesus arrested and killed for "blasphemy" and being a "false" messiah. The Bible also says that Pontius Pilate

---

[351] The Guardian "Israel threatens to pull evangelical Christian TV station aimed at Jews" by Oliver Holmes (May 10th 2020)

[352] The New York Daily News "The Passion of the Christ" by Jami Bernard (February 24th 2004)

[353] ADL.org "ADL and Mel Gibson's 'The Passion of the Christ'" (January 2nd 2013)

even offered to release Jesus, but the angry crowd of Jewish townspeople demanded Barabbas be set free instead, another prisoner who had been recently arrested for insurrection against Rome and murder.[354]

Bari Weiss, who has worked as the opinion editor for *The New York Times* and a book reviewer for *The Wall Street Journal*, insists it's a "conspiracy theory" that Jews were behind Jesus being crucified.[355] Others however, like Jewish comedian Sarah Silverman gloat, "I'm glad the Jews killed Christ. Good! I'd fucking do it again!"[356]

Of course it's not fair to blame all Jews or Jewish people living today for killing Jesus any more than it would be to blame White people in general for slavery in America's past, but it was the Jewish religious leadership at the time (the Pharisees) who conspired to have the Romans kill him, which Jewish advocacy groups like the ADL consider to be an "antisemitic trope" if you dare say it.

Yes, quoting the Bible is considered to be "antisemitic" these days, including passages like Matthew 12:14 which reads, "But the [Jewish] Pharisees went out and plotted how they might kill Jesus."

And Mark 11:18 which says, "The chief [Jewish] priests and the teachers of the law heard this and began looking for a way to kill him, for they feared him, because the whole crowd was amazed at his teaching." It wasn't the Romans who were insisting he be crucified. The

---

[354] Luke 23:19

[355] Real Time with Bill Maher "Bari Weiss: How to Fight Anti-Semitism" segment posted on the show's official YouTube channel (September 13th 2019)

[356] Sarah Silverman in her 2005 show "Jesus is Magic." Clips of the segment are currently available on YouTube and elsewhere online if you search for "Sarah Silverman Says I Would Kill Christ Again"

Bible makes that very clear. Luke 23:23-24 says "But with loud shouts they insistently demanded that he be crucified, and their shouts prevailed. So Pilate decided to grant their demand."

It's rare for Biblical dramas to become so popular, but almost ten years after *The Passion of the Christ*, the History Channel's miniseries *The Bible* was a hit in 2013, and like clockwork the same cries of "antisemitism" rang out about that as well.[357]

Very few Christians today have an understanding of the tense (and ongoing) opposition many Jews have toward Christians. Before becoming a Christian, the Apostle Paul (a religious Jew prior to his conversion) actually hunted down and killed the first followers of Jesus.[358]

Martin Luther, the monk who started the Protestant reformation by famously nailing his *Ninety-Five Theses* to the front door of his local church in 1517 starting the Protestant Reformation, is deemed an antisemite for his theological writings criticizing Judaism.

His book *On The Jews and Their Lies,* published in 1543 and sold on Amazon since it first launched in 1995, was banned sometime around the year 2020 during a purge of numerous titles Jewish groups had been pressuring the retailer to censor.[359] There are plenty of books critical of Christianity, Catholicism, and the

---

[357] The Guardian "History Channel's The Bible series is worse than reality TV" by Alan Nyuhas (March 25th 2013)

[358] Acts 22:4 "I persecuted the followers of this Way to their death, arresting both men and women and throwing them into prison"

[359] More titles that were also removed during this purge are mentioned in the chapter on Censorship, and include David Duke's autobiography *My Awakening* and his other book *Jewish Supremacism*, along with Kevin MacDonald's *Culture of Critique: Analysis of Jewish Involvement in Twentieth-Century Intellectual and Political Movement* and others.

CHRISTIANITY AND CHURCHES

Inquisition, but certain books that are critical of Judaism, Jewish secularism (JINOs), Jewish ethnocentrism (their in-group favoritism), or discussions about any "Jewish banking dynasties" have been recently censored completely from Amazon and aren't allowed to be sold. Even used copies by third parties are forbidden from being listed.[360]

In the Talmud, the recorded oral teachings of Jewish religious leaders (known as Rabbinic Judaism which has been the mainstream form of Judaism since the 6th century), it not only says that Jesus was a false messiah and blasphemer who the Pharisees proudly put to death,[361] but that Mary was a whore and an adulteress who had sex with a Roman soldier named Panthera, and that's how she became pregnant with Jesus.[362]

The Talmud is considered to be just as sacred as the Hebrew Bible (the Old Testament) by most Jews, but Christians aren't demanding the Talmud be banned, or clamoring about any "anti-Christianism" because of the theological differences they have with Jews.

While Christians may debate and discuss their disagreements, they're not framing the Jewish view as being "hate speech" or "dangerous" like Jews paint Christian beliefs and Bible verses. Most Christians aren't even aware of the Talmud and are quite shocked to learn what it says about Jesus—and that it is one of the most

---

[360] The topic of Amazon banning books is examined in detail in the chapter on Censorship.

[361] Jesus in the Talmud by Peter Schafer pages 9 and 74 (Princeton Press 2007). Peter Shafer is a professor Judaic Studies and director of the Program of Judaic Studies at Princeton University.

[362] Jesus in the Talmud by Peter Schafer pages 17, 19, 20, 98-99, 110, 112, 141, 143 (Princeton Press 2007)

sacred religious texts of modern Judaism and "the single most influential document in the history of Judaism."[363]

The diametric opposition between Judaism and Christianity softened in the early 20th century largely due to a new edition of the Bible, the Schofield Bible, an annotated version of the Bible (meaning including commentary and notes alongside the scriptures) published by Cyrus I. Scofield in 1909 which changed the view many Christians have towards Jews. It eased the tensions between the two groups by convincing Christians that God commands their uncritical support of the State of Israel, and turned most American evangelicals into Zionists (people who support Israel as a homeland exclusively for Jewish people) and now put Jews on a pedestal as "God's chosen people" or the "apple of God's eye."

This, despite Jews not believing in Jesus as the Son of God, and most ethnic Jews not even being religious at all.[364] The Bible makes it clear that God's covenant is with those who have faith in Christ—those who believe in Jesus, not people who just so happen to belong to a certain ethnic group, even if at one point in history God issued them the Ten Commandments.[365]

Christians believe that faith in Jesus (that he is God in human form and he paid the penalty for your sins, accepting the punishment on your behalf) along with genuine repentance (regret or remorse for your sins) is the only way to have salvation and come into fellowship with

---

[363] Invitation to the Talmud: Revised and Expanded Edition by Jacob Neusner page 1 (1973, 1984 Harper & Row Publishers)

[364] Haaretz "New Poll Shows Atheism on Rise, With Jews Found to Be Least Religious" (August 20th 2012)

[365] Galatians 3:29, Romans 9:6-8, 1 John 2:23

CHRISTIANITY AND CHURCHES

God;[366] and the entire premise of Christianity is that it's by *faith* alone (belief), not rituals or works—or outside actions; or anything that you can "do" (such as "being a good person," so no one can boast that they have more favorability with God than others).[367]

And this salvation certainly isn't contingent on anyone's ancestry or what ethnic group you belong to. Jesus offers fellowship with God (and access to the Kingdom of Heaven) to all of mankind—Jew and Gentile (meaning non-Jews, also called Goy or Goyim, which is a disparaging term used by some Jews to refer to non-Jews).[368]

Judaism is a very exclusive and ethnocentric religion. Notice Jews don't try to preach or spread the word to others about their God, because to them, he's *their* God, and *they* are his special people. In fact, they discourage people who aren't born (ethnically) Jewish from converting to Judaism, and many converts still aren't considered Jews according to Jewish law because if their mother isn't an (ethnic) Jew, then they're not really seen as Jewish because they have no direct genetic lineage to the ancient Israelites.[369]

This is why some people accuse Jews of being Jewish supremacists, which of course is denounced as another "antisemitic slur" because White people are the only

---

[366] There are numerous interpretations of Christianity and the Bible, and what being a Christian means. Some believe the Bible is 100% historical and literal, while others view the scriptures as allegorical or mythological but still conveying a divine message from God by symbolically representing of various psychological processes involving the Self and the Ego.

[367] Ephesians 2:8-9

[368] https://www.merriam-webster.com/dictionary/goys

[369] Chabad.org "Why Is Jewishness Matrilineal? Maternal Descent in Judaism" by Tzvil Freeman and Yehudda Shurpin

CHRISTIANITY AND CHURCHES

ethnic group that are supposed to be framed as seeing themselves superior to others. But some Jews do reveal their own superiority complex when giving the impression that they're above doing certain kinds of jobs like manual labor.[370]

One of the most famous rabbis in Israel, Ovadiah Yosef, preached that "Goyim were born only to serve us. Without that, they have no place in the world—only to serve the People of Israel...Why are gentiles needed? They will work, they will plow, they will reap. We will sit like an effendi [a member of the nobility] and eat... That is why gentiles were created."[371] When he died in 2013, he was given the largest funeral in the history of Israel.[372]

Jews, in their view, work "prestigious" jobs like being doctors and lawyers. This is not a knock against them at all. Their culture emphasizes education and success, much like Asian Americans do. But they're very sensitive to even the slightest criticism from non-Jews.

If an (ethnic) Jew who once also followed religious Judaism (an Orthodox Jew, the ones who wear the yarmulke) becomes a follower of Christ (a Christian believing in Jesus), they are often called a messianic Jew to make the distinction that while they have Jewish heritage (ethnicity) they are also a Christian.

Jesus came to fulfill the Old Testament prophesies of a Messiah (a savior), and essentially reform (or transform)

---

[370] For example, I once had a manager at a retail job who is a JINO tell me to my face that he wouldn't take out the trash at the store because he's "a tribesman."

[371] Times of Israel "5 of Ovadia Yosef's most controversial quotation" by Lazar Berman (October 9th 2013)

[372] Times of Israel "Rabbi Ovadia Yosef buried in largest funeral in Israeli history" by Gavriel Fiske (October 7th 2013)

Judaism, much like Buddha reformed Hinduism by preaching his formula for "enlightenment" to all, breaking the monopoly held by the religious leaders at the time in India, the Brahmins, who saw themselves as the authorities others needed to rely on in order to gain knowledge of God.[373]

With the coming of Jesus the Messiah, Jews were invited into God's new covenant which was also offered to all of mankind so they could do away with external rituals and other stringent practices they previously used in hopes of becoming holy and pleasing to God, and instead they could now be guided by faith alone through a spiritual transformation of their mind which automatically changes how they think and behave, bringing them into harmony with God through the Holy Spirit, a supernatural force that functions as an invisible guide and conscience.

But the Bible makes it clear that many Jews were jealous of their "chosenness" over the Gentiles (non-Jews) being offered communion with the God of Israel who they saw as *their* God—the God of (ethnic) Jews.

By God becoming a man in the form of Jesus, he also provided a way for humans to better understand him, and relate to him. He came to earth not only to reveal his instructions through parables that any man, woman, and child could understand, but to set an example for how to think and how to behave. To be the ultimate role model. And when the Holy Spirit enters a person's mind (through belief in Christ) it's like downloading a new operating system for your computer or phone, and the old animalistic (carnal) human nature is upgraded, and one

---

[373] Buddha's real name was Siddhartha Gautama—*The Buddha* is just a title meaning "the awakened one" or "the enlightened one."

becomes anointed with a spiritually-minded consciousness.

2nd Corinthians 5:17 says "Therefore, if anyone is in Christ, the new creation has come: The old has gone, and the new is here." There are many metaphors that describe this, perhaps the most common is a caterpillar transforming into a butterfly. Christians use the term *born again* to signify this transformation, and Jesus enables us to interface with the awesome and inconceivable power of God in a way that our limited brains can comprehend.

Anyone who rejects Christ as the Son of God, the Light of the World (the transmission of God's messages to mankind) also rejects God (John 2:23), so Jews who don't believe in Jesus are not God's chosen people.[374] Not anymore. Not since the new covenant—the arrival of Jesus. *Christians* are God's chosen people. This is Supersessionism because Christians superseded the Jews as God's covenanted people.

Often it's called *replacement theology* as a pejorative and is considered a "heresy" by many churches today because they don't want to be accused of "antisemitism" even though the Bible makes it very clear that Christians are God's chosen people, and ever since the early days of Christianity, *Christians* were universally understood to be just that until Zionism became a major influence in Christianity.[375]

---

[374] Matthew 21:43 says "Therefore I tell you that the kingdom of God will be taken away from you and given to a people who will produce its fruit."

[375] Zionism is the belief (and political movement) which promotes the idea that Israel should be a country exclusively for Jews, while all western democracies (such as the United States and all countries throughout Europe) are under strict demands to surrender *their* ethnic majorities by embracing multiculturalism through mass immigration and importation of other (non-White) ethnic groups.

Romans 9:6-8 says "For not all who are descended from Israel are Israel…it is not the children by physical descent who are God's children, but it is the children of the promise who are regarded as Abraham's offspring."

Galatians 3:29 also makes it clear that, "If you belong to Christ, then you are Abraham's seed, and heirs according to the promise." And your personal salvation and relationship with Christ have nothing to do with two different ethnic groups (Jews and Palestinians) fighting over a plot of land half way around the world in Israel or which one occupies any of the disputed territories.[376]

And any Christians who read the New Testament for themselves, instead of relying on what non-Christians or false preachers tell them it says, would know the true history and reasons for the differences and ongoing tensions between Christianity and Judaism.

While most Christians today don't hold any grudges against Jews despite the conflicts of the past, and instead revere them for the role they played in God's plan in the Old Testament and hope that they (along with everyone on earth) will one day come to believe in Jesus, unfortunately many Jews stand firm in their opposition to Christian culture and holidays while often masking their hostilities in hopes of not bringing any attention to themselves because of it.[377]

---

[376] The Bible calls Christians a Holy nation in 1 Peter 1:9 and in Matthew 23:37-39 it says Israel kills their prophets and their house will be left desolate until they believe in Jesus. Also the Holy Temple is now the body of believers in Christ, not some physical building in Jerusalem as noted in 1 Corinthians 6:19

[377] City Journal "Why Don't Jews Like the Christians Who Like Them?" by James Q. Wilson from The Social Order, Politics and Law magazine (Winter 2008). Article cites a Pew survey that found 42 percent of Jewish respondents expressed hostility to evangelical and fundamentalist Christians.

Tax-Exempt Churches

Most Christians don't know, but in order for churches to get tax-exempt status (meaning they don't have to pay federal or state income tax on all the donations, or property tax) the government severely limits what the pastor (or priest) can say during their sermons and restricts what kinds of political activities the church can engage in or endorse.[378] Virtually every church in the United States is held to these standards because they all operate as 501(c)(3) tax-exempt entities, as opposed to typical businesses which are set up as corporations (or sole proprietorships if they're small).

In 1954 then-senator Lyndon B. Johnson (a Democrat) successfully proposed an amendment to the tax code (called the Johnson Amendment) which prohibits all 501(c)(3) non-profit organizations from endorsing or opposing any political candidates or legislation.[379] This means that a church's tax-exempt status could be revoked if the pastor starts incorporating real world examples into their sermons and denouncing or supporting any specific candidates or legislation.[380]

You didn't think the government granted churches tax free status because they support Jesus, did you? It was to buy them off and keep them out of the way, and diminish their power to organize and influence things politically. Jesus said "Render unto Caesar what is Caesar's,"

---

[378] IRS.gov "Charities, Churches and Politics" https://www.irs.gov/newsroom/charities-churches-and-politics

[379] Ibid.

[380] WCNC "Yes, the IRS can revoke tax-exempt status for churches that endorse candidates" by Brandon Lewis and Kelly Jones (November 1st 2022)

meaning you should pay your taxes.[381] But unfortunately, most churches have sold their First Amendment rights for 30 pieces of silver. Many also don't want to drive away people who may have Liberal political views, so they try their best to keep politics out of the Church, which is one of the reasons why Christians in America have gotten so soft and afraid to denounce the widespread degeneracy in our culture.

President Obama's senior legal advisor suggested that Churches should lose their tax-exempt status if they didn't officiate gay "weddings" once the Supreme Court ruled in favor of them under his administration.[382] When Beto O'Rourke was running for president during the 2020 election season he agreed, saying that any Churches which refuse to acknowledge gay "marriage" should lose their tax-exempt status.[383] Such battles have been quietly raging for years.

The city of Houston launched an investigation into a local church back in 2014 to determine whether or not to revoke their tax-exempt status. They issued a subpoena demanding sermon notes and other documents after the lesbian mayor was alerted to the pastor's sermons denouncing a local ordinance the city was trying to pass which would have allowed those who identify as

---

[381] Life Hope & Truth ""Render Unto Caesar": What Does God Say About Taxes?" by Bruce Gore

[382] National Review "Obama's Lawyer: Religious Institutions May Lose Tax-Exempt Status If Court Rules for Gay Marriage" by Joel Gehrke (April 28th 2015)

[383] The Texas Tribune "Beto O'Rourke says religious institutions should lose tax-exempt status if they oppose gay marriage" by Patrick Svitek (October 11th 2019)

transgender to use whatever public bathrooms they wanted, no matter their biological sex.[384]

A United Methodist Church that owns a boardwalk pavilion in New Jersey lost their tax-exempt status in 2007 after they wouldn't allow a lesbian couple to use the location for their "wedding."[385] Gay "marriage" wasn't even legal at the time, but they requested to use the pavilion for their "ceremony" anyway and were denied, so they sued and the court ruled in their favor.[386]

After members of the Mormon Church helped organize support for Proposition 8 in California which banned gay "marriage" throughout the entire state back in 2008, LGBTQ groups tried to get their tax-exempt status revoked.[387] When the San Francisco archbishop issued a notice that the Catholic church would refuse then-Speaker of the House Nancy Pelosi communion because of her very vocal pro-abortion stance, #TaxTheChurch started trending on Twitter from so many people demanding their tax-exempt status be pulled.[388]

Pastor Greg Locke, a popular social media personality and head of a church in Tennessee, faced calls to have his church lose its tax-exempt status after a video went viral showing him railing against abortion, shouting, "If you vote Democrat, I don't even want you around this church!

---

[384] Fox News "City of Houston demands pastors turn over sermons" by Todd Starnes October 14th 2014)

[385] The New York Times "Group Loses Tax Break Over Gay Union Issue" by Jill Capuzzo (September 18, 2007)

[386] Ibid.

[387] CBS News "Editorial: Mormon Church Should Lose Tax Exempt Status Over Prop 8 Support" by Editorial Board, The Daily Athenaeum (November 18th 2008)

[388] The Independent "If the Catholic Church can't stay out of politics, it should start paying taxes" by Jennifer Stavros (May 24th 2022) .

You can get out! You can get out, you demon! You cannot be a Christian and vote Democrat in this nation!"[389]

After his rant made headlines he claimed that he would dissolve his church's 501(c)(3) himself, "because the government ain't gonna tell me what I can and what I can't say."[390]

Apostate Churches

Far worse than churches afraid to weigh in on political issues out of concerns that they might lose their tax-exempt status or hoping to avoid offending churchgoers (thus driving away some Democrat attendees along with their tithing) if the pastor is too overtly Conservative, are those who openly teach things or accept things that the Bible *clearly* opposes.

Most churches in America are afraid to denounce gay couples adopting children, let alone even call homosexuality a sin anymore (and especially not perverted or disgusting), but some "churches" have gone even further and hired openly gay pastors.[391] And not just "churches" in San Francisco.

---

[389] MSNBC "Pastor sparks controversy with rhetoric about Dems, Christianity" by Steve Benen (May 18th 2022)

[390] Newsweek "Pastor Who Called Democrats 'Demons' Claims He Gave Up Tax-Exempt Status" by Anders Anglesey (May 24th 2022)

[391] New York Times "Lutherans Offer Warm Welcome to Gay Pastors" by Laurie Goodstein (July 25th 2010)

CHRISTIANITY AND CHURCHES

Churches in Birmingham, Alabama,[392] Madison, Wisconsin,[393] Baptist churches in Louisville, Kentucky,[394] United Methodist churches in Texas, and more.[395] If you search Google for "Church hires openly gay pastor" there are countless news stories from local outlets about supposed "churches" across the country which are doing it.

Soon these apostate churches will likely print Bible editions that exclude various parts of scripture that the popular culture in America objects to (like verses denouncing homosexuals or pointing out that Jewish Pharisees conspired to have Jesus killed—the Romans didn't just crucify him out of the blue).[396]

A Chicago-area church announced that it was "fasting from Whiteness" for Lent—the Christian tradition in various denominations of giving something up for the period preceding Easter to commemorate the 40 days Jesus spent in the desert fasting and being tempted by Satan. Their "fast" involved "giving up" music created by White people during the worship and instead used music from Black people.[397] They even put a "Fasting from Whiteness" sign in their front lawn.

---

[392] AL.com "Birmingham church hires gay pastor; he's ready to do same-sex weddings" (June 25th 2015)

[393] Fox 47 "Church's first openly gay pastor hopes to help others find healing in faith communities" by Bradly Mallory (September 29th 2021)

[394] Baptist News "Historic Kentucky church calls gay man as co-pastor" by Mark Wingfield (August 15th 2022)

[395] Dallas Morning News "Oak Lawn United Methodist Church to self-appoint LGBTQ pastors after bishop denies request" by Nataly Keomoungkoun (June 3rd 2022)

[396] Matthew 12:14, Mark 11:18, Luke 23:23-24

[397] ABC 7 Chicago "Oak Park church 'fasting from whiteness' for Lent despite vocal backlash" by Cate Cauguiran (April 7th 2022)

Other churches across America have given sermons denouncing "White privilege" and shown solidarity with the Black Lives Matter movement.[398]

Drag shows are even being held at supposed "Christian" churches. In 2019 the Fairview Community Church in Costa Mesa, California held one which may have been the first "church" to do so.[399] A few months later that same year, South Bay Pentecostal Church in San Diego held one.[400] Followed by the Trinity Episcopal Church in Swarthmore, Pennsylvania a few months after that.[401] The Episcopal Church is an apostate organization that claims to be Christian while accepting gays and lesbians as pastors (and officially supports abortion) so it shouldn't be a surprise they're holding Drag Queen Story Hour events, but many different denominations are doing so.[402]

A private Episcopal "Christian" school in Manhattan that charges nearly $60,000 a year for tuition, forced students to attend a drag show inside its chapel. Footage of the event was posted online showing a drag queen singing and dancing up and down the aisle in between the pews.[403]

---

[398] The New Yorker "How Black Lives Matter Is Changing the Church" by Eliza Griswold (August 30th 2020)

[399] LA Times "Drag queen lends sparkle to story time at Costa Mesa church" by Hillary Davis (July 10th 2019)

[400] San Diego Union Tribune "Drag Queen Story Hour: glittery entertainment or gender-bending provocation?" by Peter Rowe (September 15th 2019)

[401] Trinity Church, Swarmouth's official website "Drag Queen Story Time at Trinity! November 3rd 2019 original post here: https://www.trinity-swarthmore.org/drag-queen-story-time.html

[402] Exposing The ELCA "ELCA Congregation Hosts Drag Queen Story Hour for Children (November 4th 2019)

[403] The New York Post "Students at ritzy NYC high school forced to attend drag show in church: report" by Patrick Reilly (August 3rd 2022)

A Lutheran church in the Chicago area hosted a drag queen story hour event at the end of 2021 where the church's pastor was the drag queen! He told the children, "I am also a boy most of the time when I'm here, but today, I'm a girl."[404] As usual, photos of the event were proudly posted on social media by the perpetrators to celebrate what they had done.[405]

More "churches" continued to follow. One in Florida called Naples United Church of Christ hosted a drag queen show for kids ages 12-18 to "help" them with the "exploration of LGBTQ-related issues facing today's youth"[406] When signing up to attend the event, children (or their parents who signed them up) were asked to include their pronouns on the registration form. The "pastor" at University Christian Church in San Diego, Caleb J. Lines, does his sermons wearing an LGBTQ rainbow-colored sash, and calls drag "holy." He also preaches that God is gay.[407]

As degenerate as drag shows are, they had always been considered exclusively an adult form of entertainment until the early 2010s when the LGBTQ community began openly targeting children. And despite what these satanic "churches" and their "pastors" say about it, the Bible is very clear on God's view of

---

[404] Daily Mail "Newly-ordained Lutheran pastor hosts DRAG Bible study class for children at woke Chicago church" by James Gordon (December 19th 2021)

[405] Christianity Daily "'Disturbing': Church Hosts 'Drag Queen Prayer Time' For Kids During Sunday Service" by Olivia Cavallaro (December 22nd 2021)

[406] Florida's Voice "Naples Church Hosting LGBT Drag Show for 12 Year-Old Children, District Not Informed of Plans to Use Schools as Transit Points" by Eric Daugherty)May 12th 2022)

[407] San Diego Reader "Pink God and Gay Jesus come to the defense of local pastor" by Walter Mencken (March 31st 2023)

crossdressing. Deuteronomy 22:5 says "The woman shall not wear that which pertaineth unto a man, neither shall a man put on a woman's garment: for all that do so are abomination unto the Lord thy God."

Aside from the perverts who get sexual gratification dressing as women (autogynephilia), crossdressing has also been used for comedic effect for generations because it's so strange to see a man dressed up as a woman or pretending to be one, and so countless films and TV shows have used the bit to get laughs.

Classics like *Some Like It Hot* (1959), *Mrs. Doubtfire* (1993), and sketch comedy shows from *In Living Color* and *Saturday Night Live* to Tyler Perry's movies used it as a staple bit, but now it's considered to be offensive and *hateful* to laugh at men who dress as women—and instead we're supposed to not just take them seriously, but put them on a pedestal as freedom fighters for "inclusion" and "diversity" in the New World Order.

Hate Crimes Against Christians

While in America it's common to be slandered and defamed for being a Christian, believers in other parts of the world like North Korea, Saudi Arabia, Iran, Afghanistan, and numerous regions in Africa, they literally risk their lives by professing belief in Jesus Christ.[408] It never makes the news in the United States, but militant Muslims in African countries (including Somalia, Nigeria, Libya, and Yemen) regularly murder them.[409]

---

[408] The Guardian "Persecution of Christians 'coming close to genocide' in Middle East" by Patrick Wintour (May 2nd 2019)

[409] BBC "Christian persecution 'at near genocide levels'" (May 3rd 2019)

Aside from being mocked and slandered by the Hollywood elite and Christianphobia allowed to flourish on the Big Tech platforms, when Christians in America are victims of hate crimes those attacks go mostly unnoticed—and are only reported in the local newspapers or in a 15-second sound bite on the local television news.

The ADL [Anti-Defamation League] claims to fight against "hate" and "bias" to "protect Democracy and ensure a just and inclusive society for all," but they aren't concerned in the least about hate against Christians. They're an anti-Christian hate group who work to protect and promote Jews, gays, transgenders, and any group of people who are non-White.

The Southern Poverty Law Center, another anti-White and anti-Christian hate group, has what they call a "hate map" on their website showing all of the groups they hate and where they're located. And this map was used by a mass shooter in 2012 to target a Christian organization called the Family Research Council which is a think tank and lobbying organization that has opposed gay "marriage" and other Leftist agendas like the LGBTQ child grooming movement.[410]

The gunman told police he intended to kill as many people as possible but was thankfully tackled by the building manager (despite being shot in the arm himself) and was able to stop what would have been a mass casualty event. The shooting soon vanished from the news, never to be mentioned again. The shooter was later

---

[410] Fox News "Christian nonprofit Family Research Council remains on SPLC's 'hate map' 10 years after terrorist attack" by Emma Colton (August 15th 2022)

convicted of terrorism charges and sentenced to 25 years in prison.[411]

An 84-page report published by the Family Research Council identified at least 420 attacks against 397 different churches between 2018 and 2022 including arson, vandalism, and bomb threats.[412] One of these involved a church in San Diego that was vandalized with satanic symbols by someone (or a group) who spray painted them on the building after the church made headlines for denouncing a local drag queen story hour event.[413]

Churches across the country were vandalized with pro-abortion messages shortly after the Supreme Court decision overturning Roe v. Wade was leaked in 2022. Churches in Wisconsin, Michigan, New York, Virginia, Oregon, Louisiana, and others were all vandalized by pro-abortion zealots.[414]

Antifa social media accounts were also posting the locations of Pregnancy Resource Centers, which are pro-life organizations that encourage pregnant women not to have abortions and offer other options like counseling to help prepare them for motherhood, or connecting them with adoption agencies to place the children with couples who will raise them as their own. Such targeting has led

---

[411] NBC News "Man gets 25 years for attack on Family Research Council headquarters" by M. Alex Johnson (September 19th 2013)

[412] The Daily Signal "An Atmosphere of Lawlessness': Attacks on Churches Nearly Triple in 4 Years, New Report Finds" by Ben Johnson (December 16th 2022)

[413] KUSI News "Chula Vista church vandalized with Satanic imagery" (September 8th 2019)

[414] America Magazine "Catholic churches vandalized by abortion-rights advocates following Supreme Court ruling" by Michael J. O'Loughlin (June 28th 2022)

to numerous cases of vandalism and arson against these facilities as well.[415]

One in Madison, Wisconsin was firebombed with a Molotov cocktail and graffiti spray painted on the building that read, "If abortions aren't safe, you aren't either."[416] Another Pregnancy Resource Center was set on fire in Peoria, Illinois during this tense time period after it was learned that Roe v. Wade was being overturned.[417]

Every Christmas there are local news reports of Nativity scenes that were set up outside of churches and peoples' homes which were destroyed, and while these crimes may make the local news, the regular occurrences of such hate crimes are ignored by the Liberal media industrial complex as a whole. But if someone drops some leaflets outside a synagogue or in a Jewish neighborhood criticizing Judaism or claiming Jewish secularists are uniquely over-represented in positions of power in the government or the media, then it's literally a national news story and gets denounced by members of Congress.[418]

World champion boxer Manny Pacquiao was assaulted while at a popular Los Angeles shopping mall called The Grove by a gay extremist who spotted him and was upset that Pacquiao had posted a Bible verse on his

---

[415] Wisconsin State Journal "Catholic churches vandalized by abortion-rights advocates following Supreme Court ruling" by Alexander Shur (May 9th 2022)

[416] New York Times "Anti-Abortion Group in Wisconsin Is Hit by Arson, Authorities Say" by Luke Vander Ploeg and Addison Lathers (May 8th 2022)

[417] WCBU.org "Authorities: Fire At Peoria Anti-Abortion Pregnancy Center Was Intentionally Set" by Tim Shelley (May 3rd 2021)

[418] The Palm Beach Post "Discovery of anti-Semitic flyers outside homes across Florida leads to call for federal probe" by Julius Whigham II (July 1st 2022)

Instagram recently denouncing sexual perversion.[419] Pacquiao obviously could have knocked the man out with one punch, but restrained himself and defused the situation. And instead of being commended for not breaking the man's face, Pacquiao was banned from the mall by the owners who denounced him as a "homophobe."[420]

In March 2023 a transgender "man" committed a mass shooting at a private Christian school in Nashville, Tennessee, killing three nine-year-old children and three adults. And during their investigation police discovered the shooter had written a detailed manifesto explaining why "he" did it, but authorities refused to publish it, or even discuss the contents of it, claiming it would be "dangerous."[421]

After several months and numerous legal challenges by those demanding police reveal the motive for the attack (and the shooter's manifesto), the courts still refused to release it, but the reason was obvious. They were trying to cover-up the fact that it was an anti-Christian hate crime committed by a transgender terrorist.

Even the Wikipedia page about the incident (titled 2023 Nashville School Shooting) respects the shooter's "preferred pronouns" referring to Audrey Hale throughout the article using he/him pronouns and calls her "Aiden" which is the masculine name "he" went by once identifying as transgender.[422]

---

[419] LGBTQ Nation "Boxer Manny Pacquiao attacked outside restaurant for antigay comments" (April 4th 2016)

[420] Los Angeles Times "Manny Pacquiao is banned from L.A.'s Grove for anti-gay comments" by Chuck Schilken (March 18th 2016)

[421] CBS News "Nashville school shooter's writings reignite debate over releasing material written by mass killers" July 25th 2023)

[422] https://en.wikipedia.org/wiki/2023_Nashville_school_shooting

The Left Embracing Satanism

The Marxist establishment doesn't just hate Christians and God, they actually admire Satan—and this isn't hyperbole or political rhetoric. They literally do. In the coming years we'll see theistic Satanism rise—not just clownish groups like the "Church of Satan" or the "Satanic Temple," but more serious groups that espouse the doctrine that Satan is actually the "good" God, and they'll proclaim the God of the Bible is the "evil" one who "enslaved" Adam and Eve as robotic animals, deprived of free will.

The great secret of most occult fraternities is that they believe Satan is the "good" God, who helped mankind break free from the prison of ignorance in the Garden of Eden by convincing Adam and Eve to eat from the Tree of Knowledge of Good and Evil. Nineteenth century occultist Helena Blavatsky, whose 1888 book *The Secret Doctrine* is credited with helping revive interest in the occult in our modern age, wrote "Satan will now be shown, in the teaching of the Secret Doctrine, allegorized as Good, and Sacrifice, a God of Wisdom."[423]

This same view is echoed by nearly all classic occult authors from Eliphas Levi and Alice Bailey, to Aleister Crowley, who wrote, "This serpent, Satan, is not the enemy of Man," but he is good, and he "made Gods of our race."[424]

An increasing number of people in the LGBTQ+ community are embracing Baphomet as one of their symbols, the hermaphroditic human/goat figure said to have been worshiped by the inner circle of the Knights

---

[423] Helena Blavatsky - The Secret Doctrine v. II page 237

[424] Aleister Crowley - Magick: In Theory and Practice page 193

Templar.[425] For hundreds of years Baphomet has been used as Satanic symbol, from people like Aleister Crowley to the Church of Satan in the 1960s to The Satanic Temple today.

And the creator of a transgender clothing line carried by Target also incorporated Baphomet into his designs because it's "a deity who themselves is mixture of genders, beings, ideas and existences. They [meaning Baphomet] reject binary stereotypes and expectations," adding "Satan respects pronouns. He loves all LGBT+ people."[426]

But the coming Luciferian religion is not just about trolling Christians by adopting satanic symbols or some abstract philosophy pondering the history of mankind and the origin of consciousness. As technology continues to advance at a breathtaking pace, Transhumanism will also rise in popularity with many people believing that through science and technology they'll be able to literally become "immortal," either through manipulating human DNA or replacing body parts as they wear out with 3D printed or lab-grown organs—or even transitioning human beings into what they're calling "inorganic life forms" by uploading the contents of one's brain into the "cloud" or external silicon databases where they can live as "gods" in a virtual world of cyberspace.

Transhumanist advocates see this as the next phase of evolution through "intelligent design" instead of by natural selection. And such ideas may sound insane and the stuff of science fiction (and they are), but there are also some very wealthy and dedicated believers who are

---

[425] Eliphas Levi - Transcendental Magic p. 307

[426] Fox News "Target customers shocked after company features pride items by Satanist partner: Devil is 'hope' and 'love'" by Kristine Parks (May 24th 2023)

literally working night and day hoping to make such ideas a reality.[427] Transhumanism and ancient occult philosophy have converged with adherents believing that they will finally be able to achieve Godhood like Satan said they could in the Garden of Eden.

Dr. Richard Seed, a geneticist who horrified the medical community by advocating for cloning human beings in the 1990s, had even more radical notions. He was a Transhumanist who once ominously stated, "We are going to become gods, period. If you don't like it, get off. You don't have to contribute, you don't have to participate, but if you are going to interfere with *me* becoming a god, you're going to have trouble. There'll be warfare."[428]

He died in 2013 at the age of 85, so things obviously didn't work out as he expected, but others are carrying on his vision. One of them is Ray Kurzweil, who has become the leading proponent of Transhumanism, and has worked for Google since 2012. He even signed up to be cryogenically frozen if he dies before technology is advanced enough to turn him into a "god," hoping to be thawed out in the future if such advancements are achieved.[429]

Elon Musk is also a Transhumanist, and his company Neuralink is developing neural interfaces, or BMIs (brain machine interfaces) in hopes of enabling humans to

---

[427] Insider "6 Billionaires who want to live forever" by Cadie Thompson (September 2nd 2015)

[428] TechnoCalyps - Part II - Preparing for the Singularity documentary by Frank Theys (2006)

[429] Wired "Ray Kurzweil's Plan: Never Die" by Kristen Philpkoski (November 18th 2002)

become super-intelligent cyborgs.[430] He has also suggested that a new religion is needed, saying, "Too many people have lost faith in the future. A new philosophy is needed"[431] and is developing an artificial intelligence entity called xAI which he says aims to "understand the true nature of the universe."[432]

This discussion is far beyond the scope of this book, but just a few years ago bringing up these issues would have been considered pure fantasy and delusional, but they're increasingly being taken seriously and the implications of such technology, if it successfully progresses, will be extremely difficult to grapple with.

Most Transhumanism proponents neglect to even begin to consider the ramifications of their goals, and are willing to naively turn their mind and body over to multinational mega-corporations who can't even be trusted with users' personal data or protecting their privacy, but they're still willing to grant these same companies physical access to their own brain through a neural interface, just like the enslaved humans in *The Matrix* films.

---

[430] Axios "Elon Musk: Humans must merge with machines" by Mike allen and Jim VanderHei (November 26th 2018)

[431] https://twitter.com/elonmusk/status/1603902562071040000

[432] TechCrunch "Elon Musk wants to build AI to 'understand the true nature of the universe'" by Kyle Wiggers (July 12th 2023)

The LGBTQ+ Agenda

All they wanted was the right to get "married" they said, which happened in 2015 when the U.S. Supreme Court dictated to the American people that the definition of marriage should be changed from a man and a woman partnered together for a lifetime committed relationship to that of two men or two women as well. This, despite a marriage being defined as a partnership between a man and a woman ever since the beginning of the human race —and this mandated redefining of marriage was the moment when our society began sliding down the slippery LGBTQ+ slope into the Twilight Zone.

Allowing two men and two women to call themselves a "married" couple wasn't enough though. Soon just a few short years later we saw the rise of "drag kids"— young boys dressed as drag queens and performing in gay bars where grown men throw dollar bills at them just like patrons do to strippers in strip clubs.[433] And then teachers began telling their elementary school students that little boys might actually be girls and vice versa. And schools started inviting drag queens to perform for students and even holding gay "Pride" parades on school grounds.[434]

These so-called "drag kids" aren't just a few isolated instances, they've become an entire industry. In 2018 ABC's flagship morning show *Good Morning America*

---

[433] The Daily Wire "11-Year-Old Boy Dressed In Drag Dances At Gay Bar, Gets Dollar Bills Thrown At Him" by Amanda Prestigiacomo (December 17th 2018)

[434] Los Angeles Times "Fight erupts at anti-Pride Day protest outside L.A. school where trans teacher's flag was burned" by Summer Lin, Andrew J. Campa, and Howard Blume (June 2nd 2023)

famously hosted "Desmond is Amazing" when he was just 11-years-old, who sashayed onto the stage to a thunderous applause.[435] He's just one of many pre-teen "drag kids" whose parents have infected social media with such material which is then celebrated and amplified by the legacy media outlets.

In 2019 YouTube, which also hosts full length films by major studios aside from user-generated content, started streaming a documentary called *Drag Kids*, not to sound the alarm about the practice, but to celebrate and promote it. Netflix produced a series called *AJ and the Drag Queen* about a 10-year-old boy who travels around with a drag queen as he performs in shows across the country.[436] In 2022 the Discovery channel produced a documentary about child drag queens—again to glorify them, not to denounce the growing trend.[437]

They feel so emboldened now since gender-benders and perverts are widely celebrated in pop culture at every Hollywood award show and boosted to go viral on the Big Tech platforms, that in 2021 the San Francisco Gay Choir (yes, that's actually the name of the organization—not just the San Francisco Choir, but the *gay* choir) released a song with lyrics about how "We're coming for your children…You think we'll corrupt your kids if our agenda goes unchecked. Funny. Just this once, you're correct." They go on, "We'll convert your children. Happens bit by

---

[435] Good Morning America YouTube channel "The 11-year-old trailblazing drag kid 'Desmond is Amazing'
(November 2nd 2018) original URL: https://www.youtube.com/watch?v=JxdvOLdG_34

[436] NewsBusters "Sick: RuPaul's New Drag Queen Dramedy Sexualizes 10-Year-Old Child as a 'Top'" by Elise Ehrhard (January 13th 2020)

[437] The Blaze "Shocking new teenage drag queen doc from Tyra Banks, Discovery+ eviscerated online as 'child abuse,' 'grooming'" by Phil Shiver (May 2nd 2022)

bit. Quietly and subtly, and you will barely notice it."[438] The chorus in the song is literally *"We're coming for your children."*

To promote their agenda even further, countless fake polls are published with highly skewed numbers attempting to show that LGBTQ people aren't just one or maybe two percent of the population (which they are), but that *twenty or thirty percent* of people are either gay or some kind of queer or transgender.[439] One such poll claimed that more freshman at Harvard and Yale identify as LGBT-whatever than consider themselves Conservative.[440]

38% of college students at Brown University in Rhode Island said they "identify" as LGBTQ as well, according to a recent poll.[441] The CDC claims that 25% of high school students identity as LGBTQ, which is utterly ridiculous.[442]

Part of the reason the percentages are so absurdly high is because not identifying as queer is seen as being homophobic these days, and many straight kids falsely check that they're some kind of LGBTQ on these surveys in order to inflate the percentages so the queers don't feel like such a small minority. It's like stuffing the ballot

---

[438] Fox News "San Francisco Gay Men's Chorus faces backlash for 'we're coming for your children' video" by Sam Dorman (July 9th 2021)

[439] Newsweek "Nearly 40 Percent of U.S. Gen Zs, 30 Percent of Young Christians Identify as LGBTQ, Poll Shows" by Paul Bond (October 20th 2021)

[440] NBC News "More Harvard, Yale freshmen identify as LGBTQ than as conservative, surveys find" by Eric Duran and Brooke Sopelsa (September 14th 2018)

[441] Fox News "38% of Brown University students identify as LGBTQ+" by Patrick Hauf (July 11th 2023)

[442] The Hill "1 in 4 high school students identifies as LGBTQ" by Lexi Lonas (April 27th 2023)

box. They're just trying to help their "team" get more votes because they feel sorry for them.

Children aren't born a boy or a girl now, they say. They are "assigned" a sex by the doctors or their parents who "assume" the child's sex because of their genitals. The subversives want kids raised "gender neutral"—meaning not making any distinction between boys and girls at all.[443] The children can later decide for themselves if they want to be a boy or a girl (or neither).

Many suspect that parents who raise their children "gender non-binary" are actually suffering from a form of Munchausen syndrome by proxy.[444] A study conducted back in 1991 published in the National Library of Medicine found that 53% of the mothers of children with gender dysphoria met the criteria for having Borderline Personality Disorder.[445]

Meanwhile all the Leftist online outlets continue to promote gender bending with an endless barrage of stories touting how men should start wearing makeup.[446] And not just to hide an unsightly blemish, but lipstick and eye shadow. And there is a sustained campaign to encourage young boys to wear dresses.[447]

It's almost impossible now to watch any major media outlet without having gays and transgenders shoved in

---

[443] NBC News "'Boy or girl?' Parents raising 'theybies' let kids decide" by Julie Compton (July 19th 2018)

[444] Christian Post "Is Munchausen syndrome by proxy driving kids to identify as trans? Psychiatrists answer" by Brandon Showalter (February 23rd 2023)

[445] Journal of the American Academy of Child and Adolescent Psychiatry. "Mothers of boys with gender identity disorder: a comparison of matched controls" by S Marantz and S Coates (March 30th 1991)

[446] The Daily Beast "Ezra Miller Shows How Gender-Fluid Lipstick Can Be —Beautifully" by Alaina Demopoulos (March 12th 2019)

[447] ABC 7 New York "Boys can be princesses, too! Photo project embraces dress-up princess play for boys" by Jina Mackin (January 14th 2021)

your face on countless TV shows, award shows, and even commercials. In 2021 *Playboy* magazine put a gay man dressed as a "bunny" on the cover, wearing heels and tights. Seriously, a gay man on the cover of *Playboy* magazine![448]

Since Pandora's Box has been opened, now men who identify as women are demanding to be allowed to use women's bathrooms, locker rooms, and showers. Transgender "women" who have been convicted of crimes have even been sent to women's prisons, where they have impregnated and even raped the (actual) women there![449] Despite being biological males and not having any "bottom surgery" (to remove their penis) they "identified" as women, and so they were sent to a women's prison![450]

And then there's the growing problem of biological men who identify as women competing in women's sports and robbing high school girls of college scholarships and robbing college athletes of their rightful place in competitions.[451] It's as if the gates of Hell have been opened and hordes of demons are running amuck, and instead of trying to contain the madness—schools, major corporations, the U.S. military, and the mainstream media are all promoting it.

---

[448] NBC News "Bretman Rock becomes Playboy's first gay male cover star" by Matt Lavietes (October 4th 2021)

[449] New York Post "Incarcerated transgender woman Demi Minor impregnates two inmates at NJ prison by Patrick Reilly (July 16th 2022)

[450] New York Post "Transgender Rikers inmate sentenced to 7 years for raping female prisoner" by Patrick Reilly (April 25th 2022)

[451] Washington Examiner "Female high school athletes fear for their future with inclusion of transgender women in sports" by Joseph Simonson (February 9th 2021)

Pride Month

Every June is the worst because now you can't escape being harassed by LGBTQ+ propaganda around every corner, whether you're scrolling through social media, channel surfing on network television, or even grocery shopping because the cultural Marxists deemed it "Pride Month," which is now basically a national holiday. It used to be called Gay Pride Month, but that wasn't "inclusive enough" since it didn't reference bisexuals, transgenders, pansexuals, and the countless other supposed "genders" and sexual orientations in the queer community.

Virtually every major brand on social media from automobile companies to banks change their profile pictures to incorporate a rainbow into their logos, and most post special messages about how much they support LGBTQ people. Nearly every professional sports team in the NFL, MLB, NBA, and even NHL now hold an annual "Pride Night" in June (or launch a promotional campaign if it's their off season) to celebrate this as well, where the teams coerce players to wear special rainbow jerseys or pins. They even have gay-themed half time shows at the games.[452]

And now there are "Pride" sections in major stores like Target and Walmart with special LGBTQ-themed clothes throughout the month of June.[453] PetSmart even sells rainbow colored "Pride" accessories for dogs and

---

[452] New York Post "Some Rays players choose not to wear LGBTQ Pride Night patches" via Associated Press (June 5th 2022)

[453] Fox Business "Walmart's Pride merchandising unchanged as Target sees backlash over new items" by Daniella Genovise (June 2nd 2023)

cats each year![454] Many major food brands from Bud Light and Kellogg's, to KIND bars and Effen Vodka all produce special gay Pride packaging for their products just like most companies do for normal holidays such as Halloween, Christmas, and Easter.[455]

In 2021 Chipotle started selling special burritos named after popular drag queens to celebrate the "holiday."[456] The following year Taco Bell announced they were sponsoring a "Drag Brunch Tour" at numerous locations and held drag shows inside their restaurants.[457] Some teachers in public schools even have their elementary school kids make Pride flags as an arts and crafts project.[458] And anyone who doesn't participate in LGBTQ Pride celebrations at schools, work, or sporting events is denounced as "homophobic" and their career can be destroyed in an instant.[459]

Targeting Children with Transgenderism

Everyone knows how impressionable young children are. Until the age of six or eight most of them believe in Santa Claus, the Easter Bunny, and the Tooth Fairy. So it wouldn't be hard at all to convince little boys that as they

---

[454] Newsweek "PetSmart Faces Boycott Calls Over Pride Collection: 'Unacceptable'" by Aleks Phillips (May 29th 2023)

[455] CNET "Pride 2022: Food and Drink Brands Giving Back to LGBTQ Causes" by Dan Avery June 24th 2022)

[456] The Food Network "Chipotle Is Hosting Its Own Drag Competition in Honor of Pride Month" by Samantha Leffler (June 1st 2021)

[457] Restaurant Business Magazine "Taco Bell will host a series of drag shows this spring" by Jonathan Maze (April 25th 2022)

[458] Huffington Post "13 Rainbow Craft Ideas To Help Kids Celebrate Pride" by Caitlin McCormack (June 14th 2018)

[459] New York Times "Toronto Blue Jays Cut Player Who Defended Anti-Queer Post" by Jesus Jimenez (June 9th 2023)

THE LGBTQ+ AGENDA

grow up they'll transform into a girl or vice versa. And since transgenders are being celebrated as if they're divine beings endowed with special powers, it seems many Liberal parents *want* their children to be transgender so they can be a symbol of how woke the family is.

The Marxist propaganda trying to normalize incorporating children into drag shows is now everywhere in media—including advertisements. Kaiser Permanente insurance featured a scene from a Drag Queen Story Hour event in one of their commercials in 2019.[460] It started off just showing people from different walks of life, noting that everyone needs health insurance, but for the obvious reason they included a quick segment of a drag queen reading to small children to further desensitize people to the idea.

Major brands like Oreo, Sprite, Pantene shampoo, and Gillette razors have produced commercials featuring and celebrating transgender kids or young adults.[461] In October 2021 the Twix candy company came out with a Halloween-themed commercial about a young boy who wanted to wear a princess dress and his babysitter (a "witch") encouraged him to do so. She even used her "magic" powers to kill another boy who was making fun of him for wearing the dress.[462]

Kraft, best known for their macaroni and cheese, sponsored the publication of a children's book about pronouns titled *His, Hers, Them & Theirs: Learning*

---

[460] News Busters "Kaiser Permanente Ad Says 'Too Bad' to Those Who Say Drag Queen Story Hour Is 'Too Much'" by Elise Ehrhard (October 9th 2019)

[461] Metro Weekly "Pantene champions LGBTQ families in ad featuring trans child with lesbian parents" by Riley Gillis (March 26th 2021)

[462] Newsweek "Why Twix's Halloween Commercial Has Divided the Internet" by Soo Kim (October 29th 2021)

Pronouns with the Bears in 2021 which was read by two drag queens online for a special Christmas-themed Drag Queen Story Hour.[463] There's even a transgender Barbie doll now, modeled after "Lavern" Cox, a transgender actor who was featured on the cover of *Time* magazine in 2014. And a drag queen Build-A-Bear modeled after RuPaul.[464]

In 2021 *Blue's Clues*, a cartoon aimed at preschoolers on Nickelodeon, aired a singalong featuring a drag queen at a Pride parade as it sung how amazing queer people are (including gender non-binary people).[465]

The Democrats' strategy to counter opposition to their new predatory behavior is to call anyone who is against grooming children a QAnon conspiracy theorist.[466] In further attempts to stifle criticism Wikipedia calls the blatant LGBTQ grooming activities a "conspiracy theory."[467]

After a few members of the Proud Boys (the American nationalist organization that often counter-protests at Marxist events) showed up to protest a drag queen story hour event at a library in the San Francisco Bay Area, the local district attorney's office launched a

---

[463] The Media Research Center "Kraft Peanut Butter Sells Kids Book On Trans Pronouns to Make Kids 'Better'" by Gabriel Hays (December 2nd 2021)

[464] CBS News "RuPaul gets a new signature Build-A-Bear (gold heels sold separately)" by Caitlin O'Kane (April 6th 2023)

[465] Washington Examiner "*Blue's Clues* song shows drag queen teaching children about gay, transgender, and nonbinary characters" by Lawrence Richard (May 29th 2021)

[466] LGBTQ Nation "It's a straight line from Q Anon's pedophilia hysteria to the GOP's groomer rhetoric" by John Gallagher (January 20th 2023)

[467] https://web.archive.org/web/20230113014449/https://en.wikipedia.org/wiki/LGBT_grooming_conspiracy_theory

"hate crime" investigation into them.[468] They weren't violent or threatening, all they did was show up and denounce the event for exposing children to sexual themes and call the drag queen a groomer.

After protesters showed up outside a gay bar in Dallas, Texas that held a drag queen event advertised to children, *Newsweek* ran a headline titled "Video of 'Anti-Groomer' Protest Outside Gay Bar Sparks Outrage," giving the impression that it was the *protest* which was the problem, not that drag queens were performing for small children inside.[469] Of course the groomers were upset about the protest so *Newsweek* took their side and portrayed them as the victims of "homophobes."

Until recently it would have been unheard of for anyone to bring children to drag shows (let alone have pre-teen children themselves dress in drag) because it was always seen as an adult form of entertainment. Drag queens often have sexual innuendo names which clearly illustrate and emphasize the adult nature of the shows. The sexual focus is also evident in the fact that all drag queens are gay (or bisexual, or some kind of queer).

Unsurprising to normal people, numerous drag queen story hour readers have been found to be convicted sex offenders or later arrested for possessing child pornography.[470] Two of the drag queens who read books to children at a Houston, Texas library were found to be

---

[468] Washington Post "Proud Boys disrupt drag-queen reading event, prompting hate-crime probe" by Kim Bellware (June 13th 2022)

[469] Newsweek "Video of 'Anti-Groomer' Protest Outside Gay Bar Sparks Outrage" by Shira Li Bartov (June 7th 2022)

[470] ABC 13 "Drag queen storytime reader once charged with child sex assault" by KTRK (March 15th 2019)

convicted child sex offenders.[471] This was only discovered after a Conservative group called Mass Resistance (formerly the Parents' Rights Coalition) investigated the drag queens who were involved. A judge in Milwaukee, Wisconsin who was the head of a local LGBTQ advocacy group called the Cream City Foundation which sponsored drag queen story hour events, was arrested for possession and distribution of child sexual abuse videos.[472]

Another reader at Drag Queen Story Hour[473] in Harrisburg, Pennsylvania was charged with 25 counts of child pornography.[474] And there are undoubtedly many more, but it would take a local journalist reporting on such arrests to take a few extra steps to look into the backgrounds of such perpetrators.

This, at the same time mainstream Liberal outlets are endorsing kink for children.[475] Kink, if you're not aware of it, is basically a synonym for sexual perversion of any and all kinds. *The Washington Post* published an op-ed by one of their writers titled, "Yes, kink belongs at Pride [celebrations]. And I want my kids to see it."[476] Photos now circulate every June showing parents who bring their small children to Pride parades which feature other

---

[471] Life Site News "Second 'Drag Queen Story Hour' library reader exposed as convicted child sex offender" by Mass Resistance (April 29th 2019)

[472] Fox News "Judge who headed 'Drag Queen Story Hour' sponsor arrested on child porn charges" by Houston Keene (March 18th 2021)

[473] check caps on all mentions.

[474] Penn Live "Central Pa. drag queen, activist charged with 25 counts of child pornography: police" by Jenna Wise (June 24th 2022)

[475] The Daily Signal "'You Should Be in Prison': Critics Slam Washington Post Article Encouraging 'Kink Culture' for Children" by Mary Margaret Olohan (July 1st 2021)

[476] Washington Post "Yes, kink belongs at Pride. And I want my kids to see it." by Lauren Rowello (June 29th 2021)

attendees wearing kink gear, including "pup masks" and others who are practically naked.

Tucking And Packing Underwear for Kids

Because an increasing number of progressive parents are either convinced their children are trans or *convincing their children they're trans*, companies are even selling special "tucking" underwear for small "transgender" children.[477] "Tucking" involves shoving the testes up inside the inguinal canals and then pulling the penis and scrotum between the legs and holding it in place with the underwear made of firm material in that area.[478] For transgender "boys" they're selling fake penises (known as "packers"). Such items were once only available on fringe websites but now they're listed for sale on Amazon and even Etsy.[479]

For "Pride Month" in June 2022, Target began selling "chest binders" (also known as compression tops) which women who want to be men use to compress and hide their breasts; and "packing underwear" which include padding to cause a bulge in the crotch to give the appearance of a penis and testicles.[480] It wasn't until the

---

[477] Etsy has an entire section called "Tucking Underwear for Kids" on their website at https://www.etsy.com/market/tucking_underwear_for_kids and Transkids.Biz is another website that sells them. https://transkids.biz/products/tuck-buddies-underwear

[478] The Daily Mail "Transgender designer is accused of 'child abuse' for selling pants that seek to 'flatten' the genitals of boys as young as four - as doctors warn the underwear could cause infertility" by Georgia Edkins and Stephan Adams (April 23rd 2022)

[479] Reduxx "Etsy Shop Selling "Tucking" Underwear For Toddlers" (March 13th 2022)

[480] CBS Austin "Target unveils pro-trans merch for kids, 'chest binders' and 'packing underwear' for 18+" by Alec Schemmel (May 12th 2022)

following year that such products caught the attention of most Conservatives, sparking calls for a boycott.

As part of Target's new LGBT Pride Collection, they also sell "tucking underwear" (or gaffs) which transgender "women" (and drag queens) use to help conceal their penis, which again is done by shoving their testicles up the inguinal canals (where they were before birth) and folding their penis downward under their legs and using a stiff front panel to keep everything in place.[481]

The head of the Health and Human Services department under Joe Biden, Xavier Becerra, supports sex change surgery for children.[482] Not "just" crossdressing the kids and using different pronouns for them. But putting them on puberty blockers and then subjecting them to gender-reassignment surgeries! They call it "health care" or "gender affirming care."

And I won't even describe what such surgeries entail, or the lifelong complications they bring. You can go and Google "vaginoplasty" or "phalloplasty" to see photos of exactly what "gender-affirming" surgeries do to people's genitals. But be warned! They are horrific, but people should know what the end of the road is for transgender patients.

When White House Press Secretary Jen Psaki was asked about the Health and Human Services director endorsing gender-reassignment surgeries for minors she confirmed that is the official stance of the Biden administration, saying it is "a best practice and potentially

---

[481] The Daily Mail "Target is slammed for selling women's bathing suits with a section to 'tuck' private parts in its new Pride collection - that includes clothes for babies and children with trans-friendly slogan" by Lewis Pennock (May 19th 2023)

[482] Fox News "Biden HHS Sec. Becerra suggests support for taxpayer-funded gender-altering procedures on children" by Andrew Mark Miller (April 7th 2022)

lifesaving."[483] The Assistant Health Secretary, Admiral "Rachel" Levine, who is a transgender "woman," is obsessed with legalizing and normalizing putting small children on puberty blockers and giving them gender-reassignment surgeries (which also literally sterilizes them).[484]

Disney Goes Gay

Even Disney, the once family friendly entertainment giant beloved by everyone for generations, has become a vehicle to deliver LGBTQ propaganda to children. A leaked Zoom meeting of Disney executives in 2022 showed them openly talking about the company's "not so secret gay agenda" with one of them bragging they were "adding in queerness" wherever they could and planned for at least 50% of the characters in their films and television series to be LGBTQ+ or racial minorities by the end of 2022.

Shortly after the leaked Zoom meeting it became clear that Disney was keeping their promise to "queer up" more characters, something that had already been happening for the last eight years, but most parents had no idea it was happening at all. Disney had been slowly yet incrementally introducing gay characters starting back in 2014 when the Disney Channel's most popular comedy at the time *Good Luck Charlie* decided to include a lesbian couple who were raising a daughter together.[485]

---

[483] CBN "Biden's Press Secretary Pushes Gender Change Procedures for Kids" by Steve Warren (April 11th 2022)

[484] ABC 7 KATV "Rachel Levine says Biden admin backs gender change therapies for kids" by Zachary Rogers (March 17th 2023)

[485] E! News "Disney Channel Introduces Its First Lesbian Couple on Good Luck Charlie" by Alyssa Toomey (January 28th 2014)

THE LGBTQ+ AGENDA

The next year (in 2015) on the Disney-owned ABC Family Channel [which has since been renamed "Freeform"] a show called *The Fosters* included a scene showing two thirteen-year-old boys kissing which was hailed as another first for the LGTBQ movement.[486]

From there, it just continued to snowball. Disney+ released an animated short called *Out* (2020) about—you guessed it—a kid who comes out to his parents as gay after he moves in with his "roommate" who turns out to be his boyfriend. He was nervous about his parents finding out the truth, but of course, they were thrilled. The film was hailed as Disney/Pixar's "first gay main character."[487]

Then they introduced their first bisexual character in their series *The Owl House* in 2020, which includes a 14-year-old girl in a leading role who used to be interested in boys, but now likes girls.[488] The show's creator is bisexual herself and bragged that she lobbied Disney to turn the character bisexual just like her, and they agreed.[489]

Again, all this started happening years before the leaked Zoom meetings where they openly talked about their agenda, which wasn't even a secret because every time they gayed up a cartoon or movie since 2014 it was celebrated as another "move forward" by the Marxist

---

[486] Breitbart "ABC Family's 'The Fosters' Airs Youngest-Ever Gay Kiss Between Two 13-Year-Old Boys" by Kipp Jones (March 4th 2015)

[487] NBC News "New short film 'Out' features Pixar's first gay main character" by Gwen Aviles (May 22nd 2020)

[488] CNN "Disney confirms its first bisexual lead character, who is also multi-cultural" by Adrianne Morales (August 15th 2020)

[489] New York Post "'The Owl House' becomes Disney's first show with bisexual lead character " by Lee Brown (August 16th 2020)

media.[490] Sadly, most Conservatives didn't notice or were too cowardly to say anything about it, but the leaked Zoom meeting in 2022 laid bare their plan for all to see.

The previous year in June 2021 for "Pride Month" they produced a special "Pride Celebration Spectacular" musical hosted by a drag queen on Disney+.[491] Two words nobody ever thought they would hear in the same sentence—Disney and drag queens. Then in 2022 Disney launched an LGBTQ Pride children's clothing line.[492] And in June 2023 they held their first LGBTQ Pride Night at their theme parks.[493] That same month they released a feature film called *Elemental* which introduced their first "gender non-binary" character, voiced by a "non-binary" actor.[494]

There's no putting the toothpaste back in the tube. Disney is a queer company, and it probably won't be long before they announce that Mickey Mouse is bisexual.

U.S. Military Goes Gay

Gays used to be banned from the U.S. military because no one wants to have a member of their unit checking them, out dreaming of having sex with them; but now our military doesn't just allow them in—they

---

[490] Entertainment Weekly "Disney Channel features its first gay couple on 'Good Luck Charlie'" by Hillary Busis (January 28th 2014)

[491] Asbury Park Press "'Drag Race' star and Disney+ queen Nina West shares why Pride is for all ages" by Alex Biese (June 25th 2021)

[492] Fox Business "Disney announces new 2022 LGBTQ+ clothing collection for kids" by Landon Mion (May 18th 2022)

[493] ABC 10 San Diego "Disneyland announces first ever Pride Night" by Claudia Amezcua (April 16th 2023)

[494] Fox News "Disney's 'Elemental,' which features 'non-binary' character, flops in opening weekend" by Jeffrey Clark (June 20th 2023)

THE LGBTQ+ AGENDA

celebrate them, and are actively recruiting them! Even during the Trump administration various branches of the military started posting messages on their social media accounts celebrating Gay Pride Month, and even posting videos of soldiers in uniform talking about how great it is to have a bunch of queers in the military.[495]

The Department of Defense has been celebrating LGBT Pride Month since 2012.[496] And now every June the different branches of the military post rainbow flags on their Instagram, Facebook, and other social media accounts along with cringeworthy messages about how they "commemorate the proud legacy of LGBT individuals who are part of the fabric of the nation and the U.S. Army."[497]

They even post videos online showing senior officers in uniform standing in front of Pride flags while announcing, "We observe LGBT pride month to mark the progress we've made" and call on all Americans to celebrate lesbians, gays, bisexuals, and transgender people.[498]

Even though President Trump is very LGBT-friendly and never really criticized the community as a whole, he did ban transgender people from serving in the military, causing every Liberal on social media to sound off about

---

[495] Army.mil "Serving with pride: LGBTQ Soldiers celebrate diversity, speak their truth" by Thmas Branding, Army News Service (June 29th 2021)

[496] Washington Post "Pentagon to Observe Gay Pride Month for First Time (by Lisa Rein (June 14th 2012)

[497] https://www.instagram.com/p/CBgjXUWDx2M

[498] U.S. Army's official Army ROTC YouTube channel. "LGBT Pride Month" - Message from the Commander (posted June 16th 2020) and posted on Facebook here: https://www.facebook.com/ArmyROTC/videos/june-is-lgbtpride-month-and-armyrotc-celebrates-the-diversity-of-our-total-force/572626036979834

what a "bigot" he is and how it's "discrimination."[499] We don't allow mentally unstable people around dangerous weapons, and since statistically about half of transgender people are suicidal, that's all the more reason they shouldn't be allowed in the military.[500] Not to mention the female soldiers don't want to have to shower with some "chick with a dick."

But once Trump was out of office and Joe Biden moved in, the woke agenda went into overdrive. First he lifted Trump's ban on transgenders, and then the U.S. Army (and other military branches) began subjecting solders to mandatory diversity, equity, and inclusion training on gender identity to indoctrinate them into accepting transgender and other queer soldiers.[501]

The Air Force then featured a transgender "woman" in a video posted online to mark the made-up Twitter holiday "Transgender Day of Visibility."[502] Lieutenant Colonel "Bree" Fam, one of the highest-ranking "openly transgender" people in the military, who works as an engineer and looks like a six-foot-tall man wearing lipstick with his hair in a ponytail.

The Army released a series of woke recruitment videos in 2021, including one featuring a girl who was proud to have been raised by "two moms," and a cartoon illustration of her story showing a scene from the lesbian

---

[499] NBC News "Trump's controversial transgender military policy goes into effect" by Hallie Jackson and Courtney Kube (April 12th 2019)

[500] NBC News "Half of transgender male teens have attempted suicide, study finds" via Reuters (September 13th 2018)

[501] Washington Free Beacon "As Russia Wages War, US Army Trains Officers on Gender Identity" by Adam Kredo (March 1st 2022)

[502] https://twitter.com/usairforce/status/1509580161376731144

"wedding."[503] She also mentioned how she had been "fighting for freedom since she was a kid" as the ad showed her marching in a gay Pride parade.

That same year the CIA also posted a series of recruiting videos featuring people who would have previously never even been considered for employment in the agency due to psychological problems, but now are being celebrated as part of the new "diversity" initiative. One woman, a "proud Latino," introduced herself as a "cisgender millennial" who said she suffers from anxiety but the CIA is so welcoming they gave her a job anyway.[504] Another video featured a queer man with a giant nose ring. Even NASA now releases videos for "Pride" month featuring employees talking about how they're gay, lesbian, transgender, and gender non-binary and "no matter what your identity is in the community, there's going to be a place for you."[505]

Since LGBT people are supposed to only be celebrated and nothing about their perverted sexual activities or unhealthy lifestyles are supposed to be criticized (like the high rate of HIV or incontinence later in life from their anuses being stretched out),[506] the issue of gay men raping other men in the military is perhaps the most forbidden topic of all. The dirty secret behind President Obama lifting the longstanding ban on gays in

---

[503] Fox News "Army recruitment video features lesbian wedding" by Fox News Staff (March 13th 2021)

[504] Newsweek "Critics Slam 'Woke' CIA Recruitment Video: 'I Am Intersectional'" by Darragh Roche (May 3rd 2021)

[505] https://twitter.com/NASA/status/1532081420520284160

[506] Reuters "Anal sex linked to increased risk of incontinence" by Lisa Rapaport (February 4th 2016)

the military is the frequency of gay soldiers raping other men.[507]

All of the focus around the issue of sexual assault in the military is on women victims (in the rare instances it's mentioned in the media at all), but the fact is that since men make up almost all of the perpetrators in sex crimes, what's always overlooked is that they're not just raping women—the gay ones are raping men. And ever since welcoming gays into the military instead of forbidding them and kicking them out if discovered (which was the policy until 2011), an epidemic of gay men sexually assaulting other men has been occurring.[508]

Such crimes are most often unreported because the victims are too embarrassed to come forward and talk about what happened.[509] Recent estimates are that 90% of male victims don't report such incidents.[510] In attempts to hide the number of men raped by gays in the military—aside from usually only focusing on the female victims—reports often group all forms of unwanted sexual contact into one figure (from groping to attempted rape, to actual rape—or penetrative assault as it's called), so most people dismiss such incidents as just hazing.[511]

And while there is hazing and bullying (the same kinds of juvenile and often perverted "pranks" seen in

---

[507] Washington Times "'Gay' rape in military underreported by Pentagon" by Rowan Scarborough (November 3rd 2015)

[508] New York Times "Men Struggle for Rape Awareness" by Roni Caryn Rabin (January 23rd 2012)

[509] Washington Times "'Gay' rape in military underreported by Pentagon" by Rowan Scarborough (November 3rd 2015)

[510] The Intercept "Culture of Silence: In U.S. Military, Sexual Assault Against Men is Vastly Underreported" by Nick Turse (November 29th 2022)

[511] ABC News "Reports of sexual assault in US military up 13%" by Luis Martinez (September 1st 2022)

college fraternities) which do technically constitute sexual assault—the rapes and attempted rapes are swept under the rug.[512]

The actual number of male rape victims in the military was estimated to be fifteen times higher than what's actually reported less than three years after gays were allowed in, according to a study by the American Psychological Association.[513] 53% of overall known sexual assault victims in the military are now male.[514] These facts are ignored by most of the media because publicizing them is not only deemed homophobic, but also a national security risk because it would undermine faith in our military and hurt recruiting efforts.[515]

The "Father" of "Gay Rights" Movement

While the gay agenda had grown into a tsunami in the 21st century, the storm had been brewing for decades as activists plotted to get LGBTQ lifestyles accepted by society as a whole. The man credited as being the "father" of the "gay rights" movement is Harry Hay, who created a secret society in the 1950s called the Mattachine Society which was named after a French group of entertainers in the 16th century who wore masks when performing. He took inspiration from Freemasonry and

---

[512] Rand Health Quarterly "Needs of Male Sexual Assault Victims in the U.S. Armed Forces" by Miriam Matthews, Coreen Farris, Margaret Tankard, Michael Stephen Dunbar (2018 Volume 8. No. 2)

[513] The Daily Mail "Male-on-male rape in the military is 15 times more prevalent than the Pentagon are reporting, according to a new study" by Khaleda Rahman (November 4th 2015)

[514] The New York Times "In Debate Over Military Sexual Assault, Men Are Overlooked Victims" by James Dao (June 23rd 2013)

[515] Yahoo News "#MenToo: The hidden tragedy of male sexual abuse in the military" by Yahoo News Photo Staff (December 31st 2019)

Communism as well because he admired Marxist ideologies regarding "oppressed" groups.[516]

Harry Hay also supported the infamous pedophile group NAMBLA, the North American Man Boy Love Association, which advocates for eliminating the age of consent laws for sexual contact with children.[517] During the Los Angeles Gay Pride Parade in 1986 he marched holding a banner that read "NAMBLA Walks With Me" because organizers had banned the group from participating in the parade and Harry Hay was upset that they were "discriminating" against NAMBLA.[518]

When he was later confronted about his support for NAMBLA he said, "If the parents and friends of gays are truly friends of gays, they would know from their gay kids that the relationship with an older man is precisely what thirteen, fourteen, and fifteen-year-old kids need more than anything else in the world."[519]

Hay himself says he had a sexual relationship with a 25-year-old adult male when he was just fourteen, and thought it was "beneficial."[520] After Hay died, David Thorstad, an admitted pederast and co-founder of NAMBLA, praised him for being "a vocal and

---

[516] The Trouble with Harry Hay: Founder of the Modern Gay Movement by Stuart Timmons pages 92-93 Alyson Publications (1990) ISBN: 978-1555831752

[517] San Diego Union-Tribune "FBI targets pedophilia advocates. Little-known group promotes 'benevolent' sex'" by Ornell R. Soto (February 14th 2005)

[518] The Phoenix "The Real Harry Hay" by Michael Bronski (July 7th 2002)

[519] The American Spectator "When Nancy met Harry" by Jeffry Lord (October 5th 2006)

[520] The Trouble with Harry Hay: Founder of the Modern Gay Movement by Stuart Timmons pages 35-36 Alyson Publications (1990) ISBN: 978-1555831752

courageous supporter of NAMBLA."[521] Hay had worked closely with the organization for years hoping to legalize and normalize pederasty just like in Ancient Greece where men engaged in sexual relations with young boys and was considered a "normal" part of the culture at the time.[522]

Harvey Milk

Harvey Milk is another gay icon celebrated for being the first openly gay man to be elected to public office, serving as a member of the Board of Supervisors in San Francisco, which is sort of like a City Council. And like virtually all of the gay men held up as heroes in the LGBTQ community for their "trailblazing" work to normalize homosexuality, Harvey Milk himself was a pederast who had a sexual relationship with a 16-year-old boy when he was a 34-year-old man.[523]

In 2008 a biographical film titled *Milk* was released starring Sean Penn which was praised by critics, and was given the Academy Award for the Best Film—and Sean Penn was given the Oscar for Best Actor.[524] Since he served (closeted) in the U.S. Navy, they later decided to celebrate him by naming a ship after him in 2021, and now sailors are forced to be stationed on the USNS [United States Naval Ship] Harvey Milk, a gigantic

---

[521] https://web.archive.org/web/20220314030036/https://www.nambla.org/hayonmanboylove.html

[522] [Box 2/folder 21] Lesbian and Gay Academic Union Records, Coll2011-041, ONE National Gay & Lesbian Archives, USC Libraries, University of Southern California

[523] The Mayor of Castro Street: A Biography of Harvey Milk by Randy Shilts (pages 30–33)

[524] Reuters "Sean Penn wins best actor Oscar for 'Milk'" by Mary Milliken (February 22nd 2009)

replenishment oiler. A Navy ship named after a pederast.[525]

And now that numerous states across the country are mandating that students be indoctrinated with "LGBTQ history" in schools, Harvey Milk is included in social studies text books—portrayed as a hero and civil rights pioneer.[526] After a school in southern California rejected a state-mandated text book because it included a section singing praises of Milk, Governor Gavin Newsom fined the school board $1.5 million dollars for violating the state's mandatory curriculum.[527]

Dr. John Money's Twisted Legacy

Since we can't go a single day without hearing about "gender identity" and the ridiculous ideas about how there are an unlimited number of "genders," it's important people understand the history of the concept and the man behind it. His name is Dr. John Money, a psychologist and "sexologist," and he's the man who is widely credited with coining the terms "gender identity" and "sexual orientation" in the 1960s which planted the seeds for the insanity that would later sweep across the country.[528]

---

[525] Pederasts claim they're not pedophiles, but instead are men attracted to adolescent boys, while pedophiles are attracted to small children, so the pederasts insist they're not molesting children, but they're "helping" young boys "discover" that they're gay.

[526] ABC 7 "Temecula Valley school board adopts textbooks that include Harvey Milk after warnings from Newsom" (July 22nd 2023)

[527] CBS Los Angeles "Gov. Newsom fines Temecula Valley school board $1.5 for rejecting new curriculum" by KCAL-News Staff (July 20th 2023)

[528] While John Money didn't originally coin the terms, he did widely popularize them. It appears that UCLA psychiatrists Robert Stoller and Ralph Greenson jointly coined "gender identity" in 1963.

John Money's concept of gender separated it from one's sex. If you look up the word *gender* in older dictionaries, the definition says something like "either the male or female division of a species," but now many dictionaries have Orwellianly changed the definition to say it has do with one's "identity" and an "individual's personal awareness," and how they "feel."

Like most (if not all) of the early LGBTQ "rights" activists, John Money also endorsed pedophilia, saying, "If I were to see the case of a boy aged ten or eleven who's intensely erotically attracted toward a man in his twenties or thirties, if the relationship is totally mutual, and the bonding is genuinely totally mutual…then I would not call it pathological in any way."[529]

He argued that pedophilia was "harmless in most instances."[530] But he is perhaps best known for recommending that a small boy (David Reimer) whose penis was accidentally cut off during a botched circumcision operation in the 1960s be raised as a girl in order to "remedy" the unfortunate situation.[531]

Dr. Money believed that gender was just a social construct and that there were no differences between boys and girls other than their genitals, so he thought that if the boy was raised as a girl that "she" would act like other girls and could *be* a girl.[532] But as David Reimer

---

[529] Paidika: The Journal of Paedophilia "Interview: John Money" (Spring 1991, vol. 2, no. 3, p. 5)

[530] Sexual Offender Treatment.org "John Money's 'Chronophilia': Untimely Sex between Philias and Phylisms" by Diederik Janssen (January 2017)

[531] The Daily Mail "The spiritual father of trans movement Dr John Money, his twisted experiment in the 1960s" by Tom Leonard (June 25th 2023

[532] Psychology Today "A Boy Raised as a Girl Killed Himself 19 Years Ago Today: Upbringing has limited power to impose gender identity." by Ari Berkowitz (May 5th 2023)

(Brenda) grew up, the brainwashing wasn't working and he rejected being raised as a girl, despite having been subjected to sexual reassignment surgery at 22 months of age which removed his testicles and fashioned a synthetic vulva (vaginoplasty).

Despite his experiment completely failing (with David Reimer not only rejecting being told he was a girl, but also committing suicide as an adult years after he resumed living as a man) and Dr. Money's hypotheses that a boy could be socialized into being a girl proving to be false, his warped ideas about "gender identity" became solidified in the LGBTQ doctrine, not to mention codified into law.

And this goes far beyond someone suffering from gender dysphoria feeling like they were born in the wrong body and wanting to change their "gender" from male to female or vice versa on their own. That was just phase one. Now they demand *no gender* be accepted as a "gender"—or the "gender non-binary" people as they're called. And these oddities aren't just found in fringe communities online. News outlets like *The New York Times* and NBC News are promoting this ideology.[533] And gender non-binary characters who use they/them pronouns are being included in children's cartoons in attempts to normalize it.[534]

Singer Sam Smith, the grammy award-winner of the chart-topping single "Stay With Me" decided to "come out" as gender non-binary in 2019, making him the most famous celebrity to do so at the time. Then two years later singer Demi Lovato did the same thing as she

---

[533] New York Times "How to Raise a Child Without Imposing Gender" by Michael Tortorello (March 7th 2019)

[534] Newsweek "Transformers' First Non-Binary Character Sparks Backlash" by Chloe Mayer (May 13th 2023)

descended into madness.[535] But it doesn't stop there—it never stops. In 2017 numerous states began issuing drivers licenses to "gender non-binary" people using a letter X instead of M or F to signify "other."[536] By 2023 nearly half of all states allowed such practice.[537]

Then people started suing to have "no gender" as an option included on birth certificates instead of just a boy or girl.[538] Thirteen different states now allow "non-binary" birth certificates to be issued.[539] In 2021 the American Medical Association recommended that a baby's sex no longer be included on birth certificates![540] As of 2023, seventeen different states allow people to amend their birth certificates to list "X" as their gender.[541]

Of course there isn't a requirement for a medical diagnosis like an MRI brain scan because there is no such thing as "no gender." All that's needed for these changes is for someone to just say they are gender "neutral" or "non-binary" or whatever the hell new term they've come up with to describe their insanity.

---

[535] USA Today "Stars like Demi Lovato, Elliot Page, Sam Smith identify as nonbinary. What does that mean?" by David Oliver (May 19th 2021)

[536] The Washington Post "Meet the first person in the country to officially receive a gender-neutral driver's license" by Perry Stein (June 30th 2017)

[537] The Hill "Here are the states where you can (and cannot) change your gender designation on official documents" by Brooke Migdon (May 31st 2022)

[538] WCAX CBS 3 Vermont parents can now use gender X marker on child's birth certificate" by Calvin Cutler (February 9th 2023)

[539] https://www.usbirthcertificates.com/articles/gender-neutral-birth-certificates-states

[540] Fox News "AMA faces backlash after opposing putting sex on birth certificates" by Sam Dorman (August 2nd 2021)

[541] The Hill "Here are the states where you can (and cannot) change your gender designation on official documents" by Brooke Migdon (May 31st 2022)

Women identifying as transgender "men" who have given birth to children are even suing the government trying to have themselves legally declared the children's *father*.[542] And it's not just a few isolated instances—this is an increasing legal battle that transgender "birthing persons" are waging.[543]

In 2017 the Dove soap company released a commercial featuring what they called "real moms" with their babies and included a transgender "woman" who fathered a child, but he not only identifies as a "woman" he also identifies as the child's mom![544] No sane society would allow someone so delusional to have custody of a child, but these sorts of things aren't just allowed to happen—it's being celebrated by a major household brand!

DeTransitioners

While transgenderism is being hailed as the next "exciting" phase of human "evolution," what's rarely talked about are the *detransitioners*, or the people who at one point in their lives decided to try portraying themselves as the opposite gender, often taking hormones and even having surgery, who then later regret their decision and decide to revert back to their original gender.

The phenomena first came to widespread attention in May 2021 when CBS's *60 Minutes* featured interviews with a group of them, causing LGBTQ activists and their

---

[542] BBC "Transgender man wants to be named father" (June 7th 2018)

[543] Chicago Tribune "In a first for Illinois, transgender man who gave birth will be listed as the father on his baby's birth certificate" by Nara Schoenberg (January 14th 2020)

[544] Newsbusters "Dove Ad Features Transgender Mom: 'No One Right Way" by Sarah Stites (April 12th 2017)

allies to completely freak out. The LGBTQ lobbying organization GLAAD slammed the *60 Minutes* report saying it was "a shameful segment fear mongering about trans youth,"[545] and were especially upset because it included some of the detransitioners explaining that they were convinced to change their gender after watching popular transgender YouTubers and joining online trans communities on Tumblr where members encourage people to change their gender if they're the slightest bit uncomfortable with their body or confused about their identity.

The Human Rights Campaign, another queer advocacy group, said it "further marginalized and victimized" transgender people.[546] They were concerned all right. Concerned that people were finally beginning to hear about the dark side of trying to change one's "gender" and how there are people who deeply regret it and are warning others not to try it. Many Leftist lunatics who live their lives online reacted as if this was the start of a transgender holocaust.

Media outlets that will even mention detransitioners cite figures that are very low, trying to downplay the number of people who regret their "transition." The supposedly small percentage of detransitioners is most likely because they don't get the celebration and adoration of those who "come out as trans." Many who detransition are embarrassed about what they had done and so they quietly revert back to their original identity and try to get on with their lives.

---

[545] The Wrap "GLAAD Slams 'Shameful' '60 Minutes' Story on Transgender Youth" by Lindsey Ellefson (May 24th 2021)

[546] Metro Weekly "60 Minutes criticized for 'dangerous' and 'dehumanizing' segment on transgender healthcare" by Rhuaridh Marr (May 26th 2021)

Rapid-Onset Gender Dysphoria

Some believe that the cause of so many young people thinking they're transgender is due to rapid-onset gender dysphoria, or a social contagion fueled by social media (and now mainstream media), and peer pressure.[547] One transgender psychologist named "Erica" Anderson (who was born a man) and who has helped hundreds of teens transition, now expresses that "she" is worried the trend has "gone too far," saying, "What happens when the perfect storm—of social isolation, exponentially increased consumption of social media, the popularity of alternative identities—affects the actual development of individual kids? We're sailing in uncharted seas."[548]

One explanation for rapid-onset gender dysphoria is that it's a maladjusted way children (especially girls) deal with being uncomfortable with their body during puberty and the pressures of being sexy, so they're repulsed by their own gender—feeling they can't compare to the cultural standards of beauty.

Often there are underlying mental health conditions which exacerbate their body image discomfort. Many are just lesbians, so they're confused about being sexually attracted to other girls and think maybe they're a boy in the wrong body because of the explosion of transgender propaganda in recent years.

Similarly many teen boys who think they're transgender are just gay (which you're not supposed to say is also abnormal and something the medical

---

[547] The Daily Caller "Growing Body of Evidence Shows 'Social Influence' Is Causing Teens To Undergo Sex Changes" by Laurel Duggan (November 25th 2022)

[548] Los Angeles Times "A transgender psychologist reckons with how to support a new generation of trans teens" by Jenny Jarvie (April 12th 2022)

community should research in order to prevent or cure, just like transgenderism).

A young woman named Chloe Cole, who at age 15 got a double mastectomy removing her breasts in order to "transition" to a boy, later changed her mind in less than a year and a half after realizing she made a mistake and is one of the more visible detransitioners.[549] Aside from giving numerous interviews detailing her story to warn others, she filed a lawsuit against Kaiser Permanente hospital in 2022 for breaching the standard of care for doing the double mastectomy on her when she was just a child.[550]

Transgender advocates argue that Conservatives being outraged over hospitals performing "sex change" surgeries or "gender affirming care" as it's called, on minors isn't happening, while at the same time denouncing those who are against it.[551]

Helena Kerschner is another young woman who speaks out about the danger of rapid-onset gender dysphoria after once identifying as a transgender man.[552] "I don't think I would have ever even considered seeing myself as a boy without the social aspects, especially if I hadn't joined these online communities specifically because there wasn't anything at the time, really in my

---

[549] New York Post "'I literally lost organs:' Why detransitioned teens regret changing genders" by Rikki Schlott (June 18th 2022)

[550] The Daily Signal "Detransition Advocate Chloe Cole Sues Doctors for 'Breaching Standard of Care'" by Dan Hart (November 16th 2022)

[551] The Daily Mail "Pink-haired Portland surgeon who performs sex-change surgery on trans CHILDREN admits they face lifetime of infertility, incontinence and sexual dissatisfaction, in now-deleted video" by James Reinl (July 14th 2023)

[552] The Christian Post "Female detransitioner says gender dysphoria must be treated like mental health issue" by Leah MarieAnn Klett (April 27th 2021)

school or in my community, that was influencing me. It was all online," she now says.[553]

A retired Navy SEAL named Chris Beck famously became a transgender "woman" in 2013, and then years later announced that he had detransitioned back to a man and now says that he destroyed his life by thinking he was transgender and is warning people about not transitioning their children if they're confused about who they are.[554]

Numerous studies have shown that the vast majority of children who suffer from gender dysphoria end up growing out of it once they go through puberty.[555] And most probably wouldn't have even questioned their gender at all if the idea hadn't been planted in their minds in the first place.

Other Possible Causes

Sigmund Freud believed homosexuality is caused by a disruption in a child's psycho-social development.[556] Other psychologists agree.[557] An article in *Scientific America* titled "Oedipus Complex 2.0: Like it or not, parents shape their children's sexual preferences" states,

---

[553] Ibid

[554] New York Post "Retired Navy SEAL Chris Beck, who came out as trans, announces detransition: 'destroyed my life'" by Emma Colton (December 11th 2022)

[555] Those who no longer experience gender dysphoria are called "desisters" because they desist as opposed to "persisters" whose dysphoria persists. Many of those who do desist later identity as gay, lesbian, or bisexual, but not as transgender.

[556] *Basic Freud: Psychoanalytic Thought for the 21st Century* by Michael Kahn, Ph.D page 77 - on the negative resolution of the Oedipus complex (2002 Basic Books)

[557] Psychoanalytic Psychology "A special oedipal mechanism in the development of male homosexuality" pages 341-359 by Lewes, K. (1998)

"This basic developmental system, one in which certain salient childhood events 'imprint' our psychosexuality, may not be terribly uncommon. In fact, that early childhood experiences mold our adult sexual preferences —specifically, what turns us on and off, however subtle or even unconscious these particular biases may be—could even be run-of-the-mill."[558]

Some studies have shown that people who were molested as children are inclined to later become child molesters themselves when they're adults.[559] So are people *born* pedophiles, or do they become pedophiles because of some horrific experience they themselves fell victim to as a child that altered their brain and perverting their desires?

It's severely politically incorrect to even remotely compare pedophiles to homosexuals, but isn't it obvious that they both suffer from a similar sexual attraction dysfunction? Scientists have even identified a high correlation between people who were molested as children and those who identify as gay when they're adults.[560]

It's not just politically incorrect to say—and if you do say it, you could easily and quickly end your career, get kicked out of school, and/or banned from social media— but gay people (and transgenders) are *not* normal. That

---

[558] Scientific American "Oedipus Complex 2.0: Like it or not, parents shape their children's sexual preferences" by Jesse Bering (August 17th 2010

[559] The British Journal of Psychiatry "Cycle of child sexual abuse: Links between being a victim and becoming a perpetrator" by M. Glasser, I. Kolvin, D. Campbell, A. Glasser, I. Leitch and S. Farrelly(January 2nd 2018)

[560] Archives of Sexual Behavior "Comparative data of childhood and adolescence molestation in heterosexual and homosexual persons" by Marie E. Tomeo, Donald I. Templer, Susan Anderson and Debra Kotler (Vol. 30, November 5, 2001)

doesn't mean you should hate them. But it doesn't mean we should ignore the scientific and obvious reality. But you're not allowed to say that they have a birth defect if they're actually "born that way" as many claim.

And you're certainly not allowed to say they have a mental disorder. Instead, the Establishment is trying to frame the issue as if there's no more of a difference between someone's sexual orientation and gender identity than there is between someone who prefers to date blondes over brunettes, or someone who is left-handed vs right-handed.

Of course there's a world of difference between what hand somebody writes with or throws a baseball with and people using body parts in ways they clearly weren't designed for (or cutting them off because they feel like they were born in the wrong body).

You're not allowed to have this conversation though, or even suggest that there is anything wrong with these people in any way, whether from a birth defect in a region of the brain that regulates sexual orientation and gender identity, or whether they developed some kind of mental disorder or maladjustment strategy to cope with the underlying issues.[561] But inquisitive people can't help but suspect that whatever is causing transgenderism and homosexuality is being covered up, and any investigation into it is violently discouraged.

---

[561] Most Christians (as well as non-Christians) think that only the Old Testament denounces homosexuality (which it does in Leviticus 20:13), but the New Testament does as well in Romans 1:26-27 and 1st Corinthians 6:9-10, so the arrival of Jesus didn't change God's stance on the behavior.

Endocrine Disruptors

Aside from rapid-onset gender dysphoria, others point to hormonal imbalances that may be caused from synthetic estrogen or what are called endocrine disruptors that are believed to ultimately result in birth defects in the brain as a fetus develops (known as the hormone theory of sexual orientation).[562]

But for well over a decade there have been concerns that these chemicals have been feminizing boys when exposed to them as they're developing in the womb. In 2005 the University of Rochester Medical Center in New York found that "Gender-bending chemicals mimicking the female hormone oestrogen can disrupt the development of baby boys" in the first human study about this after the effects had previously been widely known to occur in tests on animals.[563]

A few years later in 2009 they released a follow-up study further confirming that "Chemicals in plastics alter the brains of baby boys, making them more feminine."[564]

The findings were reported in some mainstream outlets, including *The Los Angeles Times,* which noted, "Boys born to mothers who have above-normal levels of the controversial chemicals known as phthalates in their urine are less likely to exhibit masculine behavior, a new study has found. Phthalates, which block the activity of

---

[562] Pediatric Neuroendocrinology "Sexual Hormones and the Brain: An Essential Alliance for Sexual Identity and Sexual Orientation" Volume 17 chapter 22-35 (2009) by Alicia Garcia-Falgueras and Dick F. Swaab

Trends in Cognitive Sciences "Sex-related variation in human behavior and the brain" pages 448–456 by Melissa Hines (October 2010)

[563] New Scientist "'Gender-bending' chemicals found to 'feminise' boys" by Andy Coghlan (May 27th 2005)

[564] BBC "Plastic Chemicals 'Feminise Boys'" (November 16th 2009)

male hormones such as androgens, could be altering masculine brain development."[565]

And while such findings should have caused as big of concern as the discovery of cancerous chemicals or the dangers of gun violence, these studies went mostly unnoticed.

Scientists have also found that the lower the levels of testosterone a fetus is exposed to during gestation (growth), the more feminized the child will be if it's a boy, and the more likely they are to be gay.[566] And they found that by altering the levels of testosterone in pregnant animals they can change the sexual orientation of their offspring, thus *making them* gay.[567] They even know the specific region of the brain that is affected—the third interstitial nucleus of the anterior hypothalamus, or the INAH-3, which is the part of the brain that is responsible for sexual behavior (the sexually dimorphic nucleus).[568]

Research by Ray Blanchard (who himself is gay) found that when a child is forming in utero, if there are high levels of antibodies against the NLGN4Y protein (which is involved in brain development in males), then

---

[565] Los Angeles Times "Softeners in plastics may affect masculinity in young boys, study says" by Thomas H. Maugh II (November 15th 2009)

[566] Frontiers in Neuroendocrinology "Prenatal endocrine influences on sexual orientation and on sexually differentiated childhood behavior" by Melissa Hines Volume 32, issue 2 pages 170-182 (April 2011)

[567] Frontiers in Neuroendocrinology "Hormones of choice: The neuroendocrinology of partner preference in animals" by Henley, C.L., Nunez, A.A., & Clemens, L.G. volume 32, issue 2 pages 146-154 (April 2011)

[568] Science Journal "A Difference in Hypothalamic Structure Between Heterosexual and Homosexual Men" by Simon LeVay (August 30th 1991)

the brain is also more feminized.[569] This research indicates that the more boys a woman gives birth to, the more likely they are to be gay because there is a higher level of the protein each pregnancy.[570]

Dr. Deborah Soh, author of *The End of Gender*, suggests that further researching the cause of homosexuality and transgenderism with the goal of preventing it may be "unethical" because she knows if scientists confirm it's a birth defect that could be prevented by pregnant women avoiding hormone-altering endocrine disruptors or offsetting them through medication, that would undermine LGBTQism, therefore the people who have been celebrating and promoting it will be viewed in hindsight like other medical quackery throughout history.

Before plastic food packaging was the norm, it was mostly cardboard, metal, and glass. So is it just a coincidence that as plastic food packaging containing BPA became the standard that society has seen an explosion in gay people and transgenders? Also in recent years researchers have been reporting that sperm counts have dropped 50% over the last several generations and testosterone levels in men have also been dramatically declining.[571]

Women's workout clothes have also recently been found contain as much as *40 times* the levels of BPA that has been deemed safe—since sports bras, leggings, and

---

[569] Proceedings of the National Academy of Sciences of the United States of America "Male homosexuality and maternal immune responsivity to the Y-linked protein NLGN4Y" by Anthony F. Bogaert, Malvina N. Skorska, Chao Wang, and Ray Blanchard (January 2018)

[570] The End of Gender: Debunking the Myths About Sex and Identity in Our Society by Dr. Debra Soh page 104

[571] Smithsonian Magazine "Human Sperm Counts Declining Worldwide, Study Finds" by Will Sullivan (November 22nd 2022)

athletic shirts are made of synthetic fibers (plastic) so they don't absorb sweat like cotton clothes do and instead helps wick it away.[572] The BPA in the clothes is absorbed through the skin because of the close contact, and the Center for Environmental Health sent legal notices to eight brands of popular women's clothes putting them on notice about the concerning levels of the chemical found in their clothes.[573]

Some suspect soy consumption is causing the drop in testosterone since it contains phytoestrogens or plant-based estrogen, effecting hormones levels—feminizing males.[574] Is consuming too much soy contributing to the gender-bending and sexual disorientation epidemic? Is it causing hormone imbalances in pregnant women who consume it, thus altering the brains of their baby boys?

Robert F. Kennedy Jr. made a very interesting statement during an interview on Dr. Jordan Peterson's podcast when Peterson stated he believes the apocalyptic hysteria about climate change has demoralized young people and is causing high levels of depression and loneliness. Kennedy responded that he thought that was a simplistic reason, and went on to say, "In fact, I think a lot of the problems we see in kids and particularly boys, it's probably underappreciated how much of that is coming

---

[572] CBS News "Your athletic wear could contain high levels of BPA" by CKAL-News Staff (May 18th 2023)

[573] Forbes "Worrisome BPA Levels Found In Sportswear By Nike, Adidas, Patagonia And More, Group Alleges" by Arianna Johnson (May 18th 2023)

[574] Men's Health "Is This the Most Dangerous Food For Men?" by Jim Thornton (May 19th 2009)

from chemical exposures, including a lot of the sexual dysphoria that we're seeing."[575]

He continued, "You know these kids are being overwhelmed by a tsunami, I mean they're swimming through a soup of toxic chemicals today. And many of those are endocrine disruptors. There's atrazine throughout our water supply. Atrazine by the way, if you, in a lab put atrazine in a tank full of frogs it will chemically castrate and forcibly feminize every frog in there. And ten percent of the frogs, the male frogs, will turn into fully viable females able to produce viable eggs, and if it's doing that to frogs there's a lot of other evidence that it's doing it to human beings as well."[576]

Atrazine is a common herbicide used to kill weeds in farmers' fields, golf courses, and residential lawns. And has been found in the water supply in hundreds of districts across America, which millions of people have been drinking.[577] Aside from killing weeds which it's designed to do, it has been shown to convert testosterone into estrogen.[578]

One of Alex Jones famous rants is about "chemicals in the water that turn the fricking frogs gay," referring to Atrazine, and if you can look past his histrionics, he was

---

[575] Jordan Peterson Podcast with guest Robert F. Kennedy Jr. Ep 363 (June 8th 2023) Note: YouTube censored the episode claiming it violated their terms of service because of a discussion on vaccine dangers, but the podcast is available on other platforms.

[576] Jordan B. Peterson Rekindling the Spirit of the Classic Democrat | Robert F. Kennedy Jr. | EP 363

[577] The Texas Tribune "Toxic herbicide found in many Texans' drinking water" by Carlos Anchondo (November 15th 2018)

[578] The Journal of Steroid Biochemistry and Molecular Biology "Demasculinization and feminization of male gonads by atrazine: Consistent effects across vertebrate classes" Volume 127, Issue 1-2 October 2011 Pages 64-73

making a good point. He had seen the studies and was frustrated and upset that the issue wasn't getting the attention it should and that more people weren't concerned about it.

People also made fun of him for ranting about the BPA in juice boxes feminizing boys because many couldn't look past his over the top style and didn't understand just how sophisticated his concerns were behind his theatrics hoping to get people's attention.[579]

A growing number of scientists now suspect that birth control pills may actually be causing some women to become sexually attracted to other women! The pill has long been known to come with a range of side effects from weight gain to mood swings, but now scientists are investigating anecdotal evidence that the hormone changes they cause may result in altering some women's sexual attraction.[580]

It can take eight months to a year before a woman's hormone levels return to normal after she stops taking the birth control shot.[581] In fact, it's fairly common for women who stop taking birth control to experience side effects for months, ranging from no menstrual periods, to acne and hair loss, in what's called post-birth control syndrome.[582] Is birth control medication (which is designed to alter women's hormone levels) also having

---

[579] "Alex Jones Declares War on Juice Boxes" uploaded to YouTube here: https://www.youtube.com/watch?v=L_q8F_qazbI

[580] The Daily Mail "Can birth control make you a LESBIAN? As a number of women say their homosexuality was 'woken up' after starting or coming off the Pill, studies suggest there might be some truth about the unlikely side effect" by Cassidy Morrison (November 25th 2022)

[581] Pandia Health "What Happens When You Stop Taking Birth Control? Everything You Need to Know"

[582] Healthline "Everything You Need to Know About Post-Birth Control Syndrome" by Lauren Sharkey (March 31st 2020)

effects on fetus development even after they stop taking it?

There are other factors most people are unaware of as well that are missing from virtually every discussion and debate about homosexuality and transgenderism. TMZ, the celebrity news site, published a story back in 2015 when Bruce Jenner first announced that he was transitioning into a "woman" and taking female hormones which contradicted everything the LGBT advocates had said for years about "gay conversion therapy."

TMZ reported, "Several prominent doctors in the field tell us, the hormones often change sexual preference," and referenced a study of 300 transgender people showing one third of them changed their sexual preference because of the opposite sex hormones they took.[583] They noted that the female hormones Bruce Jenner was taking would feminize not just his body, but also his brain, causing him to "think like a woman," and there was a 1/3 chance he would be sexually attracted to men as a result.

The National Center for Biotechnology Information has also reported that many transgender patients' sexual orientation (meaning the sex they're attracted to) *changes* due to undergoing hormone therapy as they're attempting to change their gender.[584] So if over 30% of people who take hormones of the opposite sex in hopes of altering their body to become more like that sex, ultimately end up also changing their sexual orientation (who they're attracted to because their brain also changes), then why

---

[583] TMZ "Bruce Jenner Sexual Preference Uncertain After Cross-Sex Hormone Therapy" (February 6th 2015)

[584] NCBI National Center for Biotechnology Information "Transgender Transitioning and Change of Self-Reported Sexual Orientation" by Matthias K. Auer, Johannes Fuss, Nina Hohne, Gunter K. Stalla, and Caroline Stevens via PLOA Online (October 9th 2014)

isn't hormone replacement therapy being explored to help children (and adults) who suffer from gender dysphoria?

If a boy thinks he's a girl, or feels like a girl, then why not give him testosterone to masculinize his brain instead of giving him cross hormones (estrogen) and then subjecting him to all kinds of horrifying surgeries trying to make him look like a woman? Is it possible that the transgender movement is looking at this entire problem from the wrong angle?

And why isn't HRT (hormone replacement therapy) being used on homosexuals to fix their sexual attraction disorder by giving them hormone boosters that correspond with their own biological sex, since that appears to be a way to reverse their same sex attraction?

Perhaps with medical advances in the future and brave scientists who aren't afraid of the social consequences of their findings we may have definitive answers to these questions and solutions to these problems.

But it's also possible that because of the ramifications of uncomfortable truths, these answers may be forever suppressed and hidden, and the scientists who pursue them smeared by disinformation campaigns as the human species continues to suffer from mass psychosis, endocrine disrupting chemical-induced birth defects, and genital-mutilating surgeries marketed as the only solution.

Immigration

If people sneak into a theater through the exits hoping to watch a movie without buying a ticket, they're kicked out immediately once they are discovered—or even arrested. If some stranger walks into your house without permission even if the door is unlocked and they start relaxing on your couch, that's trespassing—and a crime. And so is entering a country without permission, even if you find an unguarded path or sneak in by hiding in the back of a truck. But this crime is being allowed and encouraged by Democrats for various reasons, one of which you're not supposed to say out loud, but everybody knows.

Illegal immigration though our southern border has been a problem for many decades, and while some of the invaders would get deported once apprehended, once Joe Biden took over as president the word got out that the U.S. was welcoming anyone in who could make it to our southern border from anywhere in the world.

Many of the people in the massive caravans who made the long trek north from South and Central America were literally wearing Joe Biden t-shirts! When one man on the journey was asked by ABC News "Would you have tried to do this when Donald Trump was president?" He answered "Definitely not." The reporter then asked him, "Did you come here because Joe Biden was elected president?" To which he responded "Basically."[585]

---

[585] Fox News "Migrant says he came to US border because Biden was elected, would not have tried to cross under Trump" by Stephen Sorace (March 21st 2021)

IMMIGRATION

Another one interviewed by CNN said he hoped for "Patience and prayers that we can get to the U.S. because they have a new president, of course Biden. He's going to help all of us, he's giving us 100 days to get to the U.S. and give us legal paper, so we can get a better life for our kids and family."[586]

Every single day (year after year) hundreds, and often two or even three thousand people enter the United States illegally through the southern border, and the conservative estimates are that over 11 million illegal aliens currently live in the U.S. but more realistic figures are double that.[587] In the month of February 2019 alone, over 66,000 were counted by U.S. Border Patrol, the highest number in over a decade, and that doesn't include all the ones who got in without being noticed.[588] It's common for the Border Patrol to spot 1000 a day, every day, month after month flooding in.[589] And again, those figures are just the ones we know about.

The Department of Homeland Security counted 234,088 illegal aliens that were "encountered" at the border just in the month of April 2021, which was the highest total ever in one month.[590] At least two million invaded the United States in the first year Joe Biden was

---

[586] New York Post "Honduran migrant traveling to US says Biden is 'going to help all of us'" by Emily Jacobs (January 19th 2021)

[587] The Hill "Yale, MIT study: 22 million, not 11 million, undocumented immigrants in US" by Rafael Bernal (September 21st 2018)

[588] NPR "Migrant Families Arrive In Busloads As Border Crossings Hit 10-Year High" by Joel Rose and John Burnett (March 5th 2019)

[589] The Wall Street Journal "Record Immigration Surge at the Border" by Alicia A. Caldwell and Louise Radnofsky (March 5th 2019)

[590] Washington Examiner "234,088 migrants encountered at southern border in April, most in a century" by Anna Giaritelli (May 17th 2022)

president.[591] That's well over 100,000 every single month.[592] More than two million more came the next year.[593] Vice President Kamala Harris was surprisingly asked about this staggering number during an interview with Chuck Todd on NBC's *Meet the Press* and she responded with a nonsensical word salad saying, "We have a secure border in that—that is a priority for any nation, including ours and our administration."[594]

This was all part of the plan. During his campaign in 2020, Joe Biden said that as president he would call for all the migrants the Trump administration was able to block from coming in to "surge to the border."[595] Meanwhile Jonathan Greenblatt, the head of the ADL, says that the people who talk about "open borders" or "caravans" of migrants are using "White supremacist phrases."[596]

Most of them falsely claim they're seeking "asylum" or that they needed safe harbor from a hostile government they had fled—a well-known scheme used by illegal aliens to gain access to our country. Once inside they're allowed to stay under those false pretenses, and are given a court date to begin hearing their claims which is often

---

[591] Washington Times "DHS encountered a record 2 million illegal immigrants on southern border in 2021" by Stephen Dinan (January 24th 2022)

[592] CNN "More than 100,000 migrants encountered at US-Mexico border in past 3 weeks, data shows (Geneva Sands (March 9th 2021)

[593] CNN "US border encounters top 2 million in fiscal year 2022" by Priscilla Alvarez (October 22nd 2022)

[594] New York Post "Kamala Harris insists border 'secure' as illegal migrants set to pass 2M" by Emily Crane (September 12th 2022)

[595] The Daily Wire "Biden's 2019 'Surge To The Border' Comments Resurface Amid Growing Crisis" (March 18th 2021)

[596] At the Council on Foreign Relations event "The Rise of Global Anti-Semitism" (February 27th 2017) on their YouTube channel here: https://youtu.be/Q7YKE9A3I_Y?si=WjBoVBEJ84OgwE37 (at 31:52)

ten years in the future![597] In the meantime they apply for green cards, and unless they're arrested for a violent crime they'll be deemed a "lawful permanent resident" after a year, and never be deported.

Anchor Babies

The other dirty secret of the illegal immigrant invasion, aside from the astonishing number of them continuously flowing into our country, are the millions of them who have anchor babies once they're here. An anchor baby is the child of an illegal alien mother who comes here pregnant (or gets pregnant after she arrives) and then once she gives birth, the child is automatically granted citizenship, thus all but ensuring the mother will never be deported.

In 2022 there were 300,000 anchor babies born to illegal alien mothers across the U.S.[598] Analysis conducted by the Center for Immigration Studies shows that 400,000 is about the average each and every year, dating back to at least 2018. The Congressional Budget Office published a report in 2017 estimating that at least 4.5 million anchor babies are currently living in the United States.[599]

Of course *anchor baby* is considered to be a racist slur, just like *illegal alien*, because the Left tries to deter people from pointing out what's happening. The term

---

[597] New York Post "Migrants allowed into US as asylum seekers given immigration court dates into year 203" by Valentina Jaramillo and Stephanie Pagones (May 11th 2023)

[598] Breitbart "Analysis: Nearly 400K Anchor Babies Born Across U.S. Last Year, Exceeding Population of Cleveland" by John Binder (January 5th 2023)

[599] Ibid.

refers to the child anchoring the mother to our country. And as you would expect, U.S. taxpayers end up paying the hospital bills for the children to be born because the mothers don't have any insurance (or money), and then we also pay the expenses for the mother to raise the children through the various social welfare programs funded by our tax dollars since they can't afford to raise them on their own.

But it's not just *illegal* immigrants who are living off our tax dollars. Over 50% of *legal* immigrant households receive some form of government welfare—from food stamps, to housing assistance, school lunch programs, and Medicaid.[600] A report by the Center for Immigration Studies shows that 63% of non-citizens living in the U.S. use at least one form of welfare.[601]

Some Republicans have finally begun calling for an end to "birth right citizenship" which automatically grants a baby citizenship if it's born on U.S. soil, even if the mother is here illegally. The sane thing to do would be only grant citizenship to the child if the mother is here *legally*, but we live in an insane and dysfunctional society.

And of course Democrats want to legalize the 20+ million illegal aliens living here so they can be the party's new voter base. Democrats have turned their back on the working class and now pander to the welfare class who just want free stuff.

The Biden Justice Department was even planning on paying illegal aliens $450,000 each as a "settlement" for the Trump administration separating families once they

---

[600] CNBC "Report: More than half of immigrants on welfare" by Alan Gomez (September 2015)

[601] Center for Immigration Studies "63% of Non-Citizen Households Access Welfare Programs" by Steven A. Camarota and Karen Zeigler (December 2nd 2018)

were detained after crossing into the U.S. illegally![602] Only after news of the planned "settlements" made headlines did they abandon the idea.

More Preferential Treatment

Sixteen different states allow illegal aliens to get drivers licenses![603] Bank of America even allows them to get credit cards![604] In California they're given government health care through the state's Medicaid program.[605] During the 2020 election cycle all ten Democrat candidates running for president raised their hands when asked by a debate moderator if they would offer healthcare to all "undocumented" immigrants.[606]

Calling what's happening an "invasion" is considered "hate speech," because obviously *it is an invasion* and the puppet masters are desperately trying to discourage the American people from doing anything to stop it. The Department of Homeland Security under the Biden administration has even been caught secretly flying the aliens across the country in the middle of the night to disperse them throughout other regions so they're not just concentrated in border states in the South. It's for "diversity."

---

[602] Wall Street Journal "U.S. in Talks to Pay Hundreds of Millions to Families Separated at Border" by Michelle Hackman (October 8th 2021)

[603] The Hill "16 states allow undocumented migrants to obtain driver's licenses" by Brooke Migdon (February 16th 2022)

[604] NPR "Bank Defends Credit Cards for Illegal Immigrants" by Scott Horsley (February 13th 2007)

[605] Associated Press "California first to cover health care for all immigrants" by Adam Beam and Don Thompson (June 30th 2022)

[606] The Hill "All candidates raise hands on giving health care to undocumented immigrants" by Alexander Bolton (June 27th 2019)

Many of them have no desire to become Americans. They just want to take advantage of what America can offer them. They don't care about our culture, customs, holidays, or laws. They just want to create little Tijuanas within the American cities they inhabit.

Various Latino groups like La Raza (meaning *the race*, which was recently renamed to UnidosUS to sound less Latino supremacist) and MEChA (the Chicano Student Movement of Aztlan) support what's called the Reconquista movement (Spanish for *reconquest*) and openly brag about how they're plotting to take back (reconquer) territory in the American Southwest (including California, Arizona, New Mexico, and Texas) in order to make their own country called Aztlan which refers to a mythical homeland of the Aztecs.[607]

Illegal Alien Crimes

The illegal aliens aren't just using up resources they're not paying for, taking jobs away from Americans, having anchor babies that are automatically granted citizenship, and irreversibly changing our culture by making little Tijuana's within American cities, but *a lot of them also commit crimes*. And not just theft or fraud (by using stolen social security numbers to get jobs), but violent crime—and a lot of it.

Every year in America there are often hundreds of murders committed by illegal aliens who obviously shouldn't even be here to begin with.[608] These crimes

---

[607] The Washington Times "Mexican aliens seek to retake 'stolen' land" (April 16th 2006)

[608] Breitbart "Fact Check: Yes, Thousands of Americans Have Been Killed by Illegal Aliens" by John Binder (January 8th 2019)

may make the local news for 15 seconds but then it's on to the weather, so their real impact is never realized. CNN and MSNBC will do entire segments about a White person using a racial slur during an argument in a store or restaurant somewhere, but the illegal alien murders never get a mention there.

Nor on the national broadcast networks like ABC, NBC, or CBS. *The New York Times* and *The Washington Post* never report on them either and certainly wouldn't dedicate a headline to the ongoing problem, but if a White woman gets into an argument with a Black person over something and video of the incident is posted online, then the "Karen" is doxxed with a barrage of headlines and her name trends on Twitter from thousands of people denouncing her for being "racist."[609]

Aside from murder, many illegal aliens commit other crimes that should never occur because they shouldn't even be here in the first place. Burglaries, rapes, thefts, and drunk driving offenses all go virtually unnoticed by the media and Democrat lawmakers. Democrats even defend MS-13 gang members who law enforcement agencies consider to be the most violent and sadistic street gang in the world. They're the ones best known for torturing and dismembering their enemies.[610] Illegal aliens in general are estimated to commit twice as many crimes as American citizens.[611] But mentioning that is considered "xenophobic" and "racist."

---

[609] USA Today "'Citi Bike Karen' viral video shows why we shouldn't rush to judgment" by Dustin Siggins (May 23rd 2023)

[610] Newsweek "MS-13: How an FBI Informant Risked Death to Bring America's Most Brutal Gang to Justice" by Michele McPhee (June 14th 2018)

[611] Washington Times "Illegals commit crimes at double the rate of native-born: Study" by Stephen Dinan (January 26th 2018)

Often when illegal aliens are arrested for non-violent crimes like DUI or theft, they're let out of jail pending their trial because Democrat run cities (the sanctuary cities, as they're called) forbid local authorities from turning them over to ICE [Immigration and Custom Enforcement], so they're just set free back out onto the streets!⁶¹²

The Wall

Democrats used to at least pretend to be against illegal immigration, but all that changed when Donald Trump became president. They've long been planning on their new voter base being the 20 million illegal aliens living in the United States once they're given a "pathway to citizenship"—which means full citizenship within a few years of being granted amnesty.

Democrats blocked $5.7 billion in funding that President Trump wanted to complete the border wall, but gave Ukraine over $200 billion to defend *their* border.⁶¹³ Alexandria Ocasio-Cortez compares our southern border wall to the Berlin Wall and Senator Elizabeth Warren calls it "a monument to hate and division."⁶¹⁴ When he was running for president in 2020, Beto O'Rourke said he wanted to *tear the wall down!*⁶¹⁵ During Joe Biden's campaign that same year he promised if he wins "There

---

⁶¹² Huffington Post "Cities Nationwide Refuse To Cooperate With ICE's Mass Deportation Raids" by Carla Herreria Russo (June 21st 2019)

⁶¹³ NPR "Democrats Reject Trump Border Wall Proposal, Calling It A 'Non-Starter" by Ayesha Rascoe (January 19th 2019)

⁶¹⁴ Breitbart "Warren on Border Wall: We Will Not Build Trump's 'Monument to Hate and Division'" by Pam Key (February 20th 2019)

⁶¹⁵ CNN "Beto O'Rourke says he would 'take the wall down' separating El Paso and Mexico" by Eric Bradner (February 14th 2019)

will not be another foot of wall constructed in my administration."[616]

Before the Democrats embraced open borders, when Barack Obama was a U.S. Senator from Illinois back in 2005 he said, "We all agree on the need to better secure the border and to punish employers who hire illegal immigrants. Those who enter the country illegally and those who employ them disrespect the rule of law and they are showing disregard for those who are following the law. We simply cannot allow people to pour into the United States undetected, undocumented, unchecked, and circumventing the line of people who are waiting patiently, diligently, and lawfully to become immigrants in this country."[617]

When Hillary Clinton was a senator in New York she admitted, "The Mexican government's policies are pushing migration north...There isn't any sensible approach except to do what we need to do simultaneously. Secure our border—with technology, personnel, physical barriers if necessary in some places. And we need to have tough employer sanctions...if they've committed transgressions of whatever kind, they should be obviously deported."[618]

Years later when campaigning for the 2016 presidential election she said, "I voted numerous times when I was a senator to spend money to build a—uh, a barrier, to try to prevent illegal immigrants from coming

---

[616] NPR "Biden Would End Border Wall Construction, But Wouldn't Tear Down Trump's Additions" by Barbara Sprunt (August 5th 2020)

[617] Associated Press "Obama's 2005 remarks reflect strong stance on controlling immigration" (November 2nd 2018)

[618] The New American "Hillary Clinton: She Was for a Border Wall Before She Was Against It" by Joe Wolverton, II, JD (September 10th 2016)

in and I do think you have to control your borders."[619] The wall had become a dirty word since it was a major part of Donald Trump's platform, so she called it a barrier instead, but early in the 2016 race Democrats weren't yet ready to pivot to their current *no border* policy.

In 2009 Senator Chuck Schumer, one of the most powerful senators in Washington, said, "Illegal immigration is wrong, plain and simple...People who enter the United States without our permission are illegal aliens and illegal aliens should not be treated the same as people who entered the U.S. legally. When we use phrases like 'undocumented workers' we convey a message to the American people that their government is not serious about combating illegal immigration, which the American people overwhelmingly oppose."[620]

All that has changed though. Democrats now deem the term illegal alien to be on par with the n-word, and they're doing everything they can do to cater to the illegal aliens, even allowing them to vote in some local elections![621] But they're not just looking to gain the support of the 20 million of them if or when they're granted amnesty and allowed to vote in national elections. There's something else at play here as well.

---

[619] The Washington Times "Hillary Clinton: 'We need to secure our borders'" by Jessica Chasmar (November 10th 2015)

[620] The Blaze "Dems won't be pleased with recently resurfaced videos of Sen. Chuck Schumer talking tough on illegal immigration" by Sarah Taylor (December 28th 2018)

[621] CNN "New York City gives noncitizens right to vote in local elections" by Kelly Mena (December 9th 2021)

Demographic Changes

Non-Whites and the Democrats who use them to maintain their power have long anticipated White people becoming a minority in the United States (on pace to occur around 2045), but if anyone points out this trend while expressing any opposition to this impending future, then they're instantly and viciously denounced as a "White supremacist" who's promoting the "dangerous great replacement conspiracy theory."[622]

These sweeping demographic changes in the racial makeup of the United States are mostly due to the massive number of illegal aliens that have been flooding in across the southern border for decades and given safe harbor in America despite them just standing on our soil being a violation of our laws. But mass immigration is only part of it. Compounding the problem is the declining White birthrate. As far back as 2011 there were more Hispanic, Black, and Asian babies being born in America than White ones.[623]

And despite countless Democrats expressing their joy about the rapid decline of the White population in the United States, *The New York Times* says "'The Great Replacement' is a racist and misogynistic conspiracy that holds that white people face existential decline, even extinction, because of rising immigration in the West and falling birthrates among white women," adding sarcastically "caused, of course, by feminism."[624]

---

[622] NPR "The 'great replacement' conspiracy theory isn't fringe anymore, it's mainstream" by Odette Yousef (May 17th 2022)

[623] Washington Post "Census: Minority babies are now majority in United States" by Carol Morello and Ted Mellnik (May 17th 2012)

[624] New York Times "The White-Extinction Conspiracy Theory Is Bonkers" by Farhad Manjoo (March 20th 2019)

Non-Whites celebrate it as the "browning of America" while some White people uncomfortable about their looming minority status figuratively call it "White genocide" to evoke stronger emotions, but that term too is considered a dog whistle for "White supremacy." Personally, I think using "White genocide" to describe White demographic displacement is too hyperbolic and causes others to respond with an eye roll. A genocide is the mass slaughter of a group of people, and that's not what's happening.

Although the Leftist online magazine *Counter Punch* says, "White genocide would not only be good, it is necessary and even unavoidable; that is, if we are interested in the survival of the planet, humanity, and all life forms—though to be clear the phrase 'white genocide' is a bit of a misnomer."[625] It goes on to explain that they want White people divested from any thoughts about their own racial identity so White people don't organize as an ethnic group to defend their own interests and culture like all other races do—something I'll cover in detail in the next chapter on Antiwhiteism.

The Southern Poverty Law Center's president Mark Potok actually has a list hanging on the wall of his home office showing the declining percentage of White people in America starting in the 1920s through today. The chart was captured on camera for a brief moment when he was being interviewed for a documentary called *Alt-Right: Age of Rage* (2018). Obviously he made it as a visual reminder that the browning of America is going according to plan.

---

[625] CounterPunch "Why 'White Genocide' is Key to the Earth's Survival: White Genocide from Baldwin to Ciccariello-Maher" by Roberto D. Hernandez (December 30th 2016)

Some opponents of the rapidly declining White population often point to Jewish groups as being active in facilitating mass immigration to the United States and European countries for decades in order to make them more racially and ethnically diverse so that Jews aren't singled out as a sole minority or the "outsiders" within a society as they were in Nazi Germany and other parts of Europe.[626] This is why the torch-bearing marchers at the infamous Charlottesville Unite The Right event in 2017 were chanting "Jews will not replace us."

But it's not just supposed "White Nationalists" who have been talking about the White majority in the United States being demographically replaced through sustained immigration from other regions of the world—the Democrats have been openly bragging about this happening for years.

As Vice President under Barack Obama, Joe Biden had boasted about an "an unrelenting stream of immigration" that would soon make White people a minority in the United States.[627] "I'm proud of the American record on culture and economic integration of not only our Muslim communities but African communities, Asian communities, Hispanic communities, and the wave still continues. It's not going to stop. Nor should we want it to stop. As a matter of fact, it's one of the things I think we can be most proud of."[628]

---

[626] The American Jewish Committee (or AJC) is the most active Jewish pro-immigration group. Others include the National Immigration Forum, and HIAS, the Hebrew Immigrant Aid Society.

[627] Fox News "Flashback: Biden praised 'constant,' 'unrelenting' stream of immigration into US" by Adam Shaw (December 12th 2020)

[628] The Daily Caller "Biden On 'Wave' Of Immigration: 'It's Not Going To Stop" (February 18th 2015).

He continued, "Folks like me who are Caucasian of European descent—for the first time in 2017 we'll be an absolute minority in the United States of America. An absolutely minority. Fewer than 50 percent of the people in America, from then and on, will be White European stock. That's not a bad thing. That's a source of our strength."[629]

When CNN's Anderson Cooper was speaking with Jorge Ramos, a popular host on the Spanish language station Univision about the changing demographics of the United States, Cooper gloated, "The idea that, you know, Whites will not be the majority, I mean, that's—it's an exciting transformation of the country, it's an exciting evolution and you know, progress of our country in many different ways."[630]

For decades Democrats had been openly bragging how "demographic trends" are going to one day keep the Republicans from holding power. After Donald Trump became president many Democrats were concerned that his immigration plan may keep White people the country's ethnic majority for longer than they had hoped. *The Washington Post* lamented that instead of it happening in 2044, it might be pushed back to 2049.[631] MSNBC's Chris Hayes ranted, "That's what Donald Trump's plan would do—keep the nation as White as possible for as long as possible."[632]

---

[629] Ibid.

[630] Fox News "CNN's Anderson Cooper: It's 'exciting' that whites will no longer represent nation's 'majority'" by Sam Dorman (August 13th 2019)

[631] Washington Post "Trump immigration plan could keep whites in U.S. majority for up to five more years" by Jeff Stein and Andrew Van Dam (February 6th 2018)

[632] MSNBC "All In with Chris Hayes" (February 6th 2018)

IMMIGRATION

After Trump was out of office however, the globalists made up for lost time and the massive floods of illegals increased to record levels and the celebrations of the rapidly declining White majority in the United States resumed.

In April 2021 Tucker Carlson started openly discussing these issues which had been completely taboo in the Republican Party, saying one night on his Fox News show, "I know that the left and all the little gatekeepers on Twitter become literally hysterical if you use the term 'replacement;' if you suggest that the Democratic Party is trying to replace the current electorate, the voters now casting ballots, with new people, more obedient voters from the Third World. But they become hysterical because that's what's happening actually. Let's just say it—that's true."[633]

After that monologue he trended on Twitter from so many people attacking him, and the next day the ADL demanded that Fox News fire him.[634] Instead of backing down and apologizing, Tucker doubled down and in the following months would bring it up again and again. "Nothing about it is an accident, obviously. It's intentional. Joe Biden did it on purpose. But why? Why would a president do this to his own country?" he asked.[635]

"Our system cannot handle this many destitute newcomers, period. Imagine what hospitals are going to look like a year from now. How about schools? What Joe

---

[633] Tucker Carlson Tonight on Fox News (April 8th 2021)

[634] CNN "ADL calls on Fox News to fire Tucker Carlson over racist comments about 'replacement' theory" by Brian Stelter (April 9th 2021)

[635] Mediaite "Tucker Carlson Goes All In On 'The Great Replacement' Theory, Says Biden Wants To 'Change the Racial Mix Of the Country'" by Michael Luciano (September 22nd 2021)

Biden is doing now will change this country forever. So again, why is he doing it? There's only one plausible answer."[636]

Tucker then played the clip of Joe Biden which I just quoted earlier of him looking forward to Whites becoming an "absolute minority," and continued, "Biden just said it: to change the racial mix of the country. That's the reason, to reduce the political power of people whose ancestors lived here and dramatically increase the proportion of Americans newly arrived from the Third World."[637]

Tucker went on, "It's horrifying. But there's a reason Biden said it. In political terms, this policy is called the great replacement, the replacement of legacy Americans with more obedient people from far away countries. They brag about it all the time, but if you dare to say it's happening, they will scream at you with maximum hysteria. And here you have Joe Biden confirming his motive on tape with a smile on his face. No one who talks like this should ever be the president of the United States."[638]

The Left keeps calling it a conspiracy theory when it's a historic reality numerous cultures around the world have faced. White Europeans displaced the Indians (or Native Americans, "Indigenous" people, or whatever they're calling themselves these days) here in North America.

Jews displaced Palestinians in 1948 with the creation of Israel after the United Nations adopted the Zionist resolution causing over 700,000 Palestinians to be forced out of the land, an event that's called the Palestinian

---

[636] Ibid.
[637] Ibid.
[638] Ibid.

IMMIGRATION

expulsion.[639] (It's considered extremely "antisemitic" to point out this fact, by the way, so be careful when talking about it.)

Tucker responded to the ADL's calls for him to be fired for talking about this issue by pointing out the organization's own statement regarding their concerns about Jews being demographically diminished in Israel. The ADL's official stance on Zionism is that, "It is unrealistic and unacceptable to expect the State of Israel to voluntarily subvert its own sovereign existence and nationalist identity and become a vulnerable minority within what was once its own territory."[640] After Tucker highlighted their hypocrisy, they deleted that page from their website, but not before it was archived on the Wayback Machine.[641]

On Megyn Kelly's podcast, Tucker was even more candid than on his Fox News show. When she mentioned that the ADL was calling for him to be fired, he responded "Well, fuck them."[642] Tucker let the cat out of the bag, and the Left were furious that not only did he point out their plan, but by him finally talking about what had only been whispered in Republican circles out of fear of being called "White nationalists" or "Nazis," now others would feel safer pointing out the obvious too.

The very next day after one of Tucker's monologues on the issue, Charlie Kirk felt it was finally okay to say

---

[639] United Nationals (UN.org) "UN marks 75 years since displacement of 700,000 Palestinians" (May 15th 2023)

[640] https://web.archive.org/web/20210403000313/https://www.adl.org/education/resources/fact-sheets/response-to-common-inaccuracy-bi-national-one-state-solution

[641] Ibid.

[642] The Megyn Kelly Show "Tucker Carlson on the Media's Deception, the ADL's Attacks, and Armor Against Criticism" (September 24th 2021)

such an obvious fact out loud. When talking about the need for stricter border enforcement he added, "The other side has openly admitted this is about bringing in voters that they want and they like, and honestly—diminishing and decreasing White demographics in America. We're gonna say that part out loud. So many people in the corporate media are afraid to talk about it."[643]

Yeah, people in the corporate media have been afraid to talk about it. And those in Conservative Inc., including him! For years! But Tucker shattered the taboo and now others didn't feel like they had to completely avoid even hinting at the topic. The *Washington Post* soon lamented that "Half of Republicans see great replacement is real."[644]

Vice News called it "a conspiracy theory that's quickly becoming gospel on the right: that Democrats want a flood of immigrants to remake America and keep them in power."[645] Every Liberal media outlet denounced Tucker for discussing it, trying to scare others away from pointing out White people's impending minority status in the U.S. is because of mass immigration.

Some, like *The Los Angeles Times,* recommended that Republicans talking about "replacement theory" (which is a fact) be censored from social media.[646] The ADL then started calling for Tucker Carlson to be banned from

---

[643] The Charlie Kirk Show - Streamed on YouTube (September 23rd 2021)

[644] Washington Post "Nearly half of Republicans agree with 'great replacement theory'" by Philip Bump (May 9th 2022)

[645] Vice News "Racist 'Replacement Theory' Is Bleeding Into GOP Senate Campaigns" by Cameron Joseph (May 10th 2022)

[646] Los Angeles Times "After Buffalo, will social media companies finally ban great replacement theory?" by Brian Contreras (May 17th 2022)

Twitter and Facebook, and demanded that all clips of his show be deleted from the Fox News YouTube channel.[647]

Demographics Is Destiny

"Demographics is Destiny" has been a mantra for the Democrat Party for many years as they anxiously await granting amnesty to the 20 million illegal aliens living in the United States. (They deceptively underestimate the number to be "only" 11 million, but it's double that.)[648]

Politico once admitted, "The immigration proposal pending in Congress would transform the nation's political landscape for a generation or more...pumping as many as 11 million new Hispanic voters into the electorate a decade from now in ways that, if current trends hold, would produce an electoral bonanza for Democrats and cripple Republican prospects in many states they now win easily."[649]

The Center for American Progress, a Democrat think tank, openly admitted, "Supporting real immigration reform that contains a pathway to citizenship for our nation's 11 million undocumented immigrants is the only way to maintain electoral strength in the future."[650] They claim to be a "non-partisan" organization, but it was founded by John Podesta and is filled with George Soros disciples and former Clinton and Obama staffers, so they

---

[647] ADL.org "Deplatform Tucker Carlson and the 'Great Replacement' Theory" (May 24th 2022)

[648] The Hill "Yale, MIT study: 22 million, not 11 million, undocumented immigrants in US" by Rafael Bernal (September 21st 2018)

[649] Politico "Immigration reform could be bonanza for Dems" by Emily Schultheis (April 22nd 2013)

[650] Center for American Progress "Immigration Is Changing the Political Landscape in Key States" (April 8th 2013)

couldn't help but admit what "immigration reform" means to them.

For years Democrats have talked with glee about the "population growth" in Texas and other border states, which is a codeword for the influx of millions of illegal aliens. *Newsweek* magazine even ran a headline titled "America's Getting Less White, And That Will Save It."[651] As paleoconservative Pat Buchanan warned over twenty years ago in his 2002 book *The Death of the West*, "Uncontrolled immigration threatens to deconstruct the nation we grew up in and convert America into a conglomeration of peoples with almost nothing in common—not history, heroes, language, culture, faith, or ancestors."[652]

Liberal European leaders have been obsessed with needing more racial "diversity" in their countries as well. But pro-immigration activists seem to only want White European countries flooded with immigrants from South America, Africa, and the Middle East. Interestingly, nobody is demanding that Israel accept an influx of non-Jewish refugees from other Middle Eastern countries. How about more African Muslims emigrate to Israel from places like South Sudan or Somalia?

If multiculturalism is so great, then why should they not want to participate in global diversification? There aren't any cries for Japan, China, or other Asian countries to become "more diverse" by adding millions of Africans, Hispanics, or Middle Easterners either. They, like Israel, would instantly quash any such suggestions because they

---

[651] Newsweek "America's Getting Less White, And That Will Save It" by William H. Frey (December 6th 2014)

[652] The Death of the West: How Dying Populations and Immigrant Invasions Imperil Our Country and Civilization by Patrick J. Buchanan page 3 (2002 Thomas Dunne Books)

IMMIGRATION

know that flooding their countries with millions of immigrants from other cultures would replace their own.

Since BIPOCs (Black, Indigenous, People of Color) endlessly complain about European "colonizers" establishing communities and Democracies around the world, why then are they so determined to colonize North America with people from other countries? The answer of course is because they like what we built here, and instead of attempting to replicate our success in their own countries, they are coming here to live off the fruits of our labor.

But shouldn't the American people be able to maintain the dominant cultural traditions of those who founded our country and have been the foundation of our society for almost 250 years? The Founding Fathers weren't Chinese. They weren't Jews, Arabs, or Guatemalans. They were White Europeans. (So why should the United States continuously and incrementally change our culture and our customs to be more accommodating to immigrants from other regions of the world?)

Some cultures are simply not compatible with American culture. Their values, traditions, and morals are impossible to integrate into modern society. For example, some Arab cultures believe women shouldn't be able to drive a car, work at a job, or even go out into public without wearing a full burqa. Some Middle Eastern cultures even use bacha bazi boys, which are young boys they sexually abuse like the pederasts of Ancient Greece.[653] Should we really be allowing people like that into our country—especially when so many of them

---

[653] BBC "The sexually abused dancing boys of Afghanistan" by Rustam Qobil (September 8th 2010)

clearly don't abandon their native countries' old traditions and customs that are incompatible with ours?

Many people in Mexico and South America see drug kingpins like "El Chapo" and Pablo Escobar as folk heroes.[654] The locals loved them because they provided jobs! Latino gangs in virtually all parts of the United States (the American Southwest, the Pacific Northwest, the Midwest, the Mid-Atlantic region, the Northeast, and South Florida) work directly with Mexican drug cartels.[655] The MS-13 street gang, the most violent and brutal in the United States, only exists here as a result of immigrants (from El Salvador) coming to the U.S.[656]

The diversity-obsessed Leftists even oppose English as the official language for the United States, despite the Declaration of Independence and our Constitution obviously being written in English. So why shouldn't it be our nation's official language? Why should we let foreigners dictate the dominant language in our own country? Why should we have to be told to "Press one for English and numero dos for Español" when calling every customer service number? Why should we have to deal with people we can't even understand when they speak?

Imagine if millions of Americans moved to China and then opposed Chinese as the official language. Or demanded that tests in school be given in English. Or said they need more "diversity" to make China a "better, stronger" country by bringing in more non-Chinese people. If diversity is a source of strength in a society as

---

[654] Los Angeles Times "In his hometown, fugitive Mexican drug lord 'El Chapo' is a hero to many" by Deborah Bonello (August 10th 2015)

[655] Business Insider "Here's where Mexican drug cartels operate in the US, according to the DEA" by Christopher Woodly (October 25th 2017)

[656] New York Times "14 Gang Leaders Directed MS-13 'Wave of Death,' U.S. Say" by Benjamin Weiser (January 14th 2021)

Liberals always say, then why not import millions of Muslims to Israel? Or millions of Indian people or Africans to Japan? Imagine White people moving to Japan en masse and then demanding that statues of the country's founders be torn down because of how they treated other races or because the country bombed Pearl Harbor (which brought the U.S. into WWII).

Democrats' Hypocrisy Exposed

While Democrats love the flood of illegal aliens into the U.S., what they really love is them invading Republican border states like Texas, Arizona, and New Mexico, which have historically been Red states but are shifting purple and blue because of the huge numbers of Hispanics arriving.

So in April 2022 Texas Governor Greg Abbott began bussing thousands of illegal aliens into Chicago, New York City, and Washington D.C. Since he didn't have the authority to deport them, he just relocated them to Democrat strongholds which had previously declared themselves sanctuary cities to virtue signal that they're not "racist."[657]

New York City mayor Eric Adams immediately denounced the action saying the city was "nearing its breaking point" and later said the illegals "will destroy New York City."[658] Lori Lightfoot, the then-mayor of Chicago, said the city is "completely tapped out" and they have "no more space" after just a few busloads of

---

[657] CNN "Texas has bused nearly 9,000 migrants to NYC and DC as an affront to Biden's immigration policies" by Zenebou Sylla (August 27th 2022)

[658] ABC 7 New York WABC "Mayor Eric Adams says asylum seeker crisis 'will destroy New York City'" September 8th 2023)

migrants arrived from Texas.[659] The mayor of Washington D.C. (another Democrat), declared a public emergency.[660]

Then Florida Governor Ron DeSantis one-upped Governor Abbott and flew two planeloads of illegal aliens to Martha's Vineyard, a wealthy island community in Cape Cod off the coast of Massachusetts where the Obamas bought a $12 million dollar estate to retire. All hell broke loose. The residents called in the National Guard and the illegal aliens were removed from the island within 48 hours and shipped off to a military base on the mainland.[661] They "couldn't handle" the fifty migrants, local officials said, even though it was the end of summer and there were plenty of empty Airbnb rentals available for them to stay in.

The point was clear. They didn't want any illegal aliens in their community—not even a few dozen of them. Meanwhile there were 5,000 a day (every day on average) pouring across the southern border into Texas, New Mexico, Arizona, and California at the time, overwhelming countless communities in the Southwest— an ongoing problem that has been allowed to continue for years.

As Ron DeSantis said, "The minute even a small fraction of what those border towns deal with every day is brought to their front door, they go berserk, and they're so

---

[659] ABC 7 Chicago "Mayor Lightfoot says Chicago 'tapped out' of resources as marchers call for help for migrants" by Sarah Schulte and Stephanie Wade (May 1st 2023)

[660] New York Post "DC Mayor Bowser declares public emergency over thousands of bussed migrants" by Katherine Donlevy (Setember 8th 2022)

[661] Boston Herald "Migrants flown to Martha's Vineyard moved to Cape Cod military base" by Gayla Cawley (September 16th 2022)

IMMIGRATION

upset that this is happening. And it just shows you that their virtue-signaling is a fraud."[662]

Author's Note: Please take a moment to rate and review this book on Amazon.com or wherever you purchased it from to let others know what you think. This also helps to offset the trolls who keep giving my books fake one-star reviews when they haven't even read them. Almost all of the one-star reviews on my books are from NON-verified purchases which is a clear indication they are fraudulent, hence me adding this note.

These fraudulent ratings and reviews could also be part of a larger campaign trying to stop my message from spreading by attempting to tarnish my research through fake and defamatory reviews, so I really need your help to combat this as soon as possible.

Thank you!

---

[662] Fox News "DeSantis criticizes Democrats after sending migrants to Martha's Vineyard: 'Their virtue signaling is a fraud" by Timothy Nerozzi (September 15th 2022)

Antiwhiteism

White people are regularly blamed for every problem in the personal lives, communities, and countries of non-White people. And despite Martin Luther King's wish that we could become a society where people are judged on the content of their character and not the color of their skin, it's common and widely accepted for Black people to express racism against White people and continue to blame White people living today for things that other White people did hundreds of years ago.

But it's not just a few disgruntled and envious Black people who have embraced such beliefs. With the mainstreaming of the Black Lives Matter movement, antiwhiteism has become disturbingly widespread and normalized, and White people are constantly said to be keeping down "minorities" because of "White privilege" and "systemic racism," despite White people actually being a minority in the world—and even in numerous states within America.[663]

Whites have been a minority in California since the year 2000, and they're also a minority in Hawaii, New Mexico, and Texas.[664] Other states including Georgia, Nevada, and Maryland are trending to be next, and projections are that Whites will be a minority in the whole of the United States around the year 2045, according to

---

[663] Pew Research Center "Reflecting a demographic shift, 109 U.S. counties have become majority nonwhite since 2000" by Jens Manuel Krogstad (August 21st 2019)

[664] CBS News "Census: Whites no longer a majority in U.S. by 2043" (December 12th 2012)

the U.S. Census bureau.[665]   But you're not supposed to talk about that unless you frame it in glowing terms and an "exciting transformation of the country," as CNN's Anderson Cooper calls it.[666]

Jimmy Fallon's audience cheered when he said that the 2020 census showed for the first time in our nation's history the number of White people went down. He was setting up a joke, but the audience burst into applause at the setup, confusing Fallon, who looked bewildered. "Wait, what?" he said, going off script.   "That's an interesting reaction to that. I didn't want cheers or boos—I just wanted a 'interesting,' that's all I wanted." He then continued with the punchline that "Fox News declared it a national emergency."[667]

New York Times columnist Jennifer Rubin celebrated the 2020 census figures calling it "fabulous news," adding "now we need to prevent minority White rule."[668]   Many Latinos, Blacks, Jews, Native Americans, and guilt-ridden White Liberals cheer the news of White people being on the verge of becoming a minority in the United States, and anyone who dares to say they don't want it to happen are branded a "White nationalist" and a "Nazi."

But demographic displacement and becoming a racial minority in a country that was founded and built by White Europeans is just one of the complicated racial issues facing White Americans.

---

[665] Brookings Institute "The US will become 'minority white' in 2045, Census projects" by William H. Frey (March 14th 2018)

[666] Fox News "CNN's Anderson Cooper: It's 'exciting' that whites will no longer represent nation's 'majority'" by Sam Dorman (August 13th 2019)

[667] The Tonight Show starring Jimmy Fallon S8 E180 | 08/12/21 Clip posted on the show's official Twitter account here: https://twitter.com/FallonTonight/status/1426025966971854849

[668] https://twitter.com/JRubinBlogger/status/1425899248269266947

White people are openly hated by a disturbingly large segment of the non-White American population. A viral meme illustrates the situation by showing a nice White husband and wife alongside their two kids with the caption "White People: The Only Race You Can Legally Discriminate Against." But it's more than that. It's spite, envy, and hatred.

White people in America are blamed for everything from the crime problems in Black communities, to even global warming![669] There are endless stories in mainstream outlets today that complain about how there are too many White people playing golf,[670] too many White people going skiing,[671] too many White people are hiking in public parks;[672] there are too many White teachers,[673] too many White doctors,[674] and too many White airline pilots,[675] and basically just too many White people everywhere in America! So we need more "diversity" they say, which is a codeword for *less* White people.

---

[669] CNN "European colonizers killed so many Native Americans that it changed the global climate, researchers say" by Lauren Kent (February 2nd 2019)

[670] Reuters "Diversity remains golf's biggest challenge, says PGA of America CEO" by Steve Keating (August 8th 2018)

[671] Travel Weekly "Ski industry examines its lack of diversity" by Robert Silk (July 24th 2020)

[672] Washington Post "National parks are travel's next frontier in the movement for racial equality" by Kerry-Ann Hamilton (September 17th 2020)

[673] New York Post "McAuliffe laments number of white teachers ahead of Va. governor vote" by Samuel Chamberlain (November 1st 2021)

[674] Newsweek "United Airlines Sparks Debate With Pledge to Diversify Pilot Staff" by Emily Czachor (April 7th 2021)

[675] Yahoo News "86% of Air Force pilots are white men. Here's why this needs to change" by Major General Ed Thomas (October 20th 2020)

The Jewish ADL, the Ant-Defamation League (an organization originally founded to protect and defend Jews from supposed "antisemitism" but later morphed into an anti-Conservative hate group) is trying to change the very *definition* of racism. On their website they literally defined it as, "The marginalization and/or oppression of people of color based on a socially constructed racial hierarchy that privileges white people."[676]

This Orwellian word game is just one more reason why the term *antiwhiteism* needs to be part of the lexicon. When people hear the word "racism"—they've been conditioned to (wrongly) think that it's something White people do to Black people. And the ADL is perpetuating that disinformation with their false definition of the word. So when talking about anti-White racism, it's best to be specific and use the term *antiwhiteism* so people don't get the wrong impression and automatically think that the "racism" you're talking about is White people discriminating against Black people or other non-Whites.

A similar deceptive term is Critical Race Theory or CRT, which masks what's going on. It makes people think that anti-White racism is just a theory and it's too generic of a term, so call it what it is: *antiwhiteism*. Or at least always make it clear by calling it anti-White racism, instead of just "racism" to avoid the preconceptions people have been conditioned to think when they hear the word "racism."

When speaking of supposed antisemitism, the ADL's Jonathan Greenblatt told CNN, "If you demonize the Jewish people or the Jewish State, if you make these wild accusations, if you traffic in conspiracy theories, you

---

[676] https://web.archive.org/web/20220128192617/https://www.adl.org/racism

create the conditions for violence."[677] So wouldn't that mean endlessly blaming White people for all the problems in America and coining new terms like "White Privilege" and perpetuating hoaxes about "systemic White supremacy" and other lies (like police officers across the country are always beating up and shooting Black suspects) mean that those who traffic in such nonsense are actually creating an environment that puts White people at risk for violence?

It certainly does, but the Establishment always covers up hate crimes committed by Black people and perpetuates the myth that "hate crimes" are something that only White people commit. In this chapter I'll detail just a small fraction of the systemic antiwhiteism occurring in America, which is a risky thing to do because daring to stand up for White people is the quickest way to be smeared as a "White supremacist."

Every time Black people complain about White people, no matter how unfounded and ridiculous the criticism is, it's framed as an important issue that White people need to be "confronted" about and "address," but when a White person simply mentions certain pervasive problems in the Black community (no matter how tactfully) regarding crime, fatherlessness, poor grades, or the high STD rates, those concerns are immediately dismissed and vigorously opposed as more "evidence" of "racism."

The Antiwhiteism Grifters

Democrats' favorite tactic is calling White people "racist," and the Race Hustle is an entire industry with

---

[677] https://twitter.com/ADL/status/1483600090639986688

high-paid "experts" who get paid to just complain about White people all day, every day. People like Robin DiAngelo, who is credited with popularizing the term White Fragility which is used as a weapon against White people and was constructed to depict White people who are tired of hearing Black people complain about them as being a character flaw and more "evidence" that they're racist because they don't want to "acknowledge" or "address" their own "white privilege."

Ibram X. Kendi (which is a fake name to make him sound cool like Malcolm X) is another popular race grifter. His real name is Ibram Henry Rogers, and he works as an "anti-racist activist," meaning an anti-White activist. In his mind, White people are the cause of all racism in the world, and like all other Race Hustlers he ignores the racial conflicts between Black people and Latinos which are common in places like Los Angeles, especially between rival gangs. The only thing "Ibram X. Kendi" thinks about is how terrible White people are.

The *1619 Project* founder Nikole Hannah-Jones is another one. This "project" started as a feature in *The New York Times* and refers to the year 1619 when she claims Black slaves started "building America" for White people.

While there are many professional Race Hustlers, perhaps the most infamous (aside from Shaun King who looks White despite being half Black and is often mocked as "Talcum X") is Black Lives Matter co-founder Patrisse Khan-Cullors, who bought four different homes with the millions of dollars her scheme brought in.[678] Black Lives Matter (the organization) also transferred millions of

---

[678] New York Post "Inside BLM co-founder Patrisse Khan-Cullors' million-dollar real estate buying binge" by Isabel Vincent (April 10th 2021)

dollars to a "charity" run by her "wife" who then used six million dollars to buy a mansion that was the former headquarters for the Communist Party.[679]

Over $90 million dollars was given to Patrisse Khan-Cullors' Black Lives Matter organization (not to be confused with the generic "movement"—the organization is technically a legal entity in and of itself) which claims to be a "nonprofit" organization.[680] They also paid nearly a million dollars to a company run by Cullors' baby daddy for "creative services"[681] and also paid her brother over $840,000 for "security."[682]

Corporate Antiwhiteism

Under the guise of various fancy sounding terms like "diversity, equity, and inclusion" (DEI), "racial bias training," or "sensitivity and inclusivity" seminars—major American corporations are forcing their employees (and especially new hires) to undergo various classes derived from Critical Race Theory to indoctrinate them about how terrible White people are and how amazing non-Whites are (and queers).

The "anti-racism" grifters have been around for a long time, but now it's commonplace for major corporations to

---

[679] Fox News "BLM transferred millions to Canadian charity to buy mansion formerly owned by Communist Party: report" by Jon Brown (January 29th 2022)

[680] Fox News "Black Lives Matter has nearly $42 million in assets: IRS documents" by Lawrence Richard (May 17th 2022)

[681] New York Post "BLM paid co-founder's baby daddy nearly 5 times more than Trayvon Martin foundation" by Isabel Vincent and Dana Kennedy (March 17th 2022)

[682] Business Insider "A Black Lives Matter cofounder used $840,000 of the group's funds to pay her brother for 'security services" by Matthew Loh (May 19th 2022)

hire them to "teach" employees about how White people perpetuate "racism" simply by *existing* if they don't constantly prioritize Black people's thoughts and feelings. Walmart employees have been put through "training" where they're told that the United States is a "White-supremacy system" and if they're White and don't think they're racist and part of the problem, that's just more evidence of their "internalized racial superiority."[683]

Companies now include entire sections on their websites explaining their plans on how they're going to hire more people of color in the name of Diversity, Equity, and Inclusion despite favoring any particular race in the hiring process being illegal. Coca-Cola's website says, "Our plan will focus on internal and external recruitment, hiring, development and advancement of people of color."[684] They go on to openly admit that they're dedicated to only promoting Blacks, Hispanics, and Asians instead of White people.

Leaked documents show that AT&T's Diversity, Equity, and Inclusion training course labels White employees "the problem" and says that "American racism is a uniquely white trait" and Black people can't be racist.[685] They're also encouraged to take the "21-Day Racial Equity Habit Challenge" to reflect on their "white privilege," and be on the lookout for "white supremacy."[686]

---

[683] National Review "Walmart CRT Training Encourages Employees to Accept That 'White Is Not Right'" by Brittany Bernstein (October 14th 2021)

[684] https://web.archive.org/web/20230609015548/https://www.coca-colacompany.com/social/diversity-and-inclusion/internal-action

[685] New York Post "AT&T critical race theory training says white employees 'the problem'" by Lee Brown (October 29th 2021)

[686] City Journal ""White People, You Are the Problem"" by Cristopher F. Rufo (October 28th 2021)

Many major corporations now have an entire department dedicated to "Diversity, Equity, and Inclusion" and people have titles like "head of diversity," and it's their job to make sure that fewer White people (and heterosexuals) are hired to work there. LinkedIn, the employment and business-focused social media platform, now enables job recruiters to filter their searches for candidates according to race in order to help them find a more "diverse group of candidates."[687]

It used to be an unwritten rule that job applicants not include their race on their resumes to help avoid racial bias during the hiring process, but now it's encouraged for non-White people to list theirs so they can be picked as a diversity hire.

When the hiring manager of Dropbox, the Google-owned cloud storage service, posted about a new position open for product design in the U.S., she said applicants from the BIPOC (Black, indigenous, people of color) and URM communities (underrepresented minority), meaning queer people, were given priority over all others.[688] Of course that's a violation of federal law because a business can't pass up job applicants simply because of their race, but as usual, systemic antiwhiteism is ignored.

If a hiring manager of any business, whether a Fortune 500 company or a small family owned pizza place posted that they were prioritizing White applicants, then the Department of Labor would launch an investigation into them and sue them into bankruptcy, but no action is taken when White people or Christians are blatantly discriminated against. A producer for Fox News reached

---

[687] The Daily Wire "LinkedIn Allows Recruiters To Filter Job Candidates By Race" by Ben Zeisloft (April 20th 2023)

[688] ABC 15 WPDE "Tech exec prioritizes job opening to people of color, critics argue civil rights violation" by Alec Schemmel (May 10th 2022)

out to Dropbox for a comment when this story went viral, but they ignored the request proving that they're complicit in the discriminatory practices.[689]

YouTube got sued in 2018 because of their anti-White hiring policy.[690] A recruiter who worked for YouTube for nine years claims the company set quotas for hiring non-White people and recruiters were told not to even interview applicants who weren't Black, Hispanic, or women.[691] On Valentine's Day that same year, the official YouTube Twitter account tweeted, "Roses are red violets are blue, subscribe to Black creators."[692]

As noted previously, YouTube has also been hostile towards Thanksgiving, and hosts an annual event exclusively for Black YouTubers to give them extra help to build up their subscribers.[693]

Comedian Tyler Fischer was turned down by an agent because he's White, so he sued for discrimination and the talent agency quickly offered him a settlement—which he refused, saying he wanted the case to go to court, probably because a settlement would mean he would have to sign a non-disclosure agreement, preventing him from ever talking about what happened to him again.[694]

Responding to a headline in the *New York Post* that said he "claimed" the agent turned him down because he's

---

[689] https://twitter.com/gregg_re/status/1524230391825063937

[690] Wall Street Journal "YouTube Hiring for Some Positions Excluded White and Asian Men, Lawsuit Says" by Kirsten Grind and Douglas MacMillan (March 1st 2018)

[691] Ibid.

[692] https://twitter.com/YouTube/status/963900837570469888

[693] The Verge "YouTube announces 135 creators in its 2022 Black Voices Fund" by Mia Sato (January 27th 2022)

[694] New York Post "Comedian Tyler Fischer claims he was rejected by agent for being white" by Angela Barbuti (May 21st 2022)

White, Fischer said, "The entire claim is on tape and in plain English. I'm simply not allowing myself to be discriminated against for my skin color anymore. There's no such thing as 'reverse' discrimination. There's one kind and everyone is protected under the law against it."[695] He also said that "endless people" in the industry have reached out to him privately telling him the same thing has happened to them as well, but they were afraid to speak about it publicly.

It's not just corporations, but many cities are also indoctrinating their employees with antiwhiteism. Such "training" programs now mandated across the country for elected officials and their staff.[696] Many police and fire departments are requiring such programs as well.[697] These "Race and Social Justice Initiatives" teach that White staffers are "responsible" for racism and are "oppressors" of non-Whites.[698]

A teachers union in Minneapolis announced that they plan to layoff White teachers first if they have to make budget cuts, regardless of seniority—explaining in Orwellian language, "if excessing [laying off] a teacher who is a member of a population underrepresented among licensed teachers in the site [the school], the district shall excess the next least senior teacher, who is not a member

---

[695] https://web.archive.org/web/20220522003711/https://twitter.com/tythefisch/status/1528156416271425538

[696] City of Sacramento Mayor's Office of Community Engagement "Sacramento city council unanimously adopt a mandatory diversity and equity training" (May 9th 2023)

[697] WFTS "Community calls for diversity training after racism allegations at Tampa fire station" by Rochelle Alleyne (June 27th 2023)

[698] Washington Examiner "Seattle holds training session for white employees aimed at affirming 'complicity in racism' and 'undoing whiteness'" by Andrew Mark Miller (July 7th 2020)

of an underrepresented population."[699] They always try to mask their agenda by using codewords. "Excess" means to layoff, and "under represented" means if they're not White they'll be passed over, and the White teachers will be laid off instead.

Again, all of this is illegal and violates long-standing anti-discrimination laws, and the fact that such blatant racial discrimination would be adopted by so many organizations is shocking but perhaps even more disturbing are the lack of legal consequences for their actions. The Department of Labor and the Justice Department do nothing to enforce anti-discrimination laws when the discrimination is against White people.

Uber's "head of diversity" (an Asian woman) was suspended after she held an event where she tried to encourage employees to stop calling their White coworkers "Karens" (which has become an anti-White slur that Black people like to use against White women who they view as being entitled or bossy because of their "White privilege"), but Black employees felt like they were being "lectured" and "scolded" so they accused the executive of being racist *against them!*[700]

Black people feel so entitled these days in America that when a company executive tries nicely to get them to stop being racist against White people, they view *that* as racist!

---

[699] Fox News "Minneapolis teachers union agreement stipulates White teachers be laid off first, regardless of seniority" by Kelsey Koberg (August 15th 2022)

[700] CBS News "Uber diversity head put on leave over workplace event on 'Karen persona'" by Megan Cerullo (May 22nd 2023)

Black Crimes Matter

Black people in America commit more crimes than White people, Latinos, Asians and every other race.[701] It's an irrefutable fact, but because they commit more crimes (approximately *ten times* more violent crimes than White people) Blacks also get arrested and incarcerated at a much higher rate per capita than White people.[702]

But like obese people who get defensive when they're told that they should lose weight because they're at risk of having a heart attack or getting diabetes, most Black people don't want to talk about the crime problem in their communities because it involves taking a good hard look in the mirror.

Black people are arrested and incarcerated far more often than White people (and Hispanics, Asians, and every other race) because *they commit more crimes*, and it's not because of some conspiracy being carried about by police, prosecutors, and juries. It's the same reason there are dramatically more men arrested and incarcerated than women—because men commit more crimes. A lot more.

It's not that police are unfairly "targeting" men for arrest and "systemically" ignoring women who commit crime. It's obvious to everyone that men *commit more crime* than women, so it makes perfect sense that they would be arrested and incarcerated more. The *reasons* why Black men commit more crimes (particularly more violent crimes) than White people (as well as Hispanics

---

[701] U.S. Department of Justice "Race and Ethnicity of Violent Crime Offenders and Arrestees, 2018" by Allen J. Beck, Bureau of Justice Statistics (January 2021)

[702] Ibid

and Asians) is a whole other topic and beyond the scope of this book.[703] And while it's politically incorrect (or "racist," as Liberals call it) to talk about Black Crime, it's extremely taboo to talk about hate crimes committed by Black people.

When most people think of a hate crime, they think of a group of "White supremacists" attacking a random Black person for the same reason when people hear the word *racism*, they've been conditioned to automatically think of White people being prejudiced against non-White people. But Black people not only commit hate crimes against White people, Jews, Asians, and Latinos—but the media does their best to keep such attacks contained to small local news outlets in hopes of preventing people from seeing the pattern.

When they do report on such incidents, they try to hide what actually happened by insinuating that the perpetrators are White by reporting that a hate crime *did occur*, and that the "perpetrator" or "man" called the victim a racial or antisemitic slur, but they purposefully omit the race of the attackers when they're Black.

When a Black man shot up a White church in Antioch, Tennessee to get "revenge" on White people for psycho Dylann Roof's despicable attack on a Black church years earlier, his motive was covered up until the trial, and then only mentioned in local news. A note was found in the shooter's vehicle that same day which admitted he did it

---

[703] Some argue there are racial differences in aggression and impulse control, while others point to generational fatherlessness and thug culture being embraced and celebrated by Black communities.

for "vengeance" and that "10 of your kind" (meaning White people) "would die."[704]

At the time when people were posting online that the attack was suspiciously not getting any national attention, *Newsweek* claimed that it was an "alt-right conspiracy theory" that it was a "reverse Dylann Roof story," meaning the Black shooter targeted White people.[705] *The New York Times* initially reported on the shooting in a story buried on page 14 of their paper and didn't even mention the shooter's motive.[706]

While most Americans never heard of this attack, everyone remembers the endless coverage of Dylann Roof's heinous attack on churchgoers in South Carolina in 2015, which resulted in the Confederate flag being banned across the entire United States and social media companies deeming it a hate symbol; Amazon banning all sales of it, and even reruns of the 1980s classic *Dukes of Hazzard* series were pulled from TV because the famous General Lee car has the flag painted on it.[707]

Similarly, the media was obsessed with the Unite the Right rally in Charlottesville in August 2017 which would mark the end of the Alt-Right after a man who was literally a schizophrenic drove his car into a group of protesters, killing one of them and injuring others, but they always ignore Black Lives Matter violence like when

---

[704] Fox News "Tennessee church gunman hoped to kill 10 white congregants to avenge Charleston massacre, prosecutors say" by Samuel Chamberlain (May 20th 2019)

[705] Newsweek "Tennessee Church Shooting Is a 'Reverse Dylann Roof' Story, 'Alt-Right' Claims" by Michael Edison Hayden (September 28th 2017)

[706] New York Times "Shooting at a Church Near Nashville Leaves One Dead and Seven Wounded" by Christina Caron (September 24th 2017)

[707] ABC News "TV Land Pulls 'Dukes of Hazzard' Reruns" by Luchina Fisher (July 1st 2015)

Micah Xavier Johnson, a Black supremacist and supporter of the Nation of Islam, opened fire on a group of police during a Black Lives Matter rally in Dallas, Texas in 2016 killing five and wounding nine others.[708]

That story disappeared the next day, and the media *never* brought it up again, but the "White supremacists in Charlottesville" with their tiki torches is a central part of the mythos about why Joe Biden ran for president in 2020, and the car crash will be talked about in the Liberal media for an eternity.

A Black man in California was convicted of going on an anti-White murder spree, killing three random White people in Fresno in 2017 simply because they were White, and planned "to kill as many white males as possible" and advocated for the creation of a Black-only ethnostate, but that too was swept under the rug.[709] I could list more that have been covered by local news outlets (since anti-White hate crimes are always ignored by the national ones), but I'm trying to keep this book to a moderate length.

Antisemitism is always framed as coming from White supremacists, but the dirty little secret of antisemitic hate crimes is that many, if not most, are committed by Black people—particularly Black supremacists who follow the Black Hebrew Israelites' philosophy believing they are the "real" Jews. Black supremacists consider White people the Edomites, which is a reference to the Biblical story of Esau (also known as Edom) who is the twin brother of Jacob and the son of Isaac and Rebekah, who Black Hebrew Israelites consider to be the patriarch of the

---

[708] CBS News "Dallas suspect said he wanted to kill whites" (July 8th 2016)

[709] NBC News "California man convicted of murder in racist shooting spree that killed 3 in Fresno" by Phil Helsel (April 23rd 2020)

White race.[710] They often speak in code so most people have no idea what they're talking about when they rail against "the Edomites," the "White Edomite Devils," or Esau-Edom.[711]

A Black couple in New Jersey walked into a Kosher deli and started shooting, killing two people in what was a targeted attack against Jews by Black Hebrew Israelites.[712] A Black man walked into a Hanukkah party in an Orthodox Hasidic Jewish community in New York and started stabbing people, leaving five people injured.[713] As usual, all reports about the stabbing omitted the man's race and just described him as a "man" or "the suspect" to hide the fact that another Black man committed another hate crime against Jews.[714]

A Black woman in Brooklyn was arrested for slapping three Orthodox Jews while yelling "fuck you Jews" and because of the "bail reform laws" she was released from custody without having to pay any bail and three days later arrested again for assaulting more people.[715]

---

[710] The Christian Post "Was Esau-Edom white? Demolishing Hebrew Israelite lies (part 1)" by Michael Brown (March 29th 2023)

[711] Christian Research Institute "Why Do 1West "Hebrew Israelites" Call Whites "Edomites" And Chinese "Moabites" ?" by Vocab Malone (October 1st 2019)

[712] CNN "Jersey City shooters fueled by hatred of Jewish people and law enforcement, state attorney general says" by Jason Hanna and Madeline Holcombe (December 12th 2019)

[713] ABC News "5 stabbed at rabbi's Hanukkah celebration by intruder with machete-type knife" by Bill Hutchinson, Stephanie Ramos, Joshn Margolin, and Marc Nathanson (December 29th 2019)

[714] CNN "Suspect in Hanukkah celebration stabbings arrested in New York City with 'blood all over him,' source says" by Christina Maxouris, Elliot C. McLaughlin and Sarah Jorgensen (December 29th 2019)

[715] New York Post "Tiffany Harris let loose again after second alleged assault" by Tina Moore, Andrew Denney, and Aaron Feis (December 30th 2019)

A lot of the hatred Black people have towards Jews isn't from those who subscribe to the Black Hebrew Israelite philosophy, but from Black people in general who often harbor anti-Jewish sentiments from perceiving that Jewish business owners have exploited Black communities.

Malcolm X, who was a Black separatist and wanted Black people to have their own region of the United States so they could live without any White people around, said, "It is Jews right here in Harlem who run these whiskey-stores that get you drunk. It is Jews that run these old run-down stores that sell you bad food. It is Jews who control the economy of Harlem and use it for themselves and the benefit of Israel…That's not antisemitic, that's just plain intelligence."[716]

But only White people are framed as having anti-Jewish views and Blacks are always portrayed as a fellow minority group being oppressed by the White man even though antisemitism is a central part of the Nation of Islam—the Black power Muslim movement, and many Black people who aren't followers of the movement still harbor similar views.

White people are always blamed for anti-Asian hate crimes too, when surveillance footage shows they're almost all committed by Black men. After a Black man in Dallas, Texas was arrested for going on shooting sprees at various Asian businesses, specifically targeting Asians, that story vanished down the memory hole by the next

---

[716] Modern Judaism: A Journal of Jewish Ideas and Experience "White Devils, Satanic Jews: The Nation of Islam From Fard to Farrakhan" Volume 40, Issue 2 May 2020. Audio clips of this speech can be found online if you search for Malcolm X and Jews.

day and was completely forgotten.⁷¹⁷ If he was White the story would have received endless coverage on cable news and CNN would have said Donald Trump incited him because he kept calling COVID-19 the "China virus," but as usual, once the perpetrator was found to be Black, they all dropped the story.

A Black man brutally beat a 67-year-old Asian woman in Yonkers, New York, punching and stomping her more than 100 times while calling her an "Asian bitch," which was all captured on video by a security camera.⁷¹⁸ But he was just identified as a "man" in the news stories, not a Black man, even though it was a clear hate crime not just a random mugging or assault. Only those who saw the security camera footage, which was released by police and omitted in most news stories about the attack, saw that he was clearly a Black man.

"Asian man pushed onto subway tracks in Queens" read the headlines after another hate crime in the New York area, and the perpetrator was descried as only wearing a black hooded sweatshirt, while the fact that it was known he himself is a Black man was ignored, as usual, despite footage of the attacker being captured by security cameras.⁷¹⁹

In 2020, the Southern Poverty Law Center removed Black hate groups from their online list of "hate groups" because it was making the Black Lives Matter movement look bad by not just admitting Black supremacist and separatist groups exist, but showing how prevalent they

---

⁷¹⁷ Fox News "Dallas police chief: Koreatown hair salon shooting suspect 'motivated by hate'" by Louis Casiano (May 17th 2022)

⁷¹⁸ New York Post "Yonkers man hit with hate crime in 'appalling' attack on Asian woman" by Jorge Fitz-Gibbon (March 14th 2022)

⁷¹⁹ ABC 7 New York "Asian man pushed onto subway tracks in Queens" (May 24th 2021)

are. The SPLC admitted that they didn't want to "aid law enforcement in its definition of Black Identity Extremists," since the Department of Justice (under the Trump administration) finally admitted that Black hate groups pose a danger to society.[720]

They recategorized some of the groups giving them the cover of "antisemitic" groups or "general hate" groups, instead of being Black separatists or Black nationalists. There used to be *three dozen* Black hate groups on the Southern Poverty Law Center's list, including the Nation of Islam, the New Black Panther Party, the Black Hebrew Israelites, and many others, but not anymore. Admitting the reality that Black supremacist organizations exist is considered to be racist.

When discussing hate crimes, you can't ignore hate crime hoaxes, which are the vast majority of alleged "hate crimes" reported today.[721] To list the specific instances that have been confirmed hoaxes would fill up an entire book—and they do.[722] There are also numerous websites which keep a pretty good tally of the latest hate crime hoaxes, including FakeHateCrimes.org.

From a Black college Lacrosse player spray painting the n-word and a swastika on his dorm in Maryland targeting himself,[723] to a Black girl tweeting death threats to a school in New Jersey hoping to gain more sympathy

---

[720] https://www.splcenter.org/presscenter/splc-collapse-black-separatist-groups-listings-hate-map-reassigns-groups-according

[721] Wall Street Journal "Hate Crime Hoaxes Are More Common Than You Think" by Jason L. Riley (June 25th 2019)

[722] One such book is titled Hate Crime Hoax: How the Left is Selling a Fake Race War by Wilfred Reilly (2019)

[723] The Daily Mail "Black college lacrosse player, 21, is arrested for spraying N-word and swastika graffiti targeting HIMSELF and other minority students in two incidents that terrorized the campus" by Megan Sheets (December 1st 2018)

for Black Lives Matter,[724] to a Black woman writing racist notes to herself and filing a fake police report at the University of Wisconsin, Madison.[725] As *The Wall Street Journal* surprisingly admitted, "Hate crime hoaxes are more common than you think."[726]

There are countless ones which have been foiled on college campuses where mostly Blacks and gays, but sometimes Muslims and Jews, are caught faking hate crimes by spray painting graffiti, or even harming themselves and claiming they were attacked.[727] It's a common tactic that is often exposed because the hoaxers are too stupid to realize security cameras are everywhere on college campuses, but there are exponentially more hate crime hoaxes that are said to have occurred other places which go undiscovered and are reported as real in the media.

Jussie Smollett's hoax is the most famous to be exposed, but they date back decades. Al Sharpton's claim to fame was rallying behind the Tawana Brawley hoax in 1987 where a Black teenager in New York falsely accused four White men of kidnapping and raping her.[728]

The Bubba Wallace "noose" incident isn't technically a hoax because it wasn't a deliberate scheme, but instead a case of *Imaginary Racism* which is also a common

---

[724] NJ.com "Twitter threats to black Kean students made by black alum, police say" by Jessica Re3mo (December 1st 2015)

[725] The College Fix "Hoax alert: Black Illinois student criminally charged for racist notes" by Jonathan Draeger (February 7th 2022)

[726] Wall Street Journal "Hate crime hoaxes are more common than you think" by Jason L. Riley (June 25th 2019)

[727] Washington Post "An alleged hate crime at a Jewish cafe was 'the most brazen' a community had seen. It was all fake, police now say" by Meagan Flynn (April 26th 2019)

[728] Fox News "Al Sharpton doubles down on Tawana Brawley rape accusation hoax: 'Should I apologize?'" by Jeffrey Clark (January 23rd 2023)

occurrence, where Black people falsely interpret something as being "racist" because they've become paranoid from all the fear-mongering and fake news in the media (and spread through social media) about how there are supposedly "White supremacists" around every corner and that "systemic racism" is the bedrock of every American institution.

White Identity

For most of America's history White people haven't thought about themselves as a racial group because their race had been largely invisible to them, like a fish in water, since whiteness has been the dominant culture going all the way back to America's founding.

But as White people are quickly becoming a minority group (and have already become minorities in several states) they are becoming racially conscious and starting to think about themselves as an ethnic group—like Blacks, Asians, Latinos and every other race—and caring about their own interests within the multicultural communities (and states, and country) they inhabit, instead of always allowing themselves to be pushed aside in the name of diversity.

And as White people came under increasing attacks from the mainstream media, online activists, woke corporations, and others as a result of the insurgency of Black Lives Matter—*White Identity* (again, White people seeing themselves as a unique ethnic group with their own interests they want to protect or advance) has accelerated their racial consciousness and is changing how they perceive themselves in our multiracial society.

In response to this, the other ethnic groups (and self-hating Whites) along with the usual suspects in the media and Democrat Party, are frantically trying to stop this inevitable paradigm shift, equating White Identity or White collectivism with "White nationalism" and "White supremacy," deceptively conflating them as if they're the same. These increased attacks are causing a feedback loop which is only accelerating White people's awakening and involvement in ethnic collectivism. This then increases concern among non-Whites and incites more attacks against whiteness, and so on.

An assistant Professor of Political Science at Duke University named Ashley Jardina has actually been a pioneer in scholarly research into the awaking of White Identity politics and found that contrary to most people's expectations and beliefs, there is a low correlation between White Identity and racial resentment towards other races.[729]

In other words, Whites who are racially consciousness and are thinking of themselves and other White people as part of an ethic group are not racist against non-Whites. They simply want what every other racial group in America has, which is the right to not only be proud of their race, but to be able to voice support for their own in-group interests (such as preserving their culture) and to not have their civil rights be violated by being discriminated against.

The Left has stigmatized the idea of White people being concerned about their own ethnic interests to the point that it's almost always falsely equated with White supremacy. It's the biggest taboo, but if White people

---

[729] Ashley Jardina, author of White Identity Politics, during an interview with Heterodox Academy YouTube channel #52 (May 1st 2019)

keep getting systematically demonized by radical Black and Latino groups (and Jewish groups like the ADL), Whites will naturally respond by awakening to their own White Identity as a natural instinct, and will begin to collectivize and organize as an ethnic group in order to stop other races from treating them as if they are second class citizens.

Europe has seen the rise of a White Identity movement in what's called Identitarianism (or the Identitarian Movement) which is opposed to multiculturalism and promotes localism or ethnopluralism which is the idea of maintaining unique and separate ethnocultural regions. This is a reaction to the Islamization of European countries caused by the massive influx of Muslims from the Middle East as well as millions emigrating to Europe from Africa.[730]

Many of the migrants cannot assimilate into such a different culture and have no desire to. And the flood of migrants has caused massive crime waves in Sweden, Germany, France, England, and other countries who took them in.[731] Sweden is now over 8% Muslim.[732] In 2016 *Mohamed* became the most common new baby name for boys in the UK, and remained the most popular through at least 2022.[733] (It still may be, but the latest data for 2023

---

[730] The Economist "How "identitarian" politics is changing Europe" (March 28th 2018)

[731] Newsweek "Migrants in Europe Linked To Soaring Violence and Crime in Germany, Study Finds" by Grace Guarnieri (January 3rd 2018)

[732] Pew Research "5 facts about the Muslim population in Europe" by Conrad Hackett (November 29th 2017)

[733] GB News "Muhammad revealed as the most popular UK baby boy name for 2022" by Aden-Jay Wood (May 7th 2022)

wasn't released by the time this book went to print and the trend is likely continuing).[734]

London is also now 15% Muslim.[735] In 2016 the first Muslim mayor of London was elected, and many of the indigenous Europeans are extremely unhappy with such dramatic demographic changes which are resulting in a rise of White Identity throughout Europe.

Beginning in 2017 as a reaction to the rising antiwhiteism on American college campuses and social media, some members of the online forum 4Chan decided to print fliers that simply read "It's Okay To Be White" and posted them on various campuses. Instead of people ignoring such an innocuous statement, the fliers made national news and were denounced as "racist" and "neo-Nazi propaganda" by school authorities, the media, the ADL, and Southern Poverty Law Center.[736]

The fact that anyone was even upset about the fliers is strange, but catching the attention of the professional hate groups like the SPLC and ADL, and making the national news just proved the point the kids were trying to make. If they had spray painted the slogan on the side of some buildings, that would be vandalism and maybe justified making the local news, but these were ordinary 8 1/2" by 11" sheets of paper that were just taped on some light poles and stapled onto community bulletin boards.

Similar fliers reading "All Lives Matter" have occasionally been posted on college campuses and around town as well, and as you can expect, were also firmly

---

[734] Some reports claim it became the most popular baby name for boys in 2014.

[735] Office for National Statistics "Religion, England and Wales: Census 2021" (Census 2021, release date November 29th 2022)

[736] Huffington Post "'It's Okay To Be White' Signs Appear In Schools, Cities Across The U.S." by Taryn Finley (November 9th 2017)

denounced as "overtly racist" and "White supremacist propaganda."[737] In October 2022, Kanye West (who had legally changed his name to Ye) wore a White Lives Matter shirt to a fashion show in Paris alongside Candace Owens, causing everyone in the Liberal media in America to freak out. CBS News insinuated it was "racist."[738] *Rolling Stone* said it was "uncalled for."[739] And *The New York Times* ran the headline, "There Is No Excuse for Ye's 'White Lives Matter' Shirt."[740]

The ADL deems "White Lives Matter" to be a "White supremacist phrase,"[741] along with the Southern Poverty Law Center.[742] Both organizations function to smear Conservatives and Christians as racist, bigots, and homophobes; and often label organizations they hate as "hate groups," and are tirelessly trying to stop White people from embracing White Identity by equating it with White supremacy and neo-Nazis.

Even Christopher Rufo, who's held up as the world's foremost expert on Critical Race Theory by Conservatives, is firmly opposed to White people collectivizing as an ethnic group like other races, saying "I do not believe that 'white identity politics' or 'white identitarianism' is a solution; in fact, I think it would be a

---

[737] Washington Post "Law school professors say posting 'All Lives Matter' flier was an 'incident of intolerance'" by Susan Svrluga (April 4th 2016)

[738] CBS News "Kanye West faces backlash for wearing shirt with "White Lives Matter" slogan" by Caitlin O'Kane (October 4th 2022)

[739] Rolling Stone "From the Trump Supporter Who Called Slavery a Choice: Kanye West Wears 'White Lives Matter' T-Shirt" by Tomas Mier (October 3rd 2022)

[740] The New York Times "There Is No Excuse for Ye's 'White Lives Matter' Shirt" by Vanessa Friedman (October 4th 2022)

[741] https://www.adl.org/resources/hate-symbol/white-lives-matter

[742] https://www.splcenter.org/fighting-hate/extremist-files/group/white-lives-matter

major step backwards and, potentially, disastrous. We should emphasize the individual and de-emphasize racial categories, to the extent possible."[743]

He also performs mental gymnastics in order to avoid framing Critical Race Theory as "anti-White racism" out of concerns it may fuel White Identity. He argues this because "it's not exclusively anti-White," and points to the college admissions scandal over affirmative action where Asians were also passed over while Blacks were given preferential treatment, but CRT *is* specifically anti-White—it just so happens that Asians are sometimes collateral damage. The main target is obviously White people.

Rufo is married to an Asian woman, and his children look Asian, so he has a personal interest in trying to depict CRT as not being exclusively anti-White, and it would be highly unlikely that he and his wife aren't fostering in their children a strong sense of Asian identity and pride, but he cautiously advises White people not to embrace their whiteness or White Identity, saying, "White identitarianism is pathetic and disgusting."[744]

Instead, it appears Christopher Rufo wants White people to avoid any ethnic identity at all, and proposes they just view themselves as generic "Americans" and minimize their racial identity as much as possible. Of course he would never recommend Jews shed their ethnicity as the core of their identity. They're "special," and that would be antisemitic. Meanwhile he looks forward to a world in which Whites, Blacks, and Latinos are all mixed together into one homogeneous "human race," saying "I think interracial marriage is a sign of

---

[743] https://twitter.com/realchrisrufo/status/1409524324638203910

[744] https://twitter.com/realchrisrufo/status/1407206483830349856

progress, I think it's beautiful, I think it's amazing… America is going to look different in 100 years. You're not going to be able to tell 'you're Black, you're White, you're Hispanic, you're Puerto Rican, whatever.' I think ultimately that's going to be good."[745]

Ask anyone who is of mixed race about some of the complications regarding their identity and acceptance among certain peer groups and they may not sing such praises of it.[746] And ask any mixed race couple about the intercultural conflicts that arise (or persist), and they too would admit it's not always as rosy as such "diversity" is often portrayed from the outside.[747] So many people wish to retain their unique ethnicity within their families and aren't interested in their children and grandchildren becoming part of a multicultural mishmash.

But unlike every other race on the planet, White people aren't allowed to be proud of being White—or proud of the list of things White people have contributed to the world, from creating the automobile and airplanes to air-conditioning and computers. "White Pride" is considered synonymous with "White Supremacy." Wikipedia defines it as "an expression primarily used by white separatist, white nationalist, fascist, neo-Nazi and white supremacist organizations in order to signal racist or racialist viewpoints."[748]

---

[745] Timcast IRL "Kyle Rittenhouse EXTRADITED To Kenosha, DEBUNKING Critical Race Theory With Chris Rufo" (October 30th 2020) https://www.youtube.com/watch?v=A2890lBKZX0

[746] KTNV "Mental health impacts on children who struggle growing up multiracial" by Bree Guy (March 8th 2021)

[747] Marriage.com "Unique Challenges Faced by Inter-Ethnic Marriages" by Stewart Lawrence (March 9th 2021)

[748] Wikipedia entry for 'White Pride' (archived May 21st 2022) https://web.archive.org/web/20220522003016/https://en.wikipedia.org/wiki/White_pride

Of course Black Pride is defined favorably as "a movement which encourages Black people to celebrate Black culture and embrace their African heritage."[749] Similarly, the entry for Asian Pride notes that it's "a term utilized by people all over the world to celebrate their Asian ethnicity."[750]

White people just wanting to date only other White people is considered racist, and any app that would facilitate White-only dating would not only cause a national outcry by Democrats in Congress who would launch a congressional committee to investigate whoever created it, but it would be banned by the Apple and Android app stores for being "racist."[751] Meanwhile there are countless dating apps for Black people and Latinos to meet each other, not to mention Black-only beauty pageants, Black-only dorms, graduation ceremonies, and other "Black safe spaces" where they can enjoy themselves without the presence of White people.[752]

But again, if a White person just wants to date or marry another White person, that sets off alarm bells—while Blacks, Asians, Latinos, and Jews who want to do so are celebrated for maintaining their cultural heritage. And if any White people prefer to live in a predominantly White neighborhood (like Scott Adams, the creator of the *Dilbert* comic strip recommended) or want their children

---

[749] Wikipedia entry for 'Black Pride' (archived May 21st 2022) https://web.archive.org/web/20220522002847/https://en.wikipedia.org/wiki/Black_pride

[750] Wikipedia entry for 'Asian Pride' (archived May 21st 2022) https://web.archive.org/web/20220522003322/https://en.wikipedia.org/wiki/Asian_pride

[751] The Guardian "That dating site for white people? It's racist, no matter how it's justified" by Zach Stafford (January 8th 2016)

[752] Post Millennial "UC Berkeley holds segregated graduation ceremony for black students only" (May 22nd 2023)

to go to a predominantly White school, that's even worse, and they're denounced as White nationalists and Nazis.

Just for recommending that White people should live in predominantly White neighborhoods to avoid the ongoing racial strife between Whites and Blacks, Scott Adams' *Dilbert* comic strip was canceled by his syndicator after more than 30 years in publication, and overnight vanished from every newspaper around the world.[753]

Aside from the Liberal media manufacturing outrage over his comments, he was also denounced by some brand name Conservative commentators as well, including Ben Shapiro, who said that "there's a strong case" that anyone saying such "racist stuff" should have their career ended.[754]

Use Their Own Terms Against Them

One tool you can use to combat the Marxists and their incessant antiwhiteism is turning their own terminology against them by linguistically hijacking their buzzwords. When they talk about "White Fragility," point out Black Fragility—which I would define as: Discomfort and defensiveness on the part of some Black people who live in a predominantly White culture due to fixating on long since past injustices which they never experienced (and weren't experienced by anyone in their family alive today) causing them to *imagine* racism where none exists,

---

[753] NPR "Distributor, newspapers drop 'Dilbert' comic strip after creator's racist rant" by Mandalit del Barco (February 27th 2023)

[754] The Ben Shapiro Show Ep. 1677 "Musk Calls The Media Racist – And He's Right" (February 28th 2023)

and pine away for living in a culture that is predominately black instead.

When they whine about whiteness or "White normativity" then bring up their White-Envy which is when Black or other non-White people who live in a predominantly White culture feel envious of the society because their ancestors lacked the skills, knowledge, or possessions of others in the dominant culture, often resulting in resentment and demands for reparations instead of accepting personal responsibility for their own situations and working to improve their lives through hard work, discipline, and other ethical means of achieving success and happiness.[755]

When they talk about the "need" for more "diversity," call them anti-White. Don't play into their semantical games by acknowledging their made up words and ridiculous false concepts. Every time they use their cultural marxist terminology, do linguistic judo, and turn it back against them.

Doing this saves you from wasting time engaging them in an argument about why they're wrong, (and insane). And just chuckle or laugh at them, mock them, and don't even take their concerns seriously unless it's your boss and you run the risk of being fired. We should all start highlighting the systemic antiwhiteism to make it clear that anti-White racism isn't just occurring in isolated instances from a few individual Black people or organizations, but instead antiwhiteism is so pervasive it has become woven into American culture through Black Lives Matter activism and the Liberal media constantly demonizing White people and whiteness.

---

[755] A definition I came up with and posted on Gab in March 2023. https://web.archive.org/web/20230326084204/https://gab.com/MarkDice/posts/110087838443294448

And again, the term *antiwhiteism* needs to become the common word used in place of *racism* when talking about anti-White racism because of the deeply rooted associations and preconceptions people have with the word racism. Just invoking the word *racism* always conjures up a frame that it's something White people do to non-Whites, and the very word is basically an anti-White slur, so a completely different word should be used when talking about anti-White racism, or at the very least —the clear distinction should be made by describing it as *anti-White racism*, not just racism.

That is as long as the ADL, SPLC, and Wikipedia don't hijack the term and get a false definition to stick by claiming it's a "White supremacist" code word, which they will likely attempt to do just like they've done with *It's Okay to Be White*, *Cultural Marxism*, and *White Pride*. Even mentioning the percentage of Black people in relation to the percentage of violent crimes they commit in the United States (i.e. 13/50) is deemed a "numeric hate symbol."[756]

When the Left mentions "White privilege" then turn it around on them and point out that Black Privilege is actually the centerpiece in our culture now since Black people are put on a pedestal and treated as if they deserve special benefits and treatment because they've been exploiting grievances about injustices in the distant past and laying guilt trips on White people in order to subvert equal rights and blind justice. This Black Privilege often stems from false perceptions of racism where none exists, or fabricating incidents of racism in order to leverage

---

[756] The ADL has 13/50 listed as a "numeric hate symbol" because it notes that Black people are 13 percent of the U.S. population but commit 50% of the violent crime.

power over White people.[757] They try to wield this power to silence criticism or judgment about any aspect of their culture (like glorifying thugs and crime) or others pointing out the high percentage of single mothers in the Black community.

Black Privilege goes far beyond giving them jobs they're not qualified for in the name of "diversity, equity, and inclusion" (the fancy new term for affirmative action). It also grants them the benefit of often not being charged with anything when they commit crimes, or being given light sentences out of concerns that putting them in jail instead of releasing them on probation would reflect poorly on Black people as a group, so in the 21st century many are often allowed to escape justice.

Black Privilege also entails having TV shows and entire networks like BET and Fox Soul dedicated to Black-only entertainment—and having Black-only dating apps, Black-only beauty pageants, Black-only dorms at colleges, and being able to openly proclaim that Black people are the "best" and "Black is beautiful" while flying into a violent rage if a White person were to say the same thing about their race.

We all know what would happen if a White person said they wanted to live in a White-only community, or if White students said they wanted to live in White-only dorms or if a network wanted to produce a TV show that expressly doesn't include any Blacks or Latinos and instead would focus on a White family or community without any forced "diversity." All hell would break loose, but every other race can make such demands and are given those accommodations without any resistance.

---

[757] A definition I came up with and posted on Facebook in June 2023 https://www.facebook.com/photo.php?fbid=807399877410120

But beware, because cancel culture has gotten so strong that your career could be destroyed in an instant by saying many of the obvious truths mentioned in this this book—especially if you explicitly show support for White Identity (or even bring it up in any context other than denouncing it).

Not everyone is in a position to loudly or firmly push back against antiwhiteism (or LGBTQism), but we do need people who are confident they can weather the storm that may come their way if they do, or else our country and our culture will be irreparably damaged, if not destroyed.

Censorship

The World Wide Web opened up a new frontier for publishing in the 1990s where anyone could create a website from their home computer that could be seen by anyone else in the world with just a few clicks on a keyboard through their Netscape or Internet Explorer browsers. But at the time, it was difficult to build a website—and extensive computer skills (including knowing the HTML computer language) were needed, so while every major corporation eventually set one up, only a few eccentric people, computer nerds, or entrepreneurs had one.

About a decade later in the early 2000s, the advent of social media made having an online presence turn-key, and anyone with practically no computer skills or technical experience could start using the Internet to publish blogs with photos and videos, and share links to news articles with others who could then share them with their friends and followers who could do the same, and the concept of "going viral" was born. It was the next phase of the Internet revolution, or Web 2.0 as it's called. While Web 1.0 consisted of static webpages, the new era of online activity involved easy two-way communication and an interactive experience with comments, follower counts, and "likes."

While MySpace led the way, Facebook soon overtook them and quickly grew to dominate social media. At the end of 2006 Facebook opened to everyone, not just people with a college email address ending in .edu, and then

MySpace quickly died.[758] By the 2008 presidential election Facebook was already part of everyone's lives, and now on their phones thanks to the launch of the Apple App Store. When the iPhone was first released in June 2007 it had only a few apps (like email, maps, and music), but the following year the App Store was opened to 3rd party developers and enabled access to services that had previously been contained to desktop computers but were now available anywhere in the palm of your hand.[759]

Social media soon morphed from a fun novelty to a way of life. During this new social media revolution if you were a young adult and didn't have a Facebook page (or later if you were a high schooler and didn't have a Snapchat or Instagram account), then you were seen as an outcast. Social media became just as common as cellphones.

Even though Facebook, Twitter, and YouTube had become extremely popular by the 2008 presidential election, their real power still wasn't realized until a few years later. Barack Obama was the first president to have a Facebook and Twitter account, and throughout the 2008 and 2012 election cycles people used social media to argue and debate ideas and share news articles as the platforms slowly became more and more intertwined with politics and our daily lives.

But even throughout the Obama administration social media was still mostly considered to be a "neat" way to communicate with other people, and while it was certainly changing our culture, it hadn't become the center-point of it—yet.

---

[758] Huffington Post "Myspace Collapse: How The Social Network Fell Apart" by Amy Lee (June 30th 2011)

[759] Tech Crunch "iPhone App Store Has Launched" by Michael Arrington (July 10th 2008)

But by the 2016 presidential election cycle (which began in 2015), social media had become an integral part of our culture. Every celebrity, every TV show, every brand name business had Facebook and Twitter accounts. It's how major companies fielded complaints from their customers instead of the "old fashioned" way of people calling them on the phone. A new kind of celebrity was created in the form of YouTubers or "social media stars" who used the technology to go viral and gain massive audiences, often dwarfing traditional talk radio shows and television networks.

Stories that weren't chosen by editors of the major newspapers and television networks to dominate their coverage (or even get mentioned at all) could now become widely publicized from people organically sharing them, and the corporate news giants lost their ability to control the topics of conversation that the general public was having.

The *New York Times* complained that "YouTube, Reddit and Facebook have allowed fringe thinkers to bypass traditional gatekeepers and reach millions of people directly."[760] CNN's "senior media reporter" Oliver Darcy complained that social media companies have "given everybody the same ability to broadcast their views, unfiltered really, to millions and millions of people," and now "they can share it and they can tell their friends about it."[761]

After Trump beat Hillary Clinton, the entire Liberal Media Industrial Complex panicked and claimed that "fake news" being spread through Facebook by the

---

[760] The New York Times "'False Flag' Theory on Pipe Bombs Zooms From Right-Wing Fringe to Mainstream" by Kevin Roose (October 25th 2018)

[761] Live From America Podcast 067 ; Bringing Down Alex Jones With Oliver Darcy and Galen Druke via YouTube (August 13th 2018) (16:26 timecode)

Russians tricked people into not liking her, and thus not voting for her. The Establishment media aimed to take their power back and that's when the mass censorship and algorithm manipulation started. Before the 2016 election, the only posts or content that was taken down were almost exclusively things that clearly violated what were once reasonable terms of service—forbidding death threats, porn, or people just uploading full episodes of TV shows to YouTube, infringing on studios' copyrighted works.

The mainstream media lost control of the flow of information, and so they scrambled to gain back their monopoly, partnering with the Big Tech platforms to not only get *their* content artificially boosted, but also systematically *suppress* independent voices.

Immediately in the aftermath we saw an increasingly number of Conservatives having posts removed from social media and getting locked out of their accounts (or permanently banned) for posting criticism of illegal immigration, Muslim refugees, gender bending and other LGBT activities that had previously been allowed to be hotly debated and firmly denounced.

Posting basic scientific facts about gender or undisputed crime statistics about Black males became a problem. During President Trump's (first) impeachment hearings, nobody was allowed to mention the name of the "whistleblower" whose bogus allegations kicked the whole thing off after Trump asked Ukraine's President Volodymyr Zelensky about the Biden Crime Family's dealings in the country, which was spun into a story about seeking a foreign country's "help" to "interfere" in our election.

When Senator Rand Paul mentioned the name of the person widely believed to have helped get the impeachment hearing in motion (Eric Ciaramella) on the

CENSORSHIP

floor of the Senate, YouTube even removed that video, claiming it was "harassment" and an "invasion of privacy."[762]

In 2017, YouTube completely changed their search results to surface videos from mainstream media channels for most topics people look up.[763] Internally they tag brand name channels as "authoritative" so the algorithm artificially boosts them to the top of the search results even if other videos from independent "ordinary" YouTubers are more relevant and should organically be the actual top results because of their views, watch time, and the amount of engagement they have.

YouTube even created a special curated list of search terms after Liberals in the media complained about the top search results for things like abortion and the Federal Reserve.[764] They added actress Brie Larson's name to the list after "journalists" complained that the top search results for her name accompanied by the title of her latest film at the time (*Captain Marvel*) were YouTubers critical of her and the movie.[765]

Then they later hid the dislike ratings near the end of 2021 because so many people were thumbing down videos on mainstream channels that kept getting artificially boosted into people's feeds and inserted onto the trending list. They claimed it was to prevent smaller

---

[762] Axios "YouTube removes clip of Rand Paul reading alleged name of Ukraine whistleblower on Senate floor" by Rashaan Ayesh (February 13th 2020)

[763] USA Today "YouTube alters algorithm after searches for Las Vegas shooting turn up conspiracy theories" by Jessica Guynn (October 5th 2017)

[764] Breitbart "New Whistleblower Allegation: YouTube Manipulated 'Federal Reserve' Search Results in Response to MSNBC Host's Complaint" by Allum Bokhari (July 30th 2019)

[765] The Verge "YouTube fought Brie Larson trolls by changing its search algorithm" by Julia Alexander (March 8th 2019)

YouTubers from getting "bullied" by large numbers of people thumbing down their videos, but it was just another attempt to hide negative feedback about the Liberal propaganda they kept pushing.

And then another wave of censorship hit during the COVID-19 pandemic in 2020 when people opposing the mandatory lockdowns were suspended and banned from the brand name social media platforms, and people questioning the safety of the vaccine were censored as well. Even just saying that the virus leaked from the Wuhan lab wasn't allowed.

Senator Rand Paul was censored by YouTube another time for a speech he made denouncing mask mandates on the floor of the Senate.[766] Dan Bongino's channel was banned after his third strike for "COVID misinformation" because of a rant he did about masks not being effective.[767] Then just a few days later the CDC updated their "data" about masks, admitting after two years of the pandemic that cloth masks basically don't do anything.[768]

Dr. Drew, the famous Hollywood Liberal TV doctor, even got a strike from YouTube for "medical misinformation" after he discussed some of the possible side effects of the COVID-19 vaccine on his podcast.[769] He's generally pro-vaccine despite experiencing some mild side effects himself, but also said if his children were

---

[766] New York Times "YouTube suspends Rand Paul for a week over a video disputing the effectiveness of masks" by Daniel Victor (August 11th 2021)

[767] Engaget "Fox News host Dan Bongino suspended on YouTube over COVID-19 misinformation" by Mariella Moon (January 15th 2022)

[768] New York Times "The C.D.C. concedes that cloth masks do not protect against the virus as effectively as other masks" by Apoorva Mandavilli (January 14th 2022)

[769] Washington Examiner "Dr. Drew switches to Rumble after YouTube blocks him over vaccine video" by Jenny Goldsberry (April 29th 2022)

under 18, he would not have given them the COVID vaccine. The censorship was so egregious that after a medical device being used on COVID patients called the Heal Light, which consisted of a breathing tube wrapped in ultraviolet LEDs designed to kill the virus once inserted into the lungs of patents was mentioned by President Trump, the company had their YouTube channel and Twitter account censored for spreading "dangerous medical misinformation."[770]

Donald Trump mentioned that scientists were using ultraviolet light "inside the body" to kill the virus, something that the media mocked him for because anything he said they used against him. His explanation of the technology was just an off the cuff remark about some of the things that were being developed to help treat patients. So the media made it seem as if he was crazy and wanted to insert light bulbs under people's skin.[771]

Then when people starting pointing out he was referring to an actual device being tested in hospitals, the Big Tech platforms did what they could to hide that fact in order to prevent the media's mockery of him from backfiring.[772]

And while social media was the primary focus of the "thought police" looking to censor all content they disagree with, soon those who wanted to silence others began pointing to podcasts that were hosted on Apple

---

[770] The Gateway Pundit "TECH TYRANNY: Twitter Suspends Account and YouTube Removes Video of Biotech Company that Created COVID-19 Treatment Using UV Light in Lungs" by Jim Hoft (April 25th 2020)

[771] Forbes "Trump Suggests Injecting Coronavirus Patients With Light Or Disinfectants, Alarming Experts" by Matt Perez (April 23rd 2020)

[772] The Wall Street Journal "An Experimental Ultraviolet Light Treatment for Covid-19 Takes Political Heat" by Josh Disbrow (April 27th 2020)

Podcasts and Spotify.[773] The topics being censored, along with the methods and reasons for shutting down discussions kept growing.

The Next Wave of Censorship

The first wave of censorship was after the 2016 election, the second was during the COVID pandemic, and the third began immediately after the 2020 presidential election like clockwork. After four years of the Democrats coming up with countless conspiracy theories about how Donald Trump supposedly secretly worked with Russian intelligence to "steal" the 2016 election, all of a sudden claiming that *Democrats* stole the *2020* election for Joe Biden was a violation of the terms of service on all Big Tech platforms.[774]

Such claims were suddenly deemed to "undermine our Democracy" and said to be "dangerous." Exercising your First Amendment right to question the outcome of an election, or state an opinion that it was stolen, was now forbidden.

Censoring such discussions on social media was a new level of authoritarianism never seen in America. Up until that point, the only countries where people weren't allowed to question the election results were Communist countries and third world dictatorships. They claimed it might cause more civil unrest in the wake of the January 6th protest at the Capitol, but the systemic antiwhiteism and anti-police rhetoric coming from Black Lives Matter

---

[773] Associated Press "Extremists exploit a loophole in social moderation: Podcasts" by Tali Arbel (January 19th 2021)

[774] BBC "US election: YouTube to ban videos alleging widespread voter fraud" by James Clayton (December 10th 2020)

that had been inciting violence for years was still allowed to be posted and go viral.

Shortly before the 2020 election, the Big Tech platforms all censored the October surprise sprung on Democrats when the contents of Hunter Biden's laptop was published after he abandoned it at a repair shop. Aside from bizarre videos he shot of himself smoking crack and having sex with prostitutes, there were emails showing shady business deals with Ukraine and China that involved his father.[775]

So to muddy the waters hoping to hide the story, Deep State intelligence officials said it was Russian disinformation, but it was obvious at the time (and would later be undeniable) that their claims about the story being disinformation *was the disinformation.* A year and a half later, after the Biden Administration was an utter failure and Joe Biden had become an embarrassment, Liberal mainstream outlets finally admitted that the Hunter Biden laptop story is true—that the emails and explicit videos are his, but they still denied he or Joe Biden engaged in any influence peddling or illegal activity.[776]

Of course Donald Trump was banned from all brand name platforms after the January 6th protest at the Capitol got out of hand, but the Taliban (and their officials) were still able to have an official Twitter account.[777] So was Vladimir Putin and all Russian government officials and

---

[775] House Oversight Committee "Evidence of Joe Biden's Involvement in His Family's Influence Peddling Schemes" (September 13th 2023)

[776] New York Post "Washington Post joins New York Times in finally admitting emails from Hunter Biden laptop are real" by Bruce Golding (March 30th 2022)

[777] The Wrap "Twitter Refuses to Ban Taliban Accounts, Vows to Remain 'Vigilant' Moderating Content" by Samson Amore (August 17th 2021)

agencies, even after they invaded Ukraine.⁷⁷⁸ But not Donald Trump. From that point on, anytime he gave a speech or an interview, if he mentioned that he thought the 2020 election was stolen, that video would get censored from YouTube and Facebook, including his speech at CPAC in February 2021, as well as his CPAC speech the following year in 2022.⁷⁷⁹

As the 2020 election approached, numerous high-profile Democrats voiced concerns about the security of electronic voting machines and even held congressional hearings about it, but once Joe Biden was declared the supposed winner of the 2020 election, all of those concerns vanished and couldn't be raised by Republicans.

Democrats had legitimate concerns about the security and accuracy of electronic voting machines, and HBO even aired a documentary called *Kill Chain: The Cyber War on America's Elections* in March 2020 which demonstrated some of the vulnerabilities they had (anticipating a Donald Trump victory over Joe Biden, which Democrats would have blamed on Russia hacking the machines), but all those concerns went out the window—and after the election any Republican who raised them ever again was attacked as a "conspiracy theorist" and said to be spreading "dangerous misinformation."⁷⁸⁰

Surprisingly, a little over two years later Donald Trump's Twitter account was reinstated thanks to Elon

---

⁷⁷⁸ Washington Post "Why the Kremlin is still active on Facebook, Twitter and YouTube" by Christiano Lim and Will Oremus (March 17th 2022)

⁷⁷⁹ The Hill "YouTube removes CPAC content for violating 'election integrity policy'" by Chloe Folmar (March 24th 2022)

⁷⁸⁰ NBC News "Baseless GOP claims about election fraud remain dangerous for a democracy" by Chuck Todd, Mark Murray and Ben Kamisar (September 14th 2021)

Musk buying the platform, and a few months after that Facebook, Instagram, and YouTube allowed him access to his accounts again as well.[781] This, shortly after he announced he was running for reelection a second time. They probably knew that keeping the Republican frontrunner off their platforms during a presidential run would have galvanized Republicans across the country to denounce such communist-style censorship, so they reluctantly allowed him back on.

Then three months later, in June of 2023, YouTube finally lifted their ban on Republicans doubting the 2020 election results and talk of widespread voter fraud affecting the outcome.[782] YouTube claimed it was because they deemed there was no longer an "eminent" threat of people rioting again, like at the Capitol on January 6th 2021, since that tense time had long since passed and the anger dissipated.

But YouTube probably also realized that Rumble had become a viable alternative, attracting big names and even non-political channels like gamers and other content creators who thought YouTube was too saturated and wanted to try building an audience on a newer platform that was gaining momentum. Rumble even got listed on the NASDAQ stock exchange in September 2022 and has reached a market cap of two and a half billion dollars.[783] While other platforms had tried to take on YouTube, they either failed financially and ended up shutting down, or only gained niche users and audiences.

---

[781] Reuters "Trump returns to YouTube and Facebook after two-year ban" (March 17th 2023)

[782] NPR "YouTube will no longer take down false claims about U.S. elections" by Shannon Bond (June 2nd 2023)

[783] CNBC "Video platform Rumble to go public after successful SPAC vote" by Jack Stebbins (September 15th 2022)

CENSORSHIP

Rumble has grown to be a serious threat to YouTube's monopoly. While they still have policies against "hate speech," their rules regarding discussions about transgenderism and vaccines are drastically less restrictive than YouTube. And they even allow (as of November 2023) channels that have been banned from YouTube, including Alex Jones, Red Ice TV, AmRen (American Renaissance run by Jared Taylor), and Nick Fuentes.

But while Rumble promotes themselves as a "free speech" platform, they're only *freer*, and will be put to a difficult test at some point when the Apple and Android App stores pressure them to remove certain videos or channels they deem "hateful," "antisemitic," or contain what they deem "extremist" content.

Rumble is no longer a privately owned company. They have shareholders they're accountable to, and it's doubtful they will resist the ultimatum of either banning such content, or being banned from the App Stores themselves, if or when it's given. In the small chance they stand their ground and refuse to ban specific creators from their platform if threatened by the App Stores, they'll have to do what Gab.com did, and format their website so that users can visit it on their phone's browser and then just use the *Save to Home Screen* feature to create an icon on their phone that launches the website.

This workaround, pioneered by Gab's founder Andrew Torba after Gab was banned from the App Stores, allows a website to function essentially as an app on a phone, minus the push notifications. There may be some drawbacks however, such as lag-time when using certain features compared to the app itself, but it will still work—at least for now. Apple and Android may close this loophole at some point, but Gab.com has been using this method for years.[784]

Rumble will also increasingly face organized advertiser boycotts aimed at strangling them financially. After YouTube demonetized Russell Brand's channel in the wake of a coordinated campaign to cancel him, Rumble stood by him, causing brands like Burger King and HelloFresh to pull ads from the entire platform.[785] Rumble had already been the target of numerous organizations dedicated to stripping them of advertisers in hopes of shutting them down, and these groups will continue to seize on highly publicized events surrounding content creators who use the platform in order to further bully major brands (and advertising agencies) into not working with them.

Fake Fact Checkers

Facebook is the worst of all the social media platforms in terms of censorship and algorithm manipulation. What was once a great platform to keep in touch with family and friends, and a place to read interesting articles others shared, has turned into another tightly controlled corporate cog in the Left's information warfare machine.

At the end of 2016, about a month after the election when the "fake news" scare was first heating up and Democrats were blaming Hillary's loss on people posting "misinformation" about her, Facebook decided to start automatically "fact checking" things people posted,

---

[784] https://help.gab.com/faq/how-to-install-gab-app

[785] The Guardian "Firms pull ads from Rumble platform over Russell Brand videos" by Sammy Gecsoyler (September 23rd 2023)

outsourcing the operation to various organizations like Snopes and PoltiFact who were granted authority to police content so Facebook itself could claim *they* weren't censoring posts deemed to be "false" or sticking their nose into everyone's business—it's "trusted third party independent fact checkers."[786]

From this point on when anyone posted a link to a news story or YouTube video—if it triggered a "fact check," the post would be completely blurred out with a notice over it claiming it's "false" which also prevents it from going viral. But many of these "fact checks" are completely and obviously false, and the posts they censor are accurate and true. The new feature is just another way for the Establishment to further suppress information they don't want people to know.

But it's not just links that are censored. Posts just containing text are too, since Facebook automatically scans and reads everything; and if posts are detected to say things that they don't want people to say but aren't a violation of the terms of service, then they're secretly suppressed and only show up in a limited number of people's feeds who are following the page.

The Facebook "fact checks" started off to "protect civic integrity," meaning election news or falsehoods about voting, such as if someone posts that the polls in a particular area are closed when they're actually still open which could discourage people from going out to vote on their way home from work, or posts citing the wrong location of where people can vote which would send them on a wild goose chase, etc.

---

[786] Business Insider "Facebook is going to use Snopes and other fact-checkers to combat and bury 'fake news'" by Alex Heath (December 15th 2016)

That kind of misinformation was initially the target of the fact checkers, along with actual hoaxes they didn't want to go viral (such as someone claiming there was a terrorist attack in an American city, like a bombing that didn't actually happen) which many would argue may have been a good feature. But the road to hell is paved with good intentions, and the system got so out of control Facebook started censoring memes making fun of Democrats and Joe Biden.

For example, they "fact checked" a meme about gas prices being high because of President Biden that reads "Man I haven't seen gas prices this high since the last Democrat was in office." Anyone who posted it had the meme automatically grayed out and it was labeled "false" with a note claiming gas prices were high due to generic "supply issues."[787]

They even "fact check" the popular meme of Martin Luther King wearing a MAGA hat, claiming that his political affiliation isn't known.[788] Like all platforms, they use a Content ID system to automatically scan every image and video that's uploaded, and they have an entire library of memes the moderators have set to be flagged. Satirical articles from *The Babylon Bee* even get the same "fact check" in order to censor their mockery of Liberals.[789]

Another ridiculously false "fact check" that was integrated into Facebook's automatic system by *USA Today*, one of their "trusted" partners, claimed it was fake

---

[787] USA Today "Fact check: Rising gas prices due to high demand and low supply, not Biden's policies" by Miriam Fauzia (June 10th 2021)

[788] Reclaim The Net "Facebook fact-checks and censors Martin Luther King Jr. memes on MLK Day" by Tom Parker (January 20th 2020)

[789] Snopes "Did CNN Purchase an Industrial-Sized Washing Machine to Spin News?" by David Mikkelson (March 1st 2018)

news that a thug named Jacob Blake was armed at the time he got himself shot by police in Kenosha, Wisconsin. He's the thug whose shooting sparked the Black Lives Matter riots there shortly after, which led to Kyle Rittenhouse having to defend himself when he was attacked by the angry mob.

Anyone who posted that Jacob Blake was armed with a knife (which he was) had their posts flagged as "false" and penalties placed on their accounts. Not only did police say he had a knife on him at the time of the shooting, but it could be seen on video, and later during an interview with *Good Morning America* he admitted the obvious—that he was armed with a knife when police shot him.[790] But Facebook tried to protect the false narrative that another "unarmed" Black man just happened to get shot by police who must have been racist.

Facebook also "fact checked" a true claim that Donald Trump made about Kyle Rittenhouse when he said that videos showed he was trying to get away from the mob when they attacked him.[791] Anyone who followed that story closely saw those videos which went viral that same night, but Facebook was censoring posts that defended Rittenhouse or showed he acted in self-defense, deeming him a "mass shooter," and supporting or praising such individuals is a violation of their terms of service.[792]

Rittenhouse himself was banned from Facebook after his arrest, so he couldn't even defend himself on the

---

[790] Fox News "Jacob Blake admits he had a knife when he was shot by police" by Brittany De Lea (January 14th 2021)

[791] Fox News "Kyle Rittenhouse acquittal: PolitiFact blasted for fact-check saying Trump's comments on incident were 'false'" by Joseph A. Wulfsohn (November 19th 2021)

[792] Fox News "Facebook accused of pulling post about Kenosha gunman after declaring shooting 'mass murder" by Sam Dorman (September 4th 2020)

platform while the media, Democrats in Congress, and countless others online kept smearing him as a White supremacist and a mass murderer.[793]

One of the most hilarious fake "fact checks" happened after CNN made Joe Rogan look green when they aired a video he posted on Instagram announcing that he had tested positive for coronavirus. He wasn't vaccinated, so the media tried to rub it in that he got sick by making him look deathly ill by drastically altering the color of his video even though he only had mild symptoms because he got the monoclonal antibody treatment right away.

"No evidence video color was manipulated in CNN news segment," claimed the fact checkers,[794] but if you looked at the original video he uploaded to Instagram side by side with the one CNN aired (which is still up on their YouTube channel) he looks almost as green as the Incredible Hulk.[795] It's cartoonishly altered, and there's no reasonable explanation for it other than it was done on purpose, just like discoloring footage of political opponents in campaign ads—a common tactic used to cast them in a negative light.

Candace Owens sued the "fact checkers" because after receiving several "strikes" for posting supposedly false content then pages get demonetized just like YouTube channels—harming the livelihoods of content

---

[793] The Daily Caller "Democratic Rep Ayanna Pressley Calls Alleged Kenosha Shooter A 'White Supremacist Domestic Terrorist'" by Peter Hasson (August 27, 2020)

[794] Associated Press "No evidence video color was manipulated in CNN news segment" (September 10th 2021).

[795] Post Millennial "Joe Rogan accuses CNN of 'yellow journalism,' altering his COVID-19 announcement video" by Hannah Nightingale (January 10th 2022)

creators.[796] John Stossel also sued Facebook for over $2 million dollars claiming their fake "fact checks" were defamatory after they had declared several posts of his to be "false" (that were not), but a judge dismissed his lawsuit at the end of 2022 claiming that the "fact checks" are only a "subjective judgment about the accuracy and reliability of assertions."[797]

Note the judge's claims that the "fact checks" were "subjective," not *objective*. In other words, the supposed "fact checks" were just *opinions*. The judge's ruling goes on to say, "Simply because the process by which content is assessed and a label applied is called a 'fact-check' does not mean that the assessment itself is an actionable statement of objective fact."[798]

So a judge ruled that the "fact checks" are B.S. but Facebook is allowed to still use them to censor and suppress factual information, without facing any consequences. Candace Owens' lawsuit was also thrown out by a judge for similar bogus reasons.[799]

Elon Musk Tries to Save Twitter

Twitter (now rebranded as X by Elon Musk, but will still be referred to as Twitter for the sake of this discussion) often drives the news cycle. What trends on Twitter, makes headlines because lazy journalists looking

---

[796] Fox News "Candace Owens targets Facebook 3rd-party fact-checkers with lawsuit" by Louis Casiano (November 5th 2020)

[797] The Hollywood Reporter "Judge Dismisses John Stossel's Defamation Suit Against Facebook Over Fact-Checking" by Winston Cho (October 12th 2022)

[798] Ibid.

[799] Associated Press "Judge tosses suit by Candace Owens over Facebook fact checks" by Randall Chase (July 22nd 2021)

for a new story to write just have to scroll through Twitter for a few minutes and see what's trending and figure that would be a good topic since so many people are talking about it.

So, activists make it their mission to get topics or hashtags to trend in order to promote their cause, and of course for years Twitter manually inserted topics into the list to create a self-fulfilling prophecy. People thought the topic was popular because it was on the trending list, so they start tweeting about it, which then caused it to become popular.

It appears this manipulation stopped soon after Elon Musk purchased the platform, but since its launch in 2006 this was an extremely powerful method of directing news cycles, especially since Twitter has been predominantly a news platform and is a favorite for "journalists," news junkies, and political activists. Equally powerful was the platform preventing topics from trending when they were so widely tweeted about the algorithm would have organically included them on the list. Under Jack Dorsey's leadership (and later Parag Agrawal) the company regularly suppressed topics from trending that they didn't want to become bigger issues.

The platform is largely considered to be the digital public square where people argue and try to dunk on each other's stupid tweets, and its very design incentivizes dogpiling, which can instantly flood someone's mentions with an endless stream of mockery and this is why it's often used by activists to cancel people. A small group of people can easily whip up an online mob and flood a business's mentions with angry demands that someone be fired or they drop a certain product or stop advertising on certain TV shows or podcasts.

While once perhaps the least strict platform in terms of censorship, it slowly fell in lock step with the same policies of the other major platforms—banning "misgendering" transgender people (which means not using their preferred pronouns) and suspending people for "homophobic," "Islamophobic," or "antisemitic" tweets.[800]

Then in April 2022, Elon Musk—the richest man in the world at the time, made an official offer to buy Twitter for a shocking $44 billion dollars. And perhaps even more shocking—the board of directors approved the offer. But as soon as the wheels were in motion to get the legalities ironed out, the entire Liberal media machine completely freaked out over the thought of Musk, who had been clear about his support for free speech (and even saying he would reinstate Donald Trump's account), now loosening restrictions and restoring Twitter to its glory days.

The Washington Post denounced Musk's pending takeover, saying "we need regulation of social-media platforms to prevent rich people from controlling our channels of communication."[801] Of course rich people had controlled our channels of communication for nearly two decades. People like Mark Zuckerberg, and the executives at Twitter and YouTube.

What the *Washington Post* meant was they wanted the government to prevent Elon from allowing free speech—since he obviously had a very different philosophy about content moderation, and the mainstream media was scared to death that Conservatives may be able to leverage the

---

[800] BBC "Twitter's hate speech rules are expanded" by Dave Lee (December 18th 2017)

[801] The Washington Post "Elon Musk's vision of 'free speech' will be bad for Twitter" by Ellen K. Pao (April 8th 2022)

platform to promote their agenda just like Liberals had been doing on Twitter since its inception.

Axios, a popular online outlet, said "The world's richest man—someone who used to be compared to Marvel's *Iron Man*—is increasingly behaving like a movie supervillain, commanding seemingly unlimited resources with which to finance his mischief-making."[802] Allowing discussions critical of transgenderism and not using the platform to artificially amplify Liberal agendas was unthinkable to these people.

MSNBC's Ari Melber complained that Elon might amplify right-wing content, and suppress Liberals—which is obviously the very manipulation tactics the platform had been doing under the leadership of Jack Dorsey and Parag Agrawal for years.[803]

CNN's David Zurawik, who is also a professor of Media Studies at Groucher College, said Elon Musk running Twitter would be "dangerous" and pushed for government regulation of "hate speech" like in Europe. "You need regulation. You cannot let these guys control discourse in this country or we are headed to hell. We are there. Trump opened the gates of hell and now they're chasing us down."[804]

The Justice Department and the Securities and Exchange Commission launched a joint investigation into

---

[802] Axios "Elon Musk goes into full goblin mode" by Felix Salmon (April 14th 2022)

[803] Fox News "MSNBC host trashed for warning Elon Musk could use Twitter to ban political candidates: 'You absolute clown'" by Gabriel Hayes (April 26th 2022)

[804] CNN "CNN media analyst says 'we are headed to hell' without Twitter regulation" - video clip posted on their website of David Zurawik on "Reliable Sources" (May 1st 2022)

Elon Musk and his actions at Tesla.[805] Elon even became a victim of the MeToo movement, where women accuse rich and famous men of "sexual harassment" they say occurred many years earlier to essentially blackmail the men into paying them money to go away. A settlement Elon Musk had paid out from years earlier leaked to the media once he fell under the crosshairs of the Establishment for his plans to allow free speech on Twitter. Seven women would come to sue Elon for alleged "sexual harassment."[806]

Such lawsuits are common for celebrities even if they never did anything wrong because unscrupulous women figure they can get a decent settlement to make the problem go away and as counterintuitive as it may seem, it's often cheaper (and quicker) for the celebrities to pay out settlements than defend themselves in court.

Elon used to be a marvel of the world, but was now hated by half of the U.S. population who saw him as the man who would allow "Nazis" (like Donald Trump) to have Twitter accounts. And Elon would soon learn that he had dramatically underestimated the complexities of running a social media company, especially in the "woke" age of mass censorship. He never imagined the forces that would be unleashed trying to destroy him.

Elon Restores (Some) Banned Accounts

Soon after taking full ownership of the platform, Elon reinstated Donald Trump's account, although Trump had

---

[805] Reuters "Exclusive: Tesla faces U.S. criminal probe over self-driving claims" by Mike Spector and Dan Levine (October 26th 2022)

[806] Rolling Stone "'How Many Women Were Abused to Make That Tesla?'" by Stephen Rodrick (September 19th 2022)

already launched his own social media platform Truth Social, so he hesitated to return to the platform because he was under obligation to Truth Social investors to use that platform exclusively for a set period of time.[807]

Jonathan Greenblatt, the head of the ADL, denounced Elon's decision as "dangerous and a threat to American democracy," and then insinuated that Twitter should be banned from the Internet, saying, "We need to ask—is it time for Twitter to go?"[808] And he wasn't just making idle threats. Efforts were underway hoping to ban Twitter from the App Stores.[809]

Elon also restored over 12,000 accounts which had been banned under false pretenses, including poplar Conservatives, who—while not being household names, had built up rather large followings on the platform.[810] He also started releasing internal communications showing top executives who had previously run the company having discussions about banning popular accounts including Donald Trump's, as well as discussions about censoring the Hunter Biden laptop story and other (accurate) tweets about COVID-19 related issues.[811]

Elon would later say, "To be totally frank, almost every conspiracy theory that people had about Twitter

---

[807] As of the time of this writing in November 2023, he did tweet once, after his fourth indictment, posting a link to his website to help fundraise. As the 2024 election approaches he will likely use it again, at least occasionally, to gain attention.

[808] https://twitter.com/JGreenblattADL/status/1594161768905015298

[809] CNBC "Elon Musk claims Apple has threatened to remove the Twitter app" by Kif Leswing (November 28th 2022)

[810] Gizmodo "Elon Has Restored Nearly 12,000 Banned Twitter Accounts, Data Shows" by Kyle Barr (December 3rd 2022)

[811] CNN "Elon Musk speaks out on 'Twitter Files' release detailing platform's inner workings" by Ramishah Maruf (December 4th 2022)

turned out to be true."⁸¹² But despite restoring thousands of wrongfully banned accounts (including Donald Trump's) and loosening the terms of service and ending the partisan manipulation of the trending list, Elon's claims of being a "free speech absolutist" are false.⁸¹³

When a user recommended he restore Alex Jones' account, he responded "No." And then later in the day doubled down saying "too bad" when someone else in the thread tweeted that bringing back Alex Jones should be the litmus test of him allowing free speech.⁸¹⁴

When he was pressed even further about restoring Jones' account, Elon tweeted that he has "no mercy" for Jones because of his conspiracy theories surrounding the mass shooting at the Sandy Hook Elementary School.⁸¹⁵ Even though Jones' comments were insane, they weren't why he was banned from Twitter. He was banned for confronting CNN's Oliver Darcy in the halls of Congress in 2018 outside of a hearing about social media censorship which he live-streamed on Twitter through their Periscope app.⁸¹⁶ Twitter deemed it "harassment," but video of the interaction shows Jones was rather calm and wasn't even being disruptive.

Many thought perhaps Elon would change his mind in the future and allow Alex Jones back on because his

---

⁸¹² Newsmax "Musk: All 'Conspiracy' Theories About Twitter Turning 'Out to Be True'" by Nick Koutsobinas (December 25th 2022)

⁸¹³ Reuters "Twitter suspends Kanye West's account again" by Maria Ponnezhath and Eva Matthews (December 2nd 2022)

⁸¹⁴ CNN "Twitter won't restore Alex Jones' account, Elon Musk says" by Brian Fung (November 21st 2022)

⁸¹⁵ CBS News "Elon Musk says he'll never reinstate Alex Jones on Twitter" by Irina Ivanova (November 21st 2022)

⁸¹⁶ NPR "Twitter Bans Alex Jones And InfoWars; Cites Abusive Behavior" by Avie Schneider (September 6th 2018)

CENSORSHIP

policy decisions have been anything but consistent or principled, and he changes his mind more often than the way the wind blows. But a full year after taking over the platform, Alex Jones' ban remains.[817] Allowing him back on would be a PR nightmare, and even Jones has said he doesn't hold it against Elon because he's facing enough problems as it is.

But how is Twitter banning him from having an account any different than Verizon or AT&T not allowing him to have cell service because they don't like what he says? If he's not breaking the law by the things he posts (which he's clearly not) then why is he denied access to the basic communication tools available to everyone else?

He also never restored the accounts of Proud Boys founder Gavin McInnis and other high-profile controversial figures, including pro-White advocates like Jared Taylor, professor Kevin MacDonald,[818] and David Duke who all had Twitter accounts for years before eventually getting banned.[819] Nick Fuentes, a young controversial figure who built up a sizable dedicated fanbase of Conservative Zoomers (generation Z kids) had his Twitter account initially restored after Elon took over, but was permanently banned again within 24 hours after he said he loved Hitler during a Twitter Space, the group audio chat feature.[820]

---

[817] As of November 2023 when this book was originally published.

[818] Kevin MacDonald was actually banned under Elon Musk's ownership, in April 2023, and surprisingly was allowed to operate his account for years when the company was run by Jack Dorsey and Parag Agrawal.

[819] CNN "David Duke has been banned from Twitter" by Oliver Effron (July 31st 2020)

[820] The Hill "Nick Fuentes Twitter account suspended less than 24 hours after reinstatement" by Julia Shapero (January 25th 2023)

While I'm certainly not defending his incendiary rhetoric nor his support for Hitler, it is interesting to note that Leftists are allowed to praise murderous communist dictators like Joseph Stalin, Mao Zedong, and Pol Pot. Many of them are quite open about their admiration of such figures and that never seems to be a violation of the terms of service. Nor is open support for communism (which killed more people than Nazism), and while posting swastikas is strictly forbidden (unless done so with condemnation or for editorial purposes), communist and Marxist groups like Antifa are allowed to post hammer and sickle flags and openly promote their ideology.

The Future of X

The future of Twitter (famously renamed X in July 2023) remains to be seen. Elon has made some great changes (restoring thousands of accounts and loosening many of the restrictions on what people are allowed to post), but he has also made some rash and dumb decisions —like selling verification checkmarks to any account that paid $8 a month without actually verifying the identity of the accounts, leading to a wave of impersonations (and hilarious parody accounts), causing him to pause the scheme less than 24 hours later and revert back to the standard procedure of actually confirming account holders' identities before issuing the blue check signifying they're "verified."[821]

---

[821] Washington Post "Elon Musk's first big Twitter product paused after fake accounts spread" by Rachel Lerman and Cat Zakrzewski (November 11th 2022)

He once announced a new policy banning all links to content on other social media platforms because he didn't want anyone driving traffic to a competitor, only to reverse his decision (again within 24 hours) upon realizing the backlash and mockery over the idea, since it would be absurd and contrary to the core principles of social media to prevent people from linking to a Facebook post or Instagram photo.[822]

Elon often doesn't take into account feedback of others, even concerns of executives in the company who have extensive knowledge and experience before making dramatic changes that anyone else could have foreseen would cause massive problems (like selling verification checkmarks to accounts without actually verifying them) because he relies so heavily on his own instincts and intuition. This management style is often a double-edged sword extremely successful people wield because while this strategy can often work, it also leads them to further discount the doubts and concerns of others, which can result in them stumbling into obvious pitfalls that they themselves are blind to.

He wants X to be the "everything app" or a super app, which enables voice and video calls and the ability to send payments to others just like Venmo and CashApp; and perhaps even incorporate brokerage accounts for people to trade stocks, and possibly even online marketplaces like Amazon and eBay.

But because of the immense opposition to Elon allowing so many once-banned users and topics (like "misgendering" trans people, which means using pronouns other than the ones they demand people refer to

---

[822] Gizmodo "Twitter Suddenly Reverses Course on 'Policy' That Banned Links to Competing Social Media Sites" by Mark DeGeurin (December 17th 2022)

them as—something that was strictly forbidden under the previous ownership and is a violation of the terms of service on all the other Big Tech platforms), it may be difficult for him to sustain enough revenue sources to keep the app financially viable in the face of ongoing boycotts and attempts to sabotage him.

The platform experienced a massive revenue loss once Elon first took it over because many major advertisers fled out of fear it would now allow "hate speech," and "racism" would be allowed to flourish, mostly due to the Liberal media churning out a bunch of hit pieces and lying about what Elon's ownership would entail.

Then he tried to increase revenue through subscription services like Twitter Blue (now called X Premium) which gives users a verification checkmark and some other features like the ability to post longer tweets instead of the standard 280 characters, and edit them after they're posted. And despite Elon bringing aboard a new CEO from the advertising industry, Linda Yaccarino, the company continued to struggle financially.[823]

Hopefully he can maintain and grow the platform without further compromising on his support of free speech (remember, he already won't allow Alex Jones, professor Kevin MacDonald, Jared Taylor, and others to use it) and it's going to be impossible to keep everyone happy. Social media is no longer just a neat new technology for communication online. It's an information warfare tool used to drive news cycles and shape the culture, and Elon liberating it from the Big Tech oligarchs (despite his shortcomings) isn't going over very well with the powers that be.

---

[823] BBC "Twitter loses nearly half advertising revenue since Elon Musk takeover" by Jemma Dempsey (July 17th 2023)

The smears against him and the platform are relentless, with "journalists" and activist groups constantly searching for offensive or "hateful" posts and then framing stories as if "dangerous hate speech" is proliferating the entire ecosystem.

If he isn't able to make it profitable in the long term then X may end up back in the hands of another Silicon Valley social justice warrior like Mark Zuckerberg who will implement the same strict policies as usual, and go right back to using its power to shape public opinion and stifle debates in hopes of imposing their own values and agendas onto the world as they do on all the other mainstream platforms.

Coming After TV Stations

The Left weren't happy with the widespread censorship of certain topics and deplatforming of individuals from the virtual town squares of Twitter, Facebook, and YouTube, so they're trying to do more. Their agenda of stamping out influential opposition to the New World Order was working so well they decided to take things even further and hoped to get Fox News, Newsmax, and OAN taken off cable and satellite TV.

CNN's Oliver Darcy, the weasel-looking creature who worked as Brian Stelter's sidekick until he was fired in August 2022, helped amplify the idea. "Somehow, these companies have escaped scrutiny and entirely dodged this conversation. That should not be the case anymore," he said.[824]

---

[824] CNN "Analysis: TV providers should not escape scrutiny for distributing disinformation" by Oliver Darcy (January 8th 2021)

He then put out a call to action, saying "it is time TV carriers face questions for lending their platforms to dishonest companies that profit off of disinformation and conspiracy theories. After all, it was the very lies that Fox, Newsmax, and OAN spread that helped prime President Trump's supporters into not believing the truth: that he lost an honest and fair election."[825]

The editor-in-chief of *The Verge*, an online outlet owned by Vox Media, had also called for Fox News to be taken off the air several years earlier, saying, "I feel like we should be just as comfortable asking Comcast and Verizon and Charter why they continue to offer Fox News on their networks as we are about Facebook and Alex Jones."[826] At the time, few had even thought of such an idea, or weren't so bold to try, but recently the calls to pull Fox News, Newsmax, and OAN from the air have been growing.

DirecTV would later drop OAN in April 2022, which accounted for 90% of their revenue through what are called carriage fees, which are payments cable and satellite providers pay to channels on their service because being on the system is an incentive for people to subscribe.[827] Their removal was celebrated by many on the Left, including NAACP President Derrick Johnson who called it "a victory for us and the future of democracy."[828] Eliminating the free press in America is a "victory" in his mind!

---

[825] Ibid.

[826] In a tweet archived here: http://archive.fo/xb693

[827] The Washington Post "DirecTV says it will sever ties with far-right network One America News" by Timothy Bella (January 15th 2022)

[828] NAACP.org "NAACP President & CEO Derrick Johnson Releases Statement on Directv's announcement to drop One America News (OAN)" (January 15th 2020)

Compounding their problems was a lawsuit OAN faced after being sued for one billion dollars by the Dominion electronic voting machine company. Then a few months later Verizon dropped them from their TV service (called Fios) too.[829] Newsmax was dropped from DirecTV in January 2023 but later picked back up again two months later after they came to a new agreement, perhaps in part due to Republicans boycotting the company once they were dropped.

While only bringing in a small fraction of Fox News's audience at the time, Newsmax has grown into a formidable competitor to Fox and has been gaining former Fox News viewers who prefer Newsmax because programming tends to be further to the right. And after Tucker Carlson was fired without any reason being given, even more people left Fox for Newsmax.[830]

A woman named Gigi Sohn, who President Joe Biden nominated to be one of the five FCC Commissioners, had previously called Fox News "state propaganda" and suggested the Federal Communications Commission should pull the broadcast license for Sinclair media's television stations—a Conservative leaning company that owns and operates nearly 300 local news stations across America.[831]

Luckily after her hatred of Conservative media went viral, she withdrew her nomination (claiming she was the

---

[829] The Verge "One America News gets dumped by Verizon, the only major carrier it had left" by Emma Roth (July 24th 2022)

[830] Washington Post "Fox's Tucker Carlson firing is boosting Newsmax's ratings. Will it last? by Jeremy Barr (May 25th 2023)

[831] The Federalist "Biden's FCC Commissioner Nominee Gigi Sohn Wants To Nuke Right-Leaning Broadcasters From Air" by Jordan Boyd (January 18th 2022)

"victim of cruel attacks."[832] But the fact that such a Left-wing extremist would be nominated in the first place to sit as an FCC commissioner and oversee television and radio broadcast licenses is stunning.

Congresswoman Alexandria Ocasio-Cortez called on the FCC to pull Tucker Carlson off the air, claiming he "clearly incites violence," but she's so dumb she doesn't know that the Fox News channel isn't governed by the FCC, only over the air broadcast stations are (not cable). But Tucker Carlson was fired by Fox News just a few days later, which she celebrated on an Instagram livestream where she said "Deplatforming works," and used the event to fundraise.[833]

Pulling Fox News from cable systems and satellite TV providers will never happen, but it happened to OAN because they're too far to the right and their news and commentary is seen as more threatening to the Establishment's order. And it did happen to Newsmax, although they returned a few months later after the backlash, and the fact that Democrats have even proposed the idea of banning television stations is a shocking indication of just how un-American they are, and how far they're willing to go in hopes of silencing their opposition.

---

[832] CNBC "Biden FCC nominee Gigi Sohn withdraws, citing 'cruel attacks' in battle with cable and media industries" by Lauren Feiner and Ashely Capoot (March 7th 2023)

[833] National Review "'Deplatforming Works': AOC Fundraises Off of Tucker Carlson's Ouster from Fox News" by Caroline Downey (April 25th 2023)

Banning Books

While Democrats claim Republicans are "banning books" because they don't want pornographic and pedophilic material in school libraries, they're actually the ones who have been working to censor books and ban them from even being sold to adults. But as you'll see, the brand name "free speech" activists will only ring the alarm when certain books are banned from Amazon (and Barnes & Noble) and stay fearfully silent when it happens to others.

In 2018 Amazon banned a children's book called *No Dress for Timmy* which is about a boy who refuses to go along with supporting gender-bending at his school, but that didn't make any major headlines and was only mentioned in a few small blogs.[834] This was back when most brand name Conservatives were still afraid to speak out against transgenderism and drag queen story hour, so only a few YouTubers (myself included) covered this story at the time.

As the years went on however, transgenderism became a major political and cultural issue, and once Conservatives realized the queers are coming for the children, then finally the stigma around aggressively opposing the trans agenda had ended.

In 2021 Amazon banned a book titled *When Harry Became Sally* which did generate major headlines and got the attention from numerous Republican members of Congress who denounced the censorship, prompting Amazon to break their silence about deleting the book's listing saying they would now ban any book that equated

---

[834] Metro Voice "Amazon changes course again, will ban 'No Dress for Timmy'" (January 29th 2019)

transgenderism or any LGBTQ "identity" with mental illness.[835]

In 2022 a recording of an Amazon Zoom meeting was leaked showing employees complaining about Matt Walsh's children's book *Johnny The Walrus* which is about a boy who decides he wants to be a walrus, mocking the gender-bending craze.[836] One of the employees on the call broke down into tears and said the book is causing "trauma" to transgender employees and pushed for it to be banned.[837]

Then during the company's LGBTQ Pride celebration that year several employees staged a "die-in" where they laid on the ground pretending to be dead to protest the sale of "transphobic" books like *Johnny the Walrus* and *Irreversible Damage: The Transgender Craze Seducing Our Daughters* by Abigail Shrier, which discusses rapid-onset gender dysphoria.[838] Surprisingly those titles have not been banned, at least at the time this book was published at the end of 2023.

And while the brand name activists on Twitter, hosts on Fox News and Newsmax, popular YouTubers "fighting the culture war," and members of Congress denounced Amazon banning *When Harry Became Sally* and the company's new policy forbidding certain anti-LGBTQ books, they all remain silent about other material Amazon

---

[835] The Wall Street Journal "Amazon Won't Sell Books Framing LGBTQ+ Identities as Mental Illnesses" by Jeffrey A Trachtenberg (March 11th 2021)

[836] The Daily Mail "Woke Amazon staffer cries in meeting to discuss the 'trauma' caused by best seller children's book 'Johnny the Walrus' that compares being transgender to pretending to be a walrus" by Natasha Anderson (April 26th 2022)

[837] Ibid.

[838] The Daily Wire "Amazon Employees Disrupt Pride Ceremony With 'Die In' Protest Over Matt Walsh's 'Johnny The Walrus', Other 'Anti-Trans' Books" by Amanda Harding (June 2nd 2022)

(and Barnes & Noble) have banned. Professor emeritus Kevin MacDonald, a sociologist from California State University Long Beach, had his magnum opus *Culture of Critique: An Evolutionary Analysis of Jewish Involvement in Twentieth-Century Intellectual and Political Movements* banned in March 2019.[839] Another one of his books titled *Cultural Insurrections: Essays on Western Civilization, Jewish Influence, and Anti-Semitism* was banned at the same time.[840]

The books, as you can probably tell from their titles, cover a taboo topic, and despite being written by a California State University professor, they have been deemed "antisemitic" by the ADL, so both Amazon and Barnes & Noble quietly banned them. They don't just refuse to stock them—they are completely banned, and used copies aren't allowed to be listed by third parties either.[841]

They had been in stock and sold for years, but as cancel culture kept gaining momentum, the censorship of content shifted from social media platforms to podcasts, and then ultimately books. But zero mainstream Conservatives noticed or spoke out against professor MacDonald's books being banned out of fear that they would have been accused of supporting "antisemitism."

Jared Taylor's book *White Identity: Racial Consciousness in the 21st Century* was also banned from

---

[839] TruthOut.org "After Activist Pressure, Amazon Purges Dozens of Far-Right Books" by Shane Burley (March 22nd 2019)

[840] The Occidental Observer Amazon Bans Culture of Critique and Separation and Its Discontents" by Kevin MacDonald (March 12th 2019)

[841] As of November 2023 when this book, The War on Conservatives was first published.

Amazon and Barnes & Noble in 2019.[842] Since 1994 he has held his American Renaissance conference ever other year (falsely labeled a "White supremacist" gathering by the media, the SPLC, and the ADL) where he and other speakers discuss some of the problems multicultural societies face and advocate that White people should demand the same rights and opportunities as other ethnic groups in the United States.[843]

Around this same time Amazon also quietly banned David Duke's autobiography *My Awakening* and his other book *Jewish Supremacy,* which details what he believes is a Jewish supremacist belief system at the core of Jewish culture.[844] It's extremely politically incorrect to accuse members of any ethnic group other than White people of believing they are superior to others. Admitting that Black supremacy exists is called "racist," but pointing out that many Jewish people believe in their own ethnic superiority is even worse—that's "antisemitism."

Theologian Martin Luther, who is responsible for the Protestant Reformation (he famously nailed his *Ninety-five Theses* to the door of the Catholic Church in 1517 challenging them on their authority), later wrote a book very critical of Jews as well, called *On The Jews and Their Lies* which has been in print ever since it was first published in 1543, and in stock on Amazon for years until

---

[842] American Renaissance "PRESS RELEASE: Amazon Now Banning Books Based on Political Content" (February 27th 2019)

[843] See chapter on Antiwhiteism.

[844] The New York Times "In Amazon's Bookstore, No Second Chances for the Third Reich" by David Streitfeld (February 9th 2020)

around this same time when it too was banned after pressure from Jewish groups.[845]

Amazon also banned *Jewish History, Jewish Religion: The Weight of Three Thousands Years* (1994) written by Israel Shahak who is not only a Jew (or was, since he died in 2001), but he was also a Holocaust survivor who was kept at a concentration camp in Poland, and after World War II moved to Israel where he later became an organic chemistry professor at Hebrew University in Jerusalem.[846] Despite being Jewish (and a citizen of Israel) he was very critical of the human rights violations against the Palestinians, Zionism, ethnocentrism in Judaism, and Jewish supremacists.[847]

The foreword to the first edition was written by Gore Vidal and the book was endorsed by Noam Chomsky, Edward Said, and other popular human rights activists.[848] So nobody can lump him in with David Duke and other supposed "White nationalists." But Israel Shahak's book has also been deemed "antisemitic" so it was quietly deleted from Amazon after being listed for over two decades.[849]

---

[845] It's unclear exactly when the book, along with its listing and reviews were removed, but presumably it was in early 2019 when the big purge of supposed "antisemitic" and "White supremacist" titles were removed.

[846] Foreword to the First Edition, as well as the Foreword to the Second and Third Edition.

[847] Jewish History, Jewish Religion: The Weight of Three Thousands Years by Israel Shahak pages 30, 36, 107, 124 (Pluto Press 1994) ISBN: 978-0-7453-2840-9

[848] https://twitter.com/alisonweir/status/1612868601056460806

[849] The main listing, along with all of the reviews from readers has been deleted. Someone listed a used copy for sale on Amazon that slipped through the cracks but when a book goes out of print, the listing and all of the reviews stay, no matter how long the book has been out of print, which is not the case with Israel Shahak's book and the others listed in this chapter.

Anyone can order books critical of Christianity, Catholicism, Mormonism, the Jehovah Witness cult (not to mention White people and whiteness) but certain books a little too critical of Jews, Judaism, or Jewish involvement in political movements and ones that focus on "Jewish bankers" have quietly vanished.[850]

But again, none of the "free speech culture warriors" like Ben Shapiro, Charlie Kirk, Glenn Greenwald, or even Tucker Carlson denounced the censorship of these books. The brand name Conservative Twitter personalities and YouTubers who host shows funded or produced by Turning Point USA, The Blaze, The Daily Wire, and PragerU were all silent as well.

All books promoting White nationalism and the Alt-Right have also been banned, including *The White Nationalist Manifesto*, *New Right vs. Old Right*, and *The Alternative Right* by Greg Johnson which documents the rise and fall of the movement.[851] (All purged in February 2019.)[852] Another popular one in the genre called *A Fair Hearing: The Alt-Right in the Words of Its Members and Leaders* was also banned from both Amazon and Barnes & Noble.[853]

None of these books call for any violence or even suggest it, but because they're essentially pro-White,

---

[850] A History of Central Banking and the Enslavement of Mankind (2014) by Stephen Mitford Goodson is among the titles banned. Goodson was a South African banker and politician.

[851] TruthOut.org "After Activist Pressure, Amazon Purges Dozens of Far-Right Books" by Shane Burley (March 22nd 2019)

[852] Counter-Currents.com "Amazon.com Continues to Purge Counter-Currents Titles" by Greg Johnson (February 27th 2019)

[853] The exact date of its removal is uncertain, but most likely was in February 2019 when Counter-Currents books were banned, along with Jared Taylor's White Identity, and his other essays compiled in If We Do Nothing, and two books he edited: A Race Against Time, and Face to Face with Race.

they've been deemed "White supremacist" material, and the publishers are now forbidden from listing them for sale on the two biggest bookseller websites in the world. Black nationalist books however, are allowed, with several exceptions published by the Nation of Islam which were removed—not for antiwhiteism, but for "antisemitism."[854] Amazon certainly wouldn't ban Malcom X's autobiography, even though he was a Black nationalist and called for racial separatism and wanted to create a Black-only region of the United States.[855] Countless books by Black Lives Matter activists and other "Black Power" advocates argue for Black-only spaces and support racial segregation so they don't have to deal with any White people anymore—and that's just fine.

Activist groups are even targeting other, lesser known online book retailers like ThriftBooks.com, BooksAMillion.com and BetterWorldBooks.com, as well as eBay, pressuring them to ban the sale of used copies of such books.[856] To be clear, I'm not endorsing these books, the Alt-Right, or the idea of creating a White ethnostate, which is just a nostalgic pipe dream—an impossible endeavor and a fantasy held on to by those who wish to return to an era that has long since past. Anyone who believes such a thing is even remotely possible at this point in civilization is either just dreaming or delusional.

But why shouldn't people be able to read what such authors have to say? Especially since they're not calling

---

[854] Noirg.org "Amazon Bans The Secret Relationship Between Blacks & Jews" by Nation of Islam Research Group (March 16th 2019)

[855] The National Endowment for the Humanities "Malcolm X: A Radical Vision for Civil Rights" by Joe Phelan (May 5th 2017)

[856] The Jerusalem Post "'Elders Of Zion' book being sold by top booksellers" by Michael Starr (January 26th 2022)

for any kind of violence at all, and in fact specifically condemn it, arguing it would only reflect negatively on those who hold their views and ostracize others from listening to them. Most are just expressing their view as White people who are increasingly becoming marginalized and demonized simply for existing, and don't want any kind of violent conflicts at all. And you have to admit it's odd that Amazon sells literal bomb-making manuals like the *Anarchist Cookbook* (and Adolf Hitler's *Mein Kampf*) but won't allow the sale of David Duke's autobiography or Jared Taylor's book because they talk about White Identity.

In 2015, I posted a video on my YouTube channel showing me approaching random people on a southern California boardwalk and asking them if they would sign a petition demanding Amazon.com and Barnes & Noble both stop selling the *Bible* because it promotes "homophobia" and is too "offensive." Many gladly did.[857] I repeated the same experiment again over five years later with the same results.[858]

You may have seen the videos, but the analytics show that only about 15% of subscribers to a YouTube channel watch any given video that's uploaded, so I mention them here because I think it's critically important to understand just how normalized the idea of banning books has become among the Left, to the point that many of them are willing to go along with banning the Bible!

---

[857] Mark Dice YouTube Channel "Liberals Trying to Ban the Bible from Amazon.com and Barnes & Noble" (September 7th 2015) Original link: https://youtu.be/Y9WUeHHzf7s

[858] Mark Dice YouTube Channel "Woke Californians Want to BAN the BIBLE for 'Hate Speech'" (April 13th 2022) Original link: https://youtu.be/XckcMeSueMA

First Amendment Doesn't Apply

A detailed discussion of censorship on social media would fill hundreds of pages, and I documented the history of it in my previous books *The Liberal Media Industrial Complex* and *The True Story of Fake News* which you should read if you haven't already because it's important to be familiar with the different phases the platforms have gone through—and how much they have changed, and why.

When the censorship first started it was "only" social media personalities who weren't household names but who had amassed followings of hundreds of thousands of people that were getting suspended and banned. Little to no news articles were written about them when it happened. No Republican members of Congress tweeted about them. They weren't invited on Fox News for a segment to talk about it. Only others in their online community seemed to notice or care.

Those of us who saw the writing on the wall did our best to ring the alarm bell about the growing problem, but it really wasn't until the Hunter Biden laptop story was blocked on social media (and *The New York Post* suspended from Twitter) that censorship became a major concern for the Republican Party.

Because the First Amendment only protects free speech from being censored by the government and not corporations which control telecommunication technologies and social media platforms, people have little recourse and are held over a barrel by the selectively enforced "terms of service" and the whims of faceless moderators who can ban anyone they want for any reason.

Seeing the problem early on, however, were numerous entrepreneurs who staunchly support free speech so they worked to create platforms by basically cloning the features of Facebook, Twitter, and YouTube but applying the type of content moderation policies that the Big Tech platforms used to have before they started massively restricting what people are allowed to post.

And while Rumble, Odysee, BitChute, Gab, Gettr, Truth Social, MeWe, Telegram, and others haven't gained the widespread user bases of the Big Tech platforms, millions of people use them, and they are invaluable tools for free speech despite how "niche" they may be.

The Washington Post wrote an entire article complaining about Congresswoman Marjorie Taylor Greene's reach on the alt-tech platforms after her personal account was banned from Twitter in early 2022 for "repeated violations" of their COVID "misinformation" policy. *The Post* was stunned that she continued to reach hundreds of thousands of people.[859] Her Twitter account was among those later restored by Elon Musk, but that's beside the point. Facebook, YouTube, and Instagram continue to severely restrict what users can say, and who can even use their platforms.

And Rumble will likely cave to the demands of the app stores regarding banning certain individuals and content, but as we've seen with Amazon banning various controversial books, the brand name Conservatives will likely say nothing about it and go on pretending it's a "free speech" platform because they can make fun of

---

[859] The Washington Post "Twitter banned Marjorie Taylor Greene. That may not hurt her much." by Maggie Macdonald and Meghan A. Brown (January 14th 2022)

transgender people.[860] Those who touch certain third rail issues about things like White Identitarianism or Jewish power will never have their free speech rights defended by any Conservative Inc. pundits.

It's possible that we can shift the culture enough to cause the pendulum to start swinging back the other direction and get the Big Tech platforms to ease up on their censorship (at least regarding *some* issues). But it's likely they'll get even more strict and more manipulative, especially as our society becomes more polarized with each side digging in to their positions and difficult issues regarding race and transgenderism dominating the political landscape.

If they continue with the current trend, the so-called alt-tech platforms are only going to gain more users which may cause Leftists to look for their vulnerabilities, trying to get them banned from the app stores (like they already did with Gab and BitChute). Activist organizations have even gone after hosting services trying to get the websites banned too, as well as payment processors, and even banks (issues that Gab has been facing for years).[861]

They may never stop scheming, and for many years now the Left has wanted to criminalize "hate speech" in America, just like other supposed "free" countries around

---

[860] BitChute and Gab are the only true free speech platforms that allow anything that's protected by the first amendment to be posted, which is why they've both been banned from the app stores, PayPal, payment processors, and even banks.

[861] The Verge "Gab.com goes down after GoDaddy threatens to pull domain" by Sam Byford (October 28th 2018)

the world have—including Canada,[862] Germany,[863] England,[864] Scotland,[865] and others. These countries arrest people for posting "hate speech" on social media. Not death threats or harassment (which any reasonable person can agree should be illegal, and is), but things like insulting gay people, or being too critical of the Islamization of Europe from all the Muslim refugees that have flooded the West, or for posts deemed "antisemitic" (anti-Christian hate speech is always allowed though).[866]

To list the cases of people arrested for such "violations" (which include jokes) would be too long, but America should be aware that such things are happening in other western countries, and it should serve as a warning of what could happen here. There's a reason the freedom of speech is protected by the *First* Amendment—because it's the most important right we have, and it must be protected at all costs.

---

[862] Huffington Post "Think Canada Allows Freedom of Speech? Think Again" by Tom Kott (December 19, 2012)

[863] BBC "Facebook, Google and Twitter agree German hate speech deal" (December 15th 2015)

[864] Associated Press "In UK, Twitter, Facebook rants land some in jail" by Jill Lawless (November 12, 2012)

[865] Breitbart "UK Police Arrest Man For 'Offensive' Facebook Post About Migrants" by Liam Deacon (February 16th 2016)

[866] Daily Caller "Mother Arrested, Spends Seven Hours In Jail For Calling Transgender A Man" by David Krayden (February 10th 2019)

Cowardly Conservatives

Starting shortly after the turn of the 21st century most Republican members of Congress and mainstream Conservative pundits became cowards when dealing with social issues. They suddenly became afraid of being called "homophobic" for denouncing the widespread sexual perversions which are now commonplace in society, and almost as afraid to be called a "racist" for pointing out the Black Crime problem in America or denouncing antiwhiteism.

As our culture continued to rapidly decay with brazen degeneracy being thrust into the mainstream by Leftists in Hollywood and boosted by the Big Tech social media platforms, most Conservative "leaders" stayed silent, continuously self-censoring themselves hoping to avoid any backlash from the Liberal Media Industrial Complex.

Instead, all they talked about were "tax cuts for the middle class" and how they were trying to prevent jobs from being outsourced to foreign countries; and while those are great policies, their focus came at a tremendous cost to the culture which is just as important, if not more so than economics and the job market. People can usually find a new job and get by with less if they have to cut their budget, but once the culture becomes polluted, it's like a poisoned well, and anyone who drinks from it is in danger of getting sick or dying.

But after two decades of quietly watching from the sidelines as the poison was poured in, the sleeping giant of "reactionaries" finally awakened. The Left had pushed too many people too far. Although time will tell whether or not the awakening was too late. Despite Republican "firebrands" like Matt Gaetz, Marjorie Taylor Greene, and Lauren Boebert getting involved in the culture war (to some extent, at least), most politicians and political commentators are still only doing so half-heartedly and walking on eggshells hoping to avoid being labeled "far right," "homophobic," "White nationalist," and the other list of labels the Left usually tries to stick on their enemies.

One of the problems that led the Republican Establishment to become so cowardly is they morphed into a Big Tent Party, meaning one that attempts to attract as wide range of groups and voters as possible under one banner, but that means not taking a firm stance on certain issues because being "too Conservative" may scare some new people away who the party is trying to attract. "Too Conservative," meaning still supporting various issues that were core values in the Republican Party in previous generations but ones they've slowly backed away from as society has gotten more tolerant of liberalism.

So they water down their message, hoping to gain the support of first-time voters and that of moderates, independents, and some disaffected Democrats while taking for granted those who have usually supported them in the past.

The brand name Republicans, "Conservative Inc.," or the "Corporate Conservatives"—whatever name you want to attach to the Republican Establishment and their mouth pieces, have increased the size of the tent for "conservatism" so big that it became a circus. And because the Republican Party has become dramatically more socially Liberal over the last twenty years, there's a saying among *real* Conservatives (Paleoconservatives) that the only difference between Liberals and mainstream Conservatives is ten years.

The Republican Establishment functions as a political ratchet, meaning they allow the Democrats to keep moving society slowly to the left while putting up *some* resistance trying to stop it, but they rarely (if ever) turn things back to the right.

Similarly, the political commentators who work for the brand name outlets (or are trying to build up their followers on social media in hopes of one day joining them) usually function as a false opposition and pretend to be antiestablishment by criticizing a few common points of contention people often have about Congress or the media in general trying to create the impression that they're not part of the club, while either toeing the party line on every other issue or carefully avoiding going against others that are clearly core Establishment positions.[867]

Pandering To Blacks

There's an old joke about Republicans that goes: *What do you call the one Black guy at a Republican conference?—The keynote speaker!* Just like Republicans now pander to the gay community and go out of their way trying to show that they're not "homophobic" hoping to gain the support of what is just a tiny fraction of the electorate, they also pander to Black people and shamelessly try to prove that they're not "racist," playing the same game Democrats have been engaged in for decades.

---

[867] Republican Establishment positions like the fact that 35 states that have anti-BDS laws which punish American businesses if they criticize Israel; laws that are completely contrary to the principles of free speech.

Our party has great Black people like Larry Elder, David Webb, Ben Carson, Tim Scott, Byron Donalds, Candace Owens, and others, so there's no need to pander to them in hopes of showing how "diverse" the Republican Party is. If they like our ideas and our values, they'll vote Republican. There shouldn't be a focus on what the Republican Party can do "for Black people."

Older Black people tend to be socially Conservative because of their history with the church, but have historically voted Democrat for economic reasons because Democrats appeal to lower income voters through promises of social welfare programs. But seeing the Democrat Party embracing all kinds of LGBTQ nonsense should be enough to bring many of them over to the Republican side because Black people overwhelmingly do not support gay "marriage" or transgenderism. They also don't want their jobs taken by illegal aliens.

Pandering to Blacks by offering them more social welfare programs in their communities is only going to keep moving the Republican platform further to the left while marginalizing more White voters.

And sadly even Donald Trump pandered to Blacks with his "criminal justice reform" (the First Step Act) hoping to gain another few percentage of Black voters by virtue signaling that he was letting Black criminals out of prison early.[868] During his rallies the organizers strategically put people with "Blacks for Trump" shirts prominently in the background right behind him to signal to other Black people watching at home hoping to gain their support.

---

[868] The Root "91 Percent of Inmates Freed by First Step Act Were Black. Should We Give Republicans Credit?" by Michael Harriot (June 10th 2019)

Republicans even chose a token Black man named Michael Steele to be the chairman of the Republican National Committee, who later betrayed the party, joining the anti-Trump Lincoln Project and became an MSNBC contributor where he criticizes everything Republicans do. Of course he didn't vote for Donald Trump in 2016 and endorsed Joe Biden in 2020, and wants Donald Trump to go to prison.

You get what you pay for, as the saying goes. If you buy something cheap, it's usually going to break after a short period of time and need to be replaced, costing more in the long run. And if you hire a token Black person trying to show how "inclusive" you are instead of hiring whoever is best qualified for the job, regardless of their race, it's always going to backfire. The Republican Party's first major affirmative action hire, Michael Steele, went from a top leadership position to a Democrat operative in the span of just a few years. Such disastrous outcomes could easily be avoided by not even playing the diversity game.

CPAC, the biggest Conservative event in the political world, sucked up to a rapper named Young Pharaoh one year because they thought it would be cool to have a rapper on the stage in hopes of attracting more Black people to the Republican Party, but right before the event, CPAC canceled his appearance because some of his past "antisemitic" comments resurfaced.[869] And the one thing the Republican Party won't tolerate is criticism of Israel or Jews, so he was canceled. Like I said, affirmative action hires always end up being a disaster.

---

[869] CNN "CPAC cancels speaker over anti-Semitic social media comments" by Eric Bradner (February 23rd 2021)

"Conservatives" Catering to Gays

The Republican Party is now more pro-gay than the Democrat Party was just over 10 years ago.[870] Even Barack Obama and Joe Biden opposed gay "marriage" until mid 2012.[871] Although when Obama was first running for president in 2008, he and his running mate Joe Biden opposed it, but once elected they both "evolved" their position and fully endorsed it, as did the entire Democrat Party. But back then nearly every Republican was firmly against it.[872] Today however, there are probably less than a half dozen Republican members of Congress who oppose it. And instead, the Republican Party has climbed aboard the gay Pride bandwagon.

Ronna McDaniel, chairwoman of the RNC, tweeted out a "Happy Pride Month" message in June 2021, adding that the GOP is proud to have "doubled our LGBTQ support over the last four years, and we will continue to grow our big tent."[873] Fox News even started celebrating LGBTQ Pride Month in 2022 with at least nine segments that June featuring the "achievements" of queer people and highlighting how great "gay culture" is.[874]

"Meet important voices of the LGBTQ+ community. And go inside their incredible contributions," one of the promos announced.[875] One of the stories was presented

---

[870] As of the end of 2023 when this book was first published.

[871] CNN "Obama announces he supports same-sex marriage" by Phil Gast (May 9th 2012)

[872] The Washington Post "Meet the four Republicans in Congress who support gay marriage" by Sean Sullivan (April 2nd 2013)

[873] https://twitter.com/GOPChairwoman/status/1400212885595426824

[874] Newsweek "Republicans Blast Fox News for Promoting LGBTQ Pride Month" by Andrew Stanton (June 14th 2022)

[875] Ibid.

by Dana Perino who began the segment saying, "Pride Month continues as we highlight the story of Ryland Whittington whose journey of transitioning at age five has been seen by seven million people in a family YouTube video."[876]

She went on to say the family hopes their experience can help convince others to support the idea of sex changes for children.[877] Fox News also highlighted a lesbian priest in the Episcopal church[878] and commemorated the first gay major league baseball player, Glenn Burke, who came out as gay back in the 1970s (and later died of AIDS).[879] What a surprise.

Fox News also hired Caitlyn Jenner in March 2022 as a contributor who appears on Sean Hannity's show and others to comment on issues that usually have nothing to do with transgender people at all.[880] At the time neither CNN or MSNBC had any transgender contributors on salary, so Fox News was the pioneer.

Richard Grenell was the first openly gay man to serve in a cabinet position after Donald Trump appointed him to the Director of National Intelligence. And practically every time his name was mentioned by Establishment Republicans as a "great" choice for the position, it was followed by them happily highlighting "he's gay" as a virtue signal about how "diverse" and "inclusive" the Republican Party was becoming.

---

[876] https://www.foxnews.com/video/6307598106112

[877] Ibid.

[878] https://www.foxnews.com/video/6260651671001

[879] https://www.foxnews.com/video/6308785798112

[880] Fox News "Caitlyn Jenner joins Fox News as contributor: 'I am humbled by this unique opportunity'" by Brian Flood (March 31st 2022)

What did his sexual orientation have to do with his ability to be an intelligence analyst and brief the President of the United States about national security matters? His personal life should have been no more of concern than someone who's divorced, or a bachelor—or a guy who prefers to date blondes. But Republican pundits on TV couldn't be happier talking about how great it was that he's the first gay person appointed to a cabinet position by either political party (Pete Buttigieg would later be the second).

And what did Richard Grenell do for conservatism in America? He led the effort to encourage President Trump to call for the "decriminalization of homosexuality" throughout the world because various countries in Africa, the Middle East, and the Caribbean (68 total in the world) still criminalize LGBT conduct and propaganda.[881] Of all the issues facing our country and the world, that was Richard Grenell's top priority.

Charlie Kirk, founder of the Republican college club Turning Point USA and one of the most prominent voices in the Conservative movement, has been a pied piper leading the next generation of Conservatives to accept gay "marriage" and even gay men adopting children as normal.

During an interview in 2018 with YouTuber Dave Rubin, Conservative Inc.'s token gay friend, he said "I think it's cool you're married. It's great. And you should have all the same tax benefits [as heterosexual couples],

---

[881] NBC News "Acting intelligence head Richard Grenell's push to decriminalize homosexuality has yielded little" by Tim Fitzimons (February 20th 2020)

adopt children, it's great."[882] Many so-called Conservatives hold this position now, but what they fail to acknowledge is when children become involved it's not about what two consenting adults are doing in the privacy of their own bedroom anymore, it's about what they're subjecting innocent children to, and what kind of an environment they're forcing them to live in.

Charlie Kirk has also welcomed drag queens into the Republican Party, posing with one in a photo at PolitiCon in 2019 who goes by the name "Lady MAGA," a Trump-supporting drag queen, who in a normal society would have been kicked out of the event immediately, not having Charlie Kirk pose for a picture with him while smiling and giving a thumbs up.[883] We don't need any "drag queens for Trump" trying to show how queer-friendly the Republican Party is. They're the kind of people who are ruining our party.

During an event in 2019 called Culture War that Turning Point USA sponsored, an attendee asked Charlie Kirk how anal sex helps the culture war, referring to Turning Point hiring a token Black gay guy—Rob Smith (who was on stage with him at the time) and denounced Charlie's palling around with queers in attempts to paint the Republican Party as not being anti-gay. Kirk then said the question was "weird" and insinuated the guy who asked it is a closeted gay himself and struggling with his sexuality.[884]

---

[882] The Rubin Report "On Trump, The Drug War, & Gay Rights (Pt. 1) | Charlie Kirk | POLITICS | Rubin Report" (January 17th 2018) at 40:37 timestamp

[883] Big League Politics "PHOTO: TPUSA Founder Charlie Kirk Yucks It Up With Drag Queen As They Flash Kids In Libraries Across America" by Shane Trejo (October 30th 2019)

[884] The Culture War Feat. Charlie Kirk at Ohio State University (October 29th 2019)

Rob Smith echoed this attack saying, "You seem to be really interested in gay sex...I'm pretty sure if you're into that, you can go find somebody to do that with."[885] This is the same tactic gays have always used whenever someone expresses disgust with them, which if you follow their logic would mean anyone who is opposed to pedophiles is secretly a pedophile, or anyone who doesn't want to hear about their parents' sex lives is actually turned on by it.

Charlie Kirk also claims to be a Christian, yet has done more to normalize homosexuality in the Conservative movement than perhaps anyone else. The unofficial Republican Party stance is now that gays—and gay "marriage," and gay adoption, and gays buying children through surrogacy, and them serving in the military is just fine, and they only draw the line at transgenderism for children and transgenders competing in women's sports.

The Conservative Political Action Conference (CPAC) chairman Matt Schlapp was asked during an interview with a Catholic news organization called Church Militant if gay men should be allowed to adopt children, and he was so caught off guard he could barely speak. "Yes or no. Should gay men be allowed to adopt young boys?" asked the host Michael Voris. Matt Schlapp responded, "Oh boy, ya know...I don't...I don't even know what... what...does our Church fight those positions? And does the, I don't know, the, what the policy position is of the Church and..."[886]

---

[885] Ibid.

[886] Church Militant "CPAC CHAIRMAN GETS SCHLAPPED" (March 21st 2022)

The host cuts him off, "Well, the teaching of the Church is that two men shouldn't be together to begin with." Matt Schlapp responds "Yeah, I know what the Church teaches in terms of sexual ethics. But I don't know what it teaches, in terms, I don't know what it lobbies for in these legislative chambers. I would say this: Obviously, um, it is, ah, we've gotten to this position where we've gotten away from this idea that having a father and a mother is awfully important."[887]

A weak and pathetic answer from one of the most prominent "Conservatives" in America today. Less than a decade earlier such a response would end a Conservative's career, but the Republican Party has moved so far left that they now tacitly support such abominations and are scared to death to oppose them in the *extremely* rare case someone even asks them about these issues anymore.

When Dave Rubin announced he and his "husband" bought two babies from surrogates after obtaining eggs from a fertility clinic and having them artificially inseminated (one with each of their sperm), they were congratulated by many of the top brand names in the "Conservative" movement including PragerU, the prestigious Conservative institution,[888] along with The Blaze, Glenn Beck's media company,[889] Breitbart's senior editor-at-large Joel Pollak,[890] critical race theory "expert"

---

[887] Ibid.

[888] https://web.archive.org/web/20220523032505/https://twitter.com/prageru/status/1504156067428638721

[889] https://web.archive.org/web/20220523032532/https://twitter.com/BlazeTV/status/1504135771938164736

[890] https://twitter.com/joelpollak/status/1504163326380568577

Christopher Rufo,[891] Megyn Kelly,[892] Megan McCain,[893] Kat Timpf (who works on Greg Gutfeld's Fox News show),[894] and many others.

Imagine growing up as a child being raised by two gay men, and when you're old enough to start learning about where babies come from and ask them where your mom is, they tell you they don't know—and you'll never know because egg donors are completely private so those who purchase the eggs will never know, and not even the children themselves will know. That's what brand name Conservatives are now celebrating.[895]

Newsmax host Greg Kelly makes it clear in no uncertain terms that the U.S. military should go back to the old "Don't Ask, Don't Tell" policy basically forbidding gays from being allowed in the military at all because normal people don't want to get stuck in a unit with one (a Democrat policy, by the way, put in place by Bill Clinton in 1993).[896] But have any Fox News hosts made such a seemingly bold statement?

Have any Republican members of Congress said *anything* in opposition to Obama allowing gays into the military in the last ten years (or mentioned the disturbing number of rapes they're committing)? Have any of them

---

[891] https://twitter.com/realchrisrufo/status/1504158072192655360

[892] https://twitter.com/megynkelly/status/1504171771984973824

[893] https://twitter.com/MeghanMcCain/status/1504135090779172864

[894] https://twitter.com/KatTimpf/status/1504283362458054662

[895] LifeSite News "Conservatives should not applaud Dave Rubin and his gay partner's surrogate baby news" (March 16th 2022)

[896] Newsmax "Greg Kelly Reports" (May4th 2023) "Colin Powell had it right" he said, about the Don't Ask Don't Tell policy, and aired video of Powell in 1993 testifying before Congress about why the policy was necessary for a successful military. Segment uploaded to Newsmax's YouTube channel here: https://youtu.be/QpncwquA52s?si=Ya6Uoztpx2ebhKhB

dared to oppose gay men adopting children? Or buying eggs from fertility clinics and renting surrogates who they have artificially inseminated, condemning the children to a life of never knowing who their mother is, and then further condemning the children to be raised by two men as their own narcissistic science project? Of course not. They're all lukewarm cowards. They all accept it as normal.

Which begs the question, how much of the Republican base has abandoned the party and doesn't even vote anymore because they're sick of it basically just trailing the Democrat agenda by ten years? How many people got so fed up with the Republican Party steadily moving to the left that they've thrown up their hands and no longer support them out of frustration because they don't feel they represent their interests and values anymore?

Neocons vs. Paleoconservatives

Few Conservatives today know that there are actually two basic kinds of conservatives, and the movement (along with the Republican Party) split into two different factions beginning back in the 1960s, resulting in the Neocons (Neo-conservatives or *new* Conservatives) taking control. Neocons are similar to RINOs (Republican in name only) but are particularly interested in foreign policy and are known for being war hawks who use the military industrial complex to intervene in the affairs of foreign countries to further the New World Order. They are globalists as opposed to nationalists, although they portray themselves as patriotic by flexing America's military power.

Paleoconservatives, on the other hand, are true Conservatives. They're the traditionalist Americans who tend to be Christian, oppose open borders and the LGBTQ agenda, and have a strong sense of national pride. Instead of being concerned with nation building in foreign countries, they prefer a more isolationist foreign policy and focus on localism. In other words, they don't support wars in the Middle East (like the War in Iraq), not just because they're almost always started by lies, but because they don't want the United States sticking its nose in other countries' business.

There are some other nuanced differences as well, such as Paleoconservatives tend to oppose free trade which they see as harming America's manufacturing sector by allowing cheap goods to be imported from foreign countries without making them pay tariffs, and instead support what's called trade protectionism.

The term *paleo* means older or ancient, just like the paleo diet refers to a diet humans are believed to have eaten during the Paleolithic Era (a long time ago), and is used to differentiate traditionalist or classical Conservatives from the new (or neo) Conservatives—the Neocons.[897] Ben Shapiro, for example, is a staunch Neocon who supported legalizing gay "marriage." He tries downplaying that position to Conservative audiences by saying he wouldn't personally attend a gay "wedding," but he does support it as an institution.

In response to someone who claimed he didn't, he answered "I've been libertarian on same-sex marriage for years, before Obergefell. But you couldn't be bothered to Google," referring to the 2015 Supreme Court case which

---

[897] The term paleoconservative was coined in 1986 by Paul Gottfried and Thomas Fleming.

ultimately legalized it.[898] Shapiro, like all Neocons, would also support any Middle Eastern war or military action that would either directly or indirectly protect Israel.

The Neocons were the ones who concocted the weapons of mass destruction hoax and the lie that Saddam Hussein had a relationship with al-Qaeda to dupe the American people (and the rest of the world) into going along with the invasion of Iraq in 2003 to carry out their Project for the New American Century. Three years earlier, the PNAC Neocon think tank had lamented their plan would be difficult "absent some catastrophic and catalyzing event—like a new Pearl Harbor."[899] The 9/11 attacks were their "New Pearl Harbor," and two years into the War on Terror the aim shifted from Afghanistan, where Osama Bin Laden was supposedly hiding out, to Iraq.

And contrary to popular belief, this wasn't just to "steal" their oil or preserve the petrodollar.[900] One of the main reasons was to protect Israel, "America's greatest ally,"[901] but you're not supposed to say this out loud though or post it on social media.[902] That's another "antisemitic trope" they say, so be careful.

---

[898] https://twitter.com/benshapiro/status/1272904470721179648

[899] "Rebuilding America's Defenses: Strategy: Forces, and Resources for a New Century" A Report of The Project for the New American Century (September 2000) page 51

[900] Iraq had switched to selling oil in euros, which threatened the U.S dollar's dominance as the world's reserve currency.

[901] Inter Press Service "Iraq War Launched to Protect Israel" by Emad Mekay (March 29th 2004)

[902] The Guardian "Israel puts pressure on US to strike Iraq" by Jonathan Steele (August 16th 2002)

In 1981 Israel bombed a nuclear reactor in Iraq out of concerns that the country would become a nuclear power and pose a danger to them since Iraq was allied with other Arab countries in the region during the Six-Day War (or the Third Arab-Israeli War) in 1967 which broke out as a result of ongoing hostilities between Israel and their Arab neighbors ever since the U.N. mandate in 1948 officially creating the State of Israel (which resulted in kicking 700,000 Palestinians out of their homes, an event known as the Palestinian expulsion).[903]

The Israeli-Palestine conflict is far beyond the scope of this book, but basically Israel remains concerned about its Arab neighbors, and Iraq was still considered a prime threat to them because of the possibility that they may acquire nuclear weapons in the future. So when George W. Bush was beating the war drums and saying Iraq posed a threat to the United States (which it didn't) and "our allies," he was talking about Israel.[904]

This is why Republicans like Mark Levin and others consider any talk about *Neocons* to be "antisemitic" and deem the word itself to be essentially an "antisemitic slur" because they want to protect Israel from the perception of having any influence over American foreign policy, despite AIPAC [the American Israel Public Affairs Committee]—a Jewish lobbying group that advocates for pro-Israeli policies, spending over $50 million dollars a year to do just that.[905]

---

[903] The Atlantic "A 'Catastrophe' That Defines Palestinian Identity" by Hussein Ibish (May 14th 2018)

[904] Ron Paul Institute for Peace and Prosperity "The Neoconservatives, the War on Iraq, and the National Interest of Israel "by Stephen J. Sniegoski (August 23rd 2016)

[905] The Wall Street Journal "Pro-Israel Group Lobbies for U.S. Aid, Funds Congressional Trips" by Julie Bykowicz and Natalie Andrews (February 14th 2019)

And while publicly the standard political line from both Democrats and Republicans is that Israel is "America's greatest ally," privately—as the classified NSA documents leaked by Edward Snowden show, the country is considered a top espionage threat because of their "intelligence collection operations and manipulation/ influence operations against the U.S. government, military, science & technology and Intelligence Community."[906]

Also, Al-Qaeda attacked the United States on 9/11, not because they "hate our freedom" as the Operation Mockingbird assets all sung in concert, but because of our financial and military backing of Israel which angers many Muslims around the world who side with the Palestinians in the ongoing territorial disputes in the region.[907] Inside job / false flag theories aside, this was still the case. One of the most prominent "conspiracy theories" of what happened is the LIHOP hypothesis, the "let it happen on purpose" theory, which doesn't negate Al-Qaeda's hatred for America or their involvement in planning and carrying out the attacks on 9/11 (even if they were aided and directed by the CIA or other intelligence agencies).

Years later when Congressman Ron Paul said that the attacks were "blowback for decades of US intervention in the Middle East" he was attacked for "blaming America,"

---

[906] Newsweek "Israel Flagged as Top Spy Threat to U.S. in New Snowden/NSA Document" by Jeff Stein (August 4th 2014)

[907] Osama Bin Laden himself wrote in his "Letter to America" fatwa saying, "The expansion of Israel is one of the greatest crimes, and you are the leaders of its criminals. And of course there is no need to explain and prove the degree of American support for Israel. Each and every person whose hands have become polluted in the contribution towards this crime must pay its price, and pay for it heavily."

but the intelligence agencies and foreign policy experts all know the truth.[908]

This is why the Iranian government (and Muslim terrorist organizations like Al-Qaeda, ISIS, Hamas, etc.) call America the "Great Satan," and sometimes chant "Death to America."[909] No matter what side of the argument you're on (if any) regarding U.S. support for Israel, Zionism is explicitly a central part of Neoconservatism.[910]

Few people make the distinction anymore between Neocons and Paleoconservatives because the Neocons want to portray conservatism as if their kind of conservatism is the only kind, and try to frame Paleoconservatism (without using that term so people don't start looking into the Paleo/Neocon split) as an ancient relic like the idea of women being virgins on their wedding night—a political belief system that's no longer practical in our modern age.

William F. Buckley and his publication *The National Review* made it their goal to purge the Paleoconservatives from the Republican Party in the 1960s.[911] One of their prime targets was the John Birch Society which was formed in the late 1950s to oppose communism, but their hard stance against globalists, and globalist organizations like the United Nations, the Council on Foreign Relations,

---

[908] Politico "Ron Paul: U.S. triggered Sept. 11" by James Arkin (September 11th 2013)

[909] Aljazeera "Who is the 'Great Satan'? In a recent speech, Ayatollah Khamenei used metaphors to describe US influence" by Hamid Dabashi (September 20th 2015)

[910] The Neoconservative Revolution: Jewish Intellectuals and the Shaping of Public Policy by Murray Friedman (2005) Cambridge University Press

[911] The National Review "The Inside Story of William F. Buckley Jr.'s Crusade against the John Birch Society" by Alvin S. Felzenberg (June 20th 2017)

and the Bilderberg Group was seen as a hindrance to the New World Order, so the Neocons strategically worked to exile them.

The remaining Paloeconservatives who survived William F. Buckley's purge in the 1960s were mostly pushed out of mainstream Republican politics in the early 1980s as the rift continued to grow. These were people such as Pat Buchanan, Paul Gottfried, Joseph Sobran, Samuel Francis, Russell Kirk, as well as organizations like the Rockford Institute and the Philadelphia Society.[912]

The John Birch Society is still in existence today, though just a shell of its former self, and hasn't had any significant power since the 1970s. So for decades the Neocons have been the ones steering much of the Republican Party until Donald Trump came on the scene igniting a populist movement and shaking the political establishment to its core, resulting in the all-out war to impeach and imprison him.

Although the term is rarely used to describe the MAGA movement, much of it is paleoconservative. And while there are now countless "Conservative" media outlets, few make any distinctions about just what type of conservatism they promote. There are some exceptions however, including *Taki's* magazine, *The New American* (published by the John Birch Society), *The American Conservative, Chronicles: A Magazine of American Culture*, the *Intercollegiate Review*, and a few others.

There are also some organizations dedicated to the philosophy, such as the Charlemagne Institute (the publisher of Chronicles magazine), VDARE, the Family Research Council, the American Family Association, the

---

[912] A Paleoconservative Anthology: New Voices for an Old Tradition (Political Theory for Today) by Paul Gottfried (editor) 2023

Conservative Caucus, as well as the Constitution Party, the American Independent Party, and Gun Owners of America (a pro-2nd Amendment group that positions themselves further to the right than the NRA).

As mainstream conservatism in America continues to drift to the left we'll likely see a resurgence of paleoconservatism (even if it doesn't overtly use the term) as millions of Christians and Conservatives become activated and work to turn things back to the right, rejecting not just liberalism, but neoconservatism as well.

Politics as a Grift

There's a saying that every social cause starts off as a movement—then becomes a business, and then later turns into a grift (or swindle).[913] Not that long ago—in the 1990s, the Republican Party would have shunned many of the stars in "Conservative" media today. And any Republican that was afraid to take a Conservative stand on various issues (or adopted the same stance as the Democrats) would have been voted out of office.

If they started sucking up to resentful Black people who will forever hold a chip on their shoulder against Whites because of slavery 150 years ago, they would have been mocked for their pathetic pandering like Democrats. If Jews started complaining about Christmas celebrations at schools or the office, they would have been completely ignored, ridiculed, or told maybe they should move to Israel then. But today even most Christians are weak.

---

[913] Attributed to Eric Hoffer, but this is said to be a frequently misquoted statement found in his 1967 book, The Temper of Our Time, where he wrote, "What starts out here as a mass movement ends up as a racket, a cult, or a corporation."

And our weakness has only allowed our opponents to get stronger.

The moral, intellectual, and economic decay in the United States may be impossible to stop, let alone reverse, so sadly we may continue to see mainstream Republicans desperately clinging to power by adopting more positions held by Democrats. More social welfare programs for minorities, further embracing gays and transgenders; maybe even a universal basic income for those who are too lazy to hold down a job or maintain a career. At this point what has the mainstream Conservative movement even conserved?

I guess in their defense, the general population may have been slowly pushed so far left through cultural marxist Hollywood propaganda, social media molding their minds, and being raised in broken homes by single parents who were raised in a broken homes, and so on— the only way to hold onto any semblance of power on a national level may be to move left to the point where the Democrat Party used to stand as recent as the Obama administration, since Democrats have moved so far left they are literally marxists in comparison.

This problem brings us back to the Breitbart Doctrine, the idea popularized by Andrew Breitbart that politics is downstream from culture, meaning in order for political change (such as new bills to be passed into law) first the culture has to change, and people's sensibilities and tolerance for certain ideas or behaviors have to be primed to accept (or demand) them.

If there is any hope in saving America it starts in the home. It starts with building strong loving families which can then form into quality communities, which can extend into strong states, which can hopefully then come together into a strong country. But even if this is a pipe dream or a fool's errand, despite what happens to our own city, state, or country as whole, we can and must maintain our social circle of family and friends and still find joy and comfort from the simple things in life, no matter what we see on the news, social media, or coming out of Washington D.C.

Author's Note: Please take a moment to rate and review this book on Amazon.com or wherever you purchased it from to let others know what you think. This also helps to offset the trolls who keep giving my books fake one-star reviews when they haven't even read them. Almost all of the one-star reviews on my books are from NON-verified purchases which is a clear indication they are fraudulent, hence me adding this note.

These fraudulent ratings and reviews could also be part of a larger campaign trying to stop my message from spreading by attempting to tarnish my research through fake and defamatory reviews, so I really need your help to combat this as soon as possible.

Thank you!

Conclusion

Conservatives are traditionalists who realize that just because something is new, doesn't mean it's better. And when people rush into something new or try to reinvent the wheel, they often fall victim to the law of unintended consequences. Like when incandescent light bulbs were replaced by more energy efficient LED bulbs to help save electricity and reduce carbon emissions.

But in areas with a cold climate like Minnesota and New York, the snow can easily collect on the traffic lights, and since LED lights don't give off a lot of heat like the old incandescent ones, the snow doesn't melt—sometimes completely obscuring the lights at intersections and causing massive traffic problems.[914]

You've likely experienced updating your phone or computer's operating system to the "newest" and "best" software only to soon find major glitches that the developers overlooked which need to be fixed with *another* update they have to frantically release.[915] The same kinds of chaos occurs when Liberals try to overturn the natural social order and norms that the human race has been following since the beginning of time.

Marxists despise these practices because they despise everything normal. They're bitter and spiteful people who want to ruin others' fun because they themselves aren't having any. Like the fat girl at school who hates the lead cheerleader just because she's pretty and popular.

---

[914] CBS News "LED Traffic Lights Getting Bogged Down By Snow" (December 5th 2017)

[915] ZDNet "iPhone owners plagued by 'no service' bug after iOS 14.7.1 upgrade" by Adrian Kingsley-Hughes (August 19th 2021)

Or someone who keys the paint of a nice car they see parked on the street because they're envious of the owner.

They're like the three-pack a day smoker coughing and wheezing from walking up a flight of stairs who then throw a fit when they're told that if they quit smoking it would really help. Liberals are in denial about their dysfunctional beliefs and behavior, and no matter how polite or well-intended criticism or advice is, they just get angry when people resist going along with them. But their problems aren't just affecting themselves. They're making society dysfunctional from their insistence that everyone else accept and celebrate their mental illnesses, perversions, laziness, and spitefulness.

And people who aren't afflicted with such disorders often cater to those who are in order to win over their political support to feed their appetites for power. They're gullible and easy to manipulate, so Democrats cater to dumb and lazy people since the party has shifted from once supporting the working class to supporting those who don't want to work and are just looking for handouts. The sheer number of people who don't have the dedication to go to work every day is scary.

And through social media they can easily connect with each other and organize online mobs—and form them in the real world as well. It's how communism took over China and other countries. The violent mobs organized and eventually became too powerful to resist. So we have to stop them here before it's too late.

But because of their viciousness they've already scared many people into silence. Widespread cowardice on our side earlier when they were weaker is what got us here, and allowed the Left to transform much of the United States into an almost unrecognizable dystopia.

CONCLUSION

Many old Conservatives championed small government and were afraid to use its power for our own purposes because they wanted to stay "principled" by not using the levers of government at all, and instead took a laissez faire approach. And it's been a losing strategy when facing an opponent who uses every possible means to win while Conservatives sit on the sidelines and say "they're being hypocrites" or "hey, that's not fair."

Conservatives' mantra about supporting "limited government" has been nothing but an embarrassing failure as a political strategy. It's time to use the existing power structure to achieve our goals for a change and to punish our enemies. Shrinking the size of government is a pipe dream. So we might as well use it to our advantage.

Conservatives and Christians have been far too timid for far too long. It's time to start giving the Left a taste of their own medicine and playing by some of their rules. Barraging businesses that go woke by flooding their social media feeds with negative comments and memes mocking them isn't enough. Boycotting woke companies isn't enough either. While that may cost them *some* loss of revenue, many won't even notice or care. You have to tell the store clerks that what the company is doing is pathetic (or perverted). You have to make the employees feel uncomfortable—even miserable.

If they can't even get through a shift without being told off by a dozen customers every single day, they're going to complain to their managers, and the managers are going to report to the corporate office that selling woke products or promoting anti-White "diversity" initiatives or the LGBTQ agenda is causing a hostile environment in the stores by customers. Many employees may agree with us, but out of fear of losing their jobs won't say anything themselves. So it's our job as the customers, because the customer is always right—to pressure them.

And while it's not some random clerk's fault what the corporation itself is doing, they are a vessel that can relay customers' dissatisfaction to those higher up the food chain, and they are the public face of the business and what it represents. Fill their Yelp and Google listings with negative reviews. Better yet, pick up the phone and start calling local branches and sound off. And do it every time any company crosses the line. Post their phone numbers and email addresses on social media to encourage others.[916] They need to be sent a loud and sustained message. Same with the schools, and our local and state governments.

Look up your Congressman and Senators' phone numbers (and those of the mayor and city council members) and save them in your contacts like you would anyone else you frequently call. They can (and do) ignore tweets and emails, but if their office phone is ringing off the hook all week and every time their aides or interns pick it up they get an earful from upset constituents, they're not going to be able to just go about their day as usual. The Congressman, the mayor, the school (or whoever) will get the message, and as the cliché goes—the squeaky wheel gets the grease. It's usually a small but vocal and active group that causes large societal changes because most people sit on the sidelines and say or do nothing.

---

[916] Posting the publicly listed phone numbers of business, schools, or government offices is not doxxing, although with the way things are going some Big Tech platforms may remove the posts under the false guise that it's an "invasion of privacy" or "harassment."

CONCLUSION

Run for city council, mayor, and get on your local school board. Trying to fix the government by using a top down approach will have a limited effect because of how gigantic the bureaucracy is and the number of obstacles that need to be overcome to achieve major changes. As president, Donald Trump tried, and while he had some major victories (like gaining a Conservative majority in the Supreme Court), he could only shift our nation's course a few degrees.

A bottom up approach is better in many regards because it can be done by ordinary people with limited resources, and being involved in local politics usually isn't as competitive as national offices because the field is less crowded.

Taking control of our local communities is not as difficult as most people think. Just a small handful of active people can take over city councils and school boards, and most people only think about voting on election years for major positions like the president, but local positions (and midterms) are just as important.

During COVID lockdowns, for example, in 2020 and 2021 many local Sheriffs (who are elected by the voters) refused to enforce state laws dictated by governors though executive orders which mandated restaurants not allow in-person dining—even Sheriffs in some major California cities refused to enforce the rule, and allowed businesses to stay open.[917]

Look up the recommended voter guide for your city which are put together by many local Republican parties and use it as a guide to choose candidates you're not familiar with for various positions that don't have their

---

[917] Times of San Diego "Much of State Shuts Down, Though Some SoCal Sheriffs Won't Enforce Order" by Editor (December 7th 2020)

party affiliation listed next to their name on the ballot. Many positions, like school board members, judges, and sheriffs do not list whether a candidate is a Republican or a Democrat, so take advantage of the research and voter guide your local Republican Party puts together. A quick Google search should bring it up.

One of the goals of this book is to move the Overton Window, which is the spectrum of ideas about social issues and public policy that are seen as acceptable by the general public. There are a lot of issues and facts that the Republican Party, Conservatives, and Christians are afraid to talk about out loud, so I'm working to normalize those issues and introduce the terminology, concepts, and arguments to the masses so those seeds can be planted into the minds of millions and one day these truths will be so widely spoken about they'll be impossible to ignore.

We have to push (or pull) Republican lawmakers and political pundits into these discussions by bombarding them with questions, evidence, and arguments; and make addressing these issues unavoidable.

I also want people to be as well rounded as possible when it comes to media literacy. (I am a media analyst after all). Everyone should know about the Social Impact Agencies in Hollywood—the lobbying groups which work to have their clients' messages inserted into the storylines of popular shows and movies, disguising political propaganda as mere entertainment. (Something I detailed in my previous book *Hollywood Propaganda: How TV, Movies, and Music Shape Our Culture*).

Everyone should know the basic facts about Operation Mockingbird and how the "war on fake news" was launched immediately after Donald Trump beat Hillary Clinton in the 2016 election as a smokescreen to begin rolling out massive censorship on social media. (See my book *The True Story of Fake News*).

We should make sure it's common knowledge that as a result of this bogus "war on fake news" the Big Tech platforms completely changed the way they function, and how they've come to manipulate their algorithms to artificially boost certain content that reinforces their agenda, while systematically suppressing and censoring those who oppose it. People should know the history of how the mainstream media merged with the very platforms that were once created so users could bypass and replace them. (See my book *The Liberal Media Industrial Complex*).

A word of caution about becoming politically active though. Some people may want to start an organization or a group to fight for the cause, but there are enormous dangers to such an approach you should be aware of before even considering it. First of all, if a member of the group does something stupid, then the entire organization gets blamed. Not just blamed online or in the media, but it can be legally held liable.

If you or your organization holds an event or promotes a protest and someone gets hurt if violence breaks out, no matter which side started it or caused it, you may be held personally liable, either civilly or even criminally. Democrats have very well-funded law firms they use to financially cripple their opponents. And even if you win a case brought against you, the legal bills are enough to bankrupt most people just defending against them.

It may be better to become part of already well-established groups and then influence their members, and ultimately their leadership, to move them further right. Being part of a movement is often better than being part of an actual organization. One can be a supporter, leader, or an influencer in a movement while remaining completely independent, but this still puts you at risk for civil and criminal penalties if you're blamed for "inciting" violence by using political rhetoric that's too heated, or even standard political analogies talking about "fighting" or "war."

They'll get your private text messages, DMs, and emails, and use them as evidence against you just like they did to the Proud Boys and Oath Keepers.[918] And figures of speech and jokes will be framed as if you were being literal.

Be cautious about posting political messages on social media. Create anonymous accounts where possible, not using your name or your photo. And use a burner email address, not your usual one, in case the platform gets hacked and login information is published for our opponents to sift through (which does happen), allowing them to find other accounts on other platforms that use the same email address, leading them to find people's real identities.

Resist the urge to become a "famous" online personality. Many online accounts have gained hundreds of thousands of followers while keeping the identity of those who run them unknown. Teach your kids how they can ruin their life with one TikTok or Snapchat post that's deemed "racist," "antisemitic," "transphobic," etc. unless or until we end cancel culture.

Be careful not to cut off your nose to spite your face. Going on a rant and using the n-word to prove you don't care what the Thought Police say isn't worth getting fired from your job over or banned from social media. Future

---

[918] Gizmodo "Encrypted Chats, Parler Posts Indict Proud Boys Leaders for Capitol Rioting" by Dell Cameron (March 19th 2021)

CONCLUSION

potential employers will Google your name during the hiring process and even if your rant doesn't make headlines—if you're named in tweets or Facebook posts, those are going to come up during their vetting process.

Even if you use a pseudonym for your social media presence, if you show your face there is an extremely high probability your actual identity will be found. There's facial recognition software that can find other photos of you online that were posted by your family or friends. Online sleuths can be ruthless and crafty in their quest to dox people. And someone who personally knows you may take it upon themselves to alert others who you are (like a former classmate, coworker, or ex-wife).

But it doesn't even have to be something *you* post online. These days if someone goes off on a "racist" rant in public that's caught on video, that video often goes viral and ultimately the person is identified, doxxed, and fired in hopes of appeasing the angry online mob who call and harass people's employers when they're the subject of a viral controversy.[919] So even if you're not posting on social media at all, social media can ruin your career from something you say in real life. It's a brave new world.

So pick your battles wisely. Some are in better positions to fight on certain fronts than others. If you're a retired veteran with a guaranteed pension and you have nothing to lose, that's different than an aspiring young college kid who could face a lifetime of limited career options if they happen to get the attention of the wrong people by pushing the envelope on certain controversial issues. With formidable foes dedicated to shutting down anyone speaking out too loudly about certain topics,

---

[919] CNN "White woman who called police on a black man bird-watching in Central Park has been fired" by Amir Vera and Laura Ly (May 26th 2020)

people need to be careful before they end up with a target on their back. Each individual must carefully decide their own level of involvement.

And this shouldn't need to be said, but no matter how frustrated you get, no matter how angry and disgusted you feel because of the onslaught of attacks against Conservatives or our cultural or religious traditions, don't do anything violent unless it's in self-defense of an *imminent* and direct threat to your life or that of another.[920]

We've all seen how occasionally disgruntled and mentally disturbed people on the Left and the Right lash out in violence against their perceived enemies, and it always hurts whatever cause they thought they were fighting for. It gains widespread sympathy for the victims and casts whatever cause the perpetrator thought they were fighting for in an extremely negative and toxic light. So when I talk about *The War on Conservatives*—as far as our side is concerned, it's a *political* and *metaphoric* war. It's an *information* war. It's a battle of ideas, so don't be stupid like some misguided self-proclaimed "patriots" in the past who have lashed out in violence, or those who think that wearing camo and "training" with a dozen others in the woods to overthrow the government is going to have anything but disastrous consequences.

Even in situations that could be deemed self-defense, one wrong decision in a split second could cost you your freedom. Some people shoot armed robbers after they turn around and head for the door and are charged with

---

[920] Even when countering a physical attack in self-defense, you could still be charged with a crime if you go beyond proportional or reasonable force. Other factors are also involved, such as if it was an unprovoked attack, or if your assessment of the threat itself was reasonable, or if you made a reasonable attempt to avoid the confrontation to begin with.

2nd degree manslaughter because technically the threat to their life was over because the perpetrator was leaving. Violence is always ugly and should be avoided at all costs. And don't try arguing or reasoning with Marxists in the street. Like Mr. Miyagi from *The Karate Kid* said, the best way to avoid a punch is to not be there.

If you haven't read my previous books, then you should know that the rabbit hole goes much deeper, and even though some of the topics are similar, each book provides a wealth of information and can help readers gain a much better understanding of how the interconnecting relationships between media, culture, and power function.

Books are one of the best forms of spreading knowledge, even in the so-called digital age (or the information age), or rather *especially* in the information age—because there is *too much* information and too many different sources trying to constantly bombard us with messages. People are drowning in information and have a difficult time sifting through it to find quality and meaningful content while avoiding all the useless drama, and pop culture gossip, propaganda, and spam.

We need to free ourselves from the digital sewage pipe that directs most people's attention. We don't need to be slaves to whatever hit show on HBO is trending or whatever new series Netflix or Hulu just launched. We need to manage our media diets in the same way we watch what foods we eat.

It's important to continue old traditions, and always put family first. Study intimate relationships and date with the purpose of finding a life partner and getting married, not just for having fun. Too many people get stuck with someone they're incompatible with in the areas of interpersonal relationships that matter most. They don't look at whether their interests, values, and goals are actually aligned until it's too late. Then it's not just their own happiness and wellbeing that suffers, it's that of their children and grandchildren down the road who have to grow up in broken or dysfunctional homes.

We may be living in a collapsing empire. Politically, financially, intellectually, and morally. Only Republican states or red districts, local communities, small towns, neighborhoods, and families can probably be preserved at this point. The United States as a whole however, is in huge trouble. Perhaps when things get so bad, the pendulum will start to swing back the other direction and society at large may begin healing. But it may not. The America we all knew and loved may be gone. We appear to be following the Tytler Cycle of Civilizations and in the end-stage of Democracy.[921]

But we can carry on the same principles in our own lives that the founding fathers established starting in 1776, in hopes of one day restoring the Republic, no matter how many generations it may take. And more importantly follow the examples set forth by Christ so that we may have the hope of glory.

---

[921] The Tytler Cycle of Civilizations lists the phases as: From bondage to spiritual faith; to great courage; to liberty to abundance to complacency to apathy to dependence back into bondage

Printed in Poland
by Amazon Fulfillment
Poland Sp. z o.o., Wrocław